Land Above the Trees

LAND ABOVE

A Guide

THE TREES

to American Alpine Tundra

by ANN H. ZWINGER
and BEATRICE E. WILLARD, Ph.D.

WITH LINE DRAWINGS BY ANN H. ZWINGER

PERENNIAL LIBRARY

Harper & Row, Publishers
New York, Cambridge, Philadelphia, San Francisco, Washington
London, Mexico City, São Paulo, Singapore, Sydney

For William T. Haymond,
who gave his daughter a love of detail
and a sense of nature

For Stephen H. and Beatrice A. Willard,
who gave their daughter a firsthand love
of nature and beauty

Portions of this work originally appeared in *The American West* and *Natural History*.

A hardcover edition of this work was originally published in 1972 by Harper & Row, Publishers, Inc.

First PERENNIAL LIBRARY edition published 1986.

Library of Congress Cataloging-in-Publication Data

Zwinger, Ann.
   Land above the trees.

   Bibliography: p.
   Includes index.
   1. Mountain ecology—United States. 2. Alpine flora—United States. I. Willard, Beatrice E. II. Title.
QH104.Z94   1986   574.5′2644′0973   86-12047
ISBN 0-06-091365-7 (pbk.)

86 87 88 89 90 MPC 10 9 8 7 6 5 4 3 2 1

Contents

Preface

The alpine tundra of the United States has never been described for the interested novice. There are numerous accounts of the tundra in the Alps—of its flowers, of adventures climbing on it, of general description—in three languages. But in North America, this single major vegetation type has been overlooked until now. This book brings together for the first time in one place most of what is known about the alpine tundra of the United States.

A visitor to Trail Ridge in Rocky Mountain National Park once exclaimed, "Oh, there's nothing that grows above the trees!" As you will discover in the following pages, there is very much that "grows above the trees." But it takes close looking, a scaling down of anticipations from the trees, shrubs and grasses with which we are so familiar, to plants that barely rise above the surface of the ground. It takes getting down on hands and knees—or even stomach—to examine a mini-forest at your toes. Such an effort is often welcome because a low profile is the warmest in the harsh arctic climate of the tundra.

This climate is no doubt another reason why so few people have studied the alpine tundra until recently. Accessibility is a third, although in Colorado roads have reached to the summits of Pikes Peak and Mount Evans for several decades. But in other regions, the tundra is quite remote, reached only by a good stiff hike of several hours.

Ever since spending fourteen wonderful months roaming in the Alps and other high mountains of the Continent on a Ford Foundation fellowship, I have wanted to unlock the treasures of this world for all to enjoy. Studying Trail Ridge tundra for five years in an effort to understand its every mood and action, while determining what visitors were doing to it, was the first step toward this goal. The second was meeting Ann Zwinger in 1968, when she asked me to check the technical ecology of her first book, *Beyond the Aspen Grove*. Immediately I recognized her exceptional talent for conveying scientific facts to lay people in vivid terms and a most delightful manner—both by words and by delicate, accurate drawings. We agreed that we would work together on a book on the alpine tundra, an undertaking we both viewed with enthusiasm.

To this end we have been working intensely for three years. For me, it was a novel and delightful way to write a book—to be able to sit back and let someone else put my years of research and experience into words. All I had to do was orally interpret scientific findings, while Ann recorded them in text and drawings.

This relationship was complemented and greatly enhanced by her husband, Herman, who, with his camera, captured on film various tundra scenes and moods. In his plane—*Icarus International Airline*—he flew us to representative mountain ranges of the United States for field forays.

We have chosen to visit and describe seven specific alpine tundra sites in the Continental United States—Colorado Rockies; Sierra Nevada of California; White Mountains in the Great Basin on the Nevada-California border; Mounts Hood and Rainier in the Cascades of Oregon and Washington; the Olympic Mountains of Washington; and Mount Washington in New Hampshire's White Mountains—out of perhaps a dozen Alpine areas in all. There is great similarity of process among these ranges, but each has differences of plant and animal species and of physical environment. These sites include all the definitive processes, and we are sure that further site descriptions, such as Northern and far Southern Rockies, San Francisco Peaks of Arizona, and the Wallowa ("Blue") Mountains of Oregon, would have added only a very small increment of information. In all cases, we have included these omitted areas in the species list. Alaskan tundra is a world of its own, mainly arctic or arctic-alpine, and deserves treatment as such.

There is more attention and information given concerning the Colorado Rockies because Colorado has a larger extent of alpine tundra than any other section of the country; the character of the Colorado tundra is more complex, with a greater number of species, communities and processes; more definitive ecological studies have been made of the tundra of Colorado than any other part of the country; and it is the tundra most easily accessible to visitors.

Researching and preparing this book has been an exciting experience for me, and I hope you will share my enthusiasm for a fascinating world apart, a dramatic world composed of extremes of sizes, of process, of climate, of adaptation to environment, of remoteness. And I also hope you will share our concern for the need to protect this world from the damage and destruction—sometimes unconscious but often irreparable—by men and their machines.

Beatrice E. Willard, Ph.D.
President, Thorne Ecological Institute
Boulder, Colorado
December, 1971

Acknowledgments

Dr. Willard and Mrs. Zwinger especially wish to thank Dr. John W. Marr and Dr. William S. Osburn for reading and commenting upon the entire manuscript while in preparation, a Herculean task. They thank the following for help in special areas: Dr. Carl Sharsmith for the Sierra Nevada; Dr. Lawrence C. Bliss for the Olympic Mountains and Mount Washington in New Hampshire; Dr. Harold Mooney for the White Mountains of California; Dr. Jerry Franklin for the Cascade Mountains.

Dr. William A. Weber, of the University of Colorado Museum, checked plant identifications, as did Mrs. Ruth Ashton Nelson, who also checked the drawings for accuracy. Dr. Clait Braun of the Colorado Game and Fish Department contributed valuable information and field experience from his research on white-tailed ptarmigan. Dr. Roger Anderson provided a listing of Colorado alpine lichens. Miss Katherin Bell generously shared her unpublished research on kobresia.

Members of the Park Service and U.S. Forest Service were always of great help. We especially wish to thank Superintendent John Townsley and Chief Naturalist Norman Bishop of Rainier National Park; Ranger Richard Harris of White Mountain National Forest and Supervisor Philbrick at Mount Washington.

For hospitality along the way, we are grateful to Mr. and Mrs. Robert Lee and Mrs. Stephen H. Willard.

Dr. Willard wishes to thank personally Mrs. Milford Davis for extensive and dedicated work on the references and plant lists; Dr. Samuel Bamberg and Dr. Jack Major for use of an unpublished plant list; Miss Miriam Colson for identification of sedges; Mrs. R. A. Nelson for reading and commenting on the manuscript and Dr. D. Ferrel Atkins for the naturalist's point of view. She is grateful to Mr. William E. Larson, Jr., and Mrs. Jane O'Keefe for assistance on the plant table.

Mrs. Zwinger wishes to thank personally Anne Cross and Janet LeCompte for reading and comment, and especially Timmie Lou Rixon for extended work on the manuscript in preparation. Comfortable facilities for drawing were provided by Jim Burrow of Ravencrest, Estes Park, Colorado; Mr. Richard Whipple of The Dana Place, Jackson, New Hampshire; and Mrs. Stephen Willard at Mammoth Lakes, California. This was much appreciated by the illustrator. Sidney Novis helped beyond thanks in technical matters of illustration and layout. Mr. Dennis L. Lynch, Pikes Peak District Ranger, gave information and assistance in the Pikes Peak area. Mr. D. E. George and his staff of the National Weather Service at Peterson Field, Colorado Springs, gave background information on the vagaries of local mountain weather. Guy Burgess, Jr., leader of the Rocky Mountain Rescue Service, shared experience and skill. Miss Louise Keber and staff of Copy Cat Reproductions helped greatly.

No undertaking of this length is done without the support of one's family. I especially want to thank Sara, who tirelessly labeled drawings and alphabetized the index; Herman for his patience and many hours of time; Jane and Susan for their interest and concern.

Dr. Willard and Mrs. Zwinger appreciate the professional advice of Marie Rodell and their editor, M. S. Wyeth, Jr., and Mrs. Zwinger is especially grateful for the encouragement and guidance of Mr. Peter Mollman, Dorothy Schmiderer and Lesley Krauss at Harper & Row.

Introduction

Tundra is a word that describes an area, a kind of vegetation, and a specific ecosystem. It is a word that characterizes the land beyond treelimit, whether it be the marshy grasslands of the Arctic with permanently frozen soils, or the high alpine reaches. The word's origin is clouded: the Lapp *tundar* means a marshy plain; the Finnish *tunturi* indicates an arctic or barren hill; the Russian *tundra* means a land of no trees and may derive from either.

There are over nine million square miles of tundra in the Northern Hemisphere, and of this forty percent is alpine. This word derives, of course, from the Alps, where some of the most thoroughly studied and familiar tundra lies. Alpine tundra lies in the region above the limit of trees and below the line of perpetual snow on all high mountains. All tundra vegetation is more uniform in aspect and composition throughout its extent than any other major vegetation type on earth. The same plant species can be found growing in Lapland, the Alps, Alaska or Colorado. The rolling, open, treeless landscape; the soil patterns caused by frost action; and the carpet of low plants can make an arctic or alpine ecologist feel remarkably at home, whether in Kamchatka, New Hampshire, India or California.

This book is concerned only with the alpine tundra of the contiguous United States. These are isolated areas of limited extent and unlimited fascination. This alpine tundra is a unique and singular world.

I find myself here because I am happiest in the mountains, and because of Marie Rodell and Bettie Willard.

Marie Rodell, literary agent and friend, suggested writing a book about alpine tundra, which had intrigued her for many years. Dr. Beatrice E. Willard, to be perfectly proper about Bettie, is an alpine ecologist. I met Bettie when she read the manuscript of a book I had written on montane ecology for the layman. Since little has been published for the lay reader in her field of American alpine ecology, she suggested collaboration on a book about it for which her theses on Rocky Mountain alpine tundra would serve as basic reference, and for which she would contribute consultation and advice, provide a list of references, glossary, and plant lists, and check for scientific accuracy. I would write and do any necessary further research for the text and draw illustrations, and my husband, Herman, in conjunction with Bettie and others, would supply color photographs.

Usually I can find Bettie sitting on a granite outcrop, notebook in hand, listing the plant species at her feet. She carefully notes the flowering stage and vigor of each, commenting upon its frequency and exact habitat, adding to her compendium of field notes, for she has studied alpine tundra in the Alps, England, and Scandinavia, as well as throughout the West. She has also conducted studies for the National Park Service on the impact of visitor use on the ecosystems of Rocky Mountain National Park, of increasing importance as the number of visitors to Park areas increases.

Since the beginning of this book several years ago, we have flown thousands of miles across the country, from the White Mountains of California to the White Mountains of New England. We have hiked and scrambled thousands of vertical feet, lunched on canned sausage and carrots in rock piles at 14,000 feet under the watchful eye of a weasel, snacked on dried fruit and nuts beside alpine streams at 12,000 feet, hurried nervously through electrical storms with crackling lightning all about at 13,000 feet, and have been sunburned by an unfiltered sun on a halcyon October day when it is hard to believe that it will ever snow.

We have been privileged to see this vast view of the United States alpine areas because Herman is a professional pilot as well as photographer. For the nongeographically oriented, like me, flying 4000 to 6000 feet above a landscape is to see a geography book illustration in three-dimensional color. Cirques where glaciers spawned; alluvial fans where mountain streams have left their deposits; snow patterns that deeply influence the vegetation patterns of the alpine tundra: all are diagrammed clearly and precisely in a way that they are not when seen from the ground or from a high-altitude commercial jet. And when one knows the pilot, sometimes he can even be persuaded to make a second pass for a better look.

Herman came to this alpine world by default: after listening to me rhapsodize about its incredible colors and patterns, his photographer's curiosity led him to suffer the problems of alpine photography. There must be enough light to stop the camera down because there is always enough wind to wobble the most carefully composed shot. Clouds scud across the sky with such rapidity and frequency that light changes constantly, and the pure colors of alpine flowers are dulled and brightened again within a second. If one gets up on the tundra early enough in the morning to avoid the wind and insure clear skies, it is more than likely cold enough to make lying on the ground a misery. Some of the flower colors are so intense that someone who has never experienced alpine colors invariably reacts by protesting that nothing could be *that* blue, and what kind of a filter was used to produce it?

There are quite likely more alpine areas in the United States than one could hike to in a lifetime, areas of total wilderness reachable only by long climbs requiring proper equipment and stamina. But some alpine areas are accessible by serviceable roads: Trail Ridge Road in Rocky Mountain National Park, the summit roads of Pikes Peak and Mount Evans, Mount Washington in New Hampshire and Obstruction Point in Olympic National Park.

We have gone to the alpine tundra both by hiking into the high country and by driving. I prefer the former. But because of the physical and physiological difficulty of working at high altitude, we have to a large extent utilized the more easily accessible areas. After one has hiked and scrambled precipitous miles upward with a twenty to forty-five pound pack, one is either too debilitated to photograph or draw, or it's already snowing. We have found that the remote areas generally follow the ecological patterns of the more accessible areas, and that there are still hundreds of isolated unstudied areas open for research. Although the more traveled areas sometimes offer less in untouched wilderness, they are the ones that most interested laymen will see and enjoy.

In order to make this book as useful as possible for those who want more detailed information about the alpine tundra, a glossary as well as a list of references for further reading are included. In addition, the reader may wish to consult *The Ecology and Phytosociology of the Tundra Curves, Trail Ridge, Colorado* (Boulder: University of Colorado, 1960), M.A. thesis by Dr. Beatrice E. Willard; *Phytosociology of the Alpine Tundra of Trail Ridge, Rocky Mountain National Park, Colorado* (Boulder: University of Colorado, 1963), Ph.D. dissertation by Dr. Beatrice E. Willard; *Grand Canyon: Daily Log and Guide Book* (Boulder, Colo.: XI Int. Bot. Cong., Field Trip No. 1, August 1–23, 1969), by W. A. Weber and Dr. Beatrice E. Willard; and *Ecology of Winter Snow-Free Areas of the Alpine Tundra of Niwot Ridge, Boulder County, Colorado* (Boulder: University of Colorado, 1958), by W. S. Osborn, Jr. A total listing of all alpine plants, including those not covered in this book, in alphabetical order by both common and scientific names, with identification data, will be found at the end of the book.

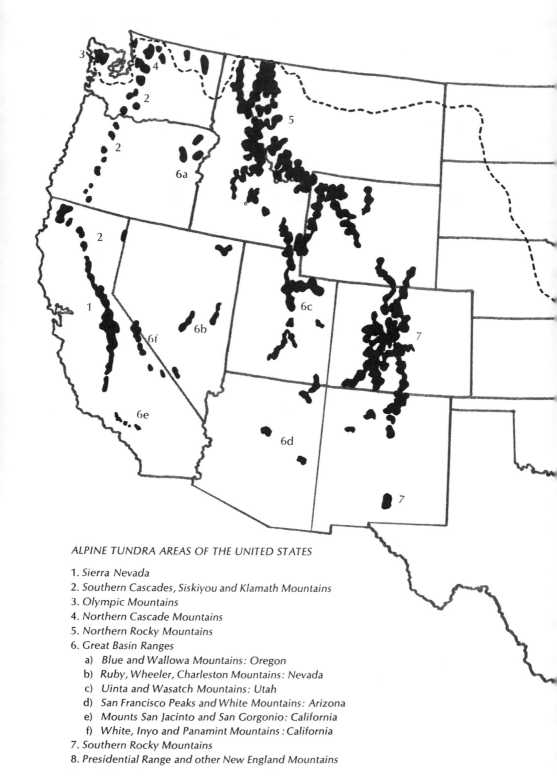

ALPINE TUNDRA AREAS OF THE UNITED STATES

1. *Sierra Nevada*
2. *Southern Cascades, Siskiyou and Klamath Mountains*
3. *Olympic Mountains*
4. *Northern Cascade Mountains*
5. *Northern Rocky Mountains*
6. *Great Basin Ranges*
   a) *Blue and Wallowa Mountains: Oregon*
   b) *Ruby, Wheeler, Charleston Mountains: Nevada*
   c) *Uinta and Wasatch Mountains: Utah*
   d) *San Francisco Peaks and White Mountains: Arizona*
   e) *Mounts San Jacinto and San Gorgonio: California*
   f) *White, Inyo and Panamint Mountains: California*
7. *Southern Rocky Mountains*
8. *Presidential Range and other New England Mountains*

Dotted line indicates extent of continental glaciation;
nearly all alpine areas had mountain glaciers.

Part One
THE ALPINE WORLD

1 : The Alpine Environment

At 8:30 on a July morning the temperature by my pocket thermometer is 38 degrees F. At 14,000 feet the breeze is light but sharply chill. In the early morning the alpine tundra has a beginning-of-the-world quality, a sense of sparseness and lucidity.

At high altitude, there is nothing between you and the sky: no tree branches, no filtering haze, no dulling pollution. Voices are often lost in the constant shushing of the wind. The tundra is a solitary world where one can feel very much alone and overwhelmed. It offers little welcome. It is a breathless place (above 11,500 feet in the southern Rockies) where rapid physical movement is an exertion, often an impossibility. The air contains less oxygen, leading not only to shortness of breath but sometimes to headache, extreme fatigue, nausea and disorientation. It is no place for anyone with a heart condition.

The alpine tundra is a land of contrast and incredible intensity, where the sky is the size of forever and the flowers the size of a millisecond. There are no trees to put one's arms around, against which to measure one's height. There are no houses or man-made mementos that give scale. The only objects larger than small are boulders. It is a strangely empty land. Few animals are in evidence. The plants are all small to infinitesimal, and in many instances relatively sparse. There is no in-between in the alpine tundra. And for humans, who live in an in-between-sized world, comprehension takes time.

The clarity of light confuses one's sense of scale. Faraway mountains are so sharp in outline that they seem much closer. The intense brightness of the light is untempered by large shadows, large buildings, or large trees. It bathes the mountains and creates a dazzling luculent landscape. There is twice as much ultraviolet radiation and twenty-five percent more light here than at sea level; the former makes sunburn cream indispensable, and the latter makes sunglasses necessary—the reflection of light off snow in the wintertime can damage vision, producing snowblindness. And psychologically, the great wash of light illuminating the alpine tundra gives one a sense of encompassing comprehension verging on euphoria.

Although it is midsummer, new snow from yesterday's storm lies opaque and white between the rocks of weathered granite at my feet. The high altitude is responsible for these summer snowfalls. The thin air holds less heat than at lower elevations; it is about thirty degrees cooler here than in the foothills, easily making the difference between rain at 6000 feet and snow up here. Although I have on a down jacket and two pairs of wool socks, I already regret not having put on an extra sweater and hood.

The ground sparkles as if sequined. At high altitudes, cold air, radiation cooling and evaporation combine to chill the snow's surface, while sunlight penetrates enough to melt the subsurface layers. When these two opposing factors of chill and heat are precisely balanced, the moisture from the thawing layer beneath the surface refreezes at the surface in a sheen of thin ice. The ice then acts as a greenhouse to trap heat and promote further melting beneath, so that there are ice bridges spanning hollows in the melting snow surface, creating a gleaming meadow. Where the snow supports beneath have melted, shattered splinters of ice lie like small piles of glass, the debris from a miniature greenhouse.

This midsummer snowstorm is of more value than harm on the

tundra. Had it fallen at 6000 feet where we live, it would have dis-
couraged most of the perennials in the garden and damaged most of
the annuals. Up here where plants are adapted to the cold it provides
precious water for all the plants beneath it. Generally the storms that
coat the alpine tundra from late March into summer are upslope
storms, characterized by a local weatherman as "weather in the weeds"
because visibility is reduced to nothing. As the air circulates in a coun-
terclockwise direction around the low pressure areas that frequently
form in northern New Mexico, it pulls in maritime subtropical Gulf of
Mexico air. When the wet winds back up against the east face of the
Rockies we are in for heavily overcast days. At lower altitudes it may
rain, but when the moist air extends up over the Continental Divide
into high elevations, the high mountains can be smothered with snow:
in April 1921 a record seventy-six inches fell in this area.

Upslope storms are usually gentle and persistent, sifting down very
moist snow, in contrast to the winter blizzards which come slashing
out of the north and west, dry and sharp, blowing the snow off almost
as quickly as it is deposited. Upslope storms come like a benediction,
with little wind and generous moisture, clinging and seeping down
into the thirsty tundra soils.

At this altitude the newly formed crystals are crisp and exquisite,
but in the warmth of summer they soon lose their spidery tracery and
metamorphose into rounded granular particles. As the delicate
branches of the crystals disintegrate, they become amorphous grains,
sliding together in a closely packed layer.

Walking up to the summit just now, I felt my boots crunch in the still-
cold snow. A southeast-facing boulder was totally coated with thick
clear ice, but beneath the ice running water made dark droplets, like
little tadpoles racing downslope, playing tag, catching each other in
continuous playful arabesques. Boulders lying below snow patches
shone with slender serpentine slivers where water plaited downward,
the dull rock enlivened by the quicksilver sparkle. A few feet farther
up the seepage was so slow that there was no glisten, just a change in
the surface color of the granite that said "damp," and the mosses were
embedded in crystal. At the top of the water trail a pika sampled the

morning breeze, alert and wary, a little handful of an animal. As soon as it heard a footstep it piped its distinctive warning and popped off its sentinel station, disappearing among the boulders.

But here on the summit not even a fly is about yet. The rocks are firmly ice-locked and on their tops hand-sized depressions still hold frozen puddles, hard mirrors with white suns. There are three small puddles in a descending row, locking the rock lichens in a glass case. Entrapped air bubbles radiate out from the center of the ice, diagrammed in tiny dotted white lines. On the bottom puddle an ice handle projects five inches upward at an angle pointing due northwest, making a crystal sundial. I cannot imagine how it was formed, although I know it must have something to do with the storm coming from the southeast. It is an evanescent timepiece, due to disappear this morning, while the rock remains nearly unchanged, telling its time in centuries, not hours.

Snow is always part of the alpine view at high altitudes. The jagged profile is of western mountain ranges solidly white in the winter, and bears vestiges of snow all summer, remnants of the great glaciers that carved and sculpted their flanks. The massive glaciers of the past were blocked out during the Pleistocene Ice Age, thousands of years ago. As more and more snow sifted onto the high peaks, it compressed the under layers into ice. As the ice froze to the rock base, any slight melting permitted water to seep into hairline cracks. Anyone who has seen a bottle of frozen milk with its cap raised on a column of white ice recognizes the formidable expansion power of ice on even a small scale.

In the tightly confined rock walls, the freezing water exerted enough force to quarry out huge boulders. As the glacier began to move, it gouged the mountain side with its own rocks, snatched out from the walls as grinding tools, joined with the scouring pressure of the ice itself. When the basin of the cirque was full, the ice moved downslope, sculpting the mountain landscape. Large ice sheets remain today only in Greenland, Alaska, Iceland and Antarctica, and mountain glaciers persist only in high cirques that receive enough snow to support them.

Over the last two million years, glaciers packed the valleys and pushed debris and rocks to the farthest extent of their passing. When they retreated they dumped moraines of rocks once held fast in icy paws, clawing reluctantly backwards, until now all that remains of their crunching passage are the U-shaped valleys, morainal lakes, and huge white thumbprints on hundreds of high-scooped cirques where they began. Even where the mountains are too low to retain snow all summer, as in the eastern mountains, the evidence of glacial passage remains on rock scratched and striated by scraping ice, moraines lying like spent dragons, and great gulfs chewed out of mountain flanks.

Many high alpine areas remained above the ice that wedged through the valleys below. But the cold and dampness marked these areas as clearly as the glaciers had marked their landscape. Much alpine tundra is more rolling and gentle than one somehow expects to see above tree line. It has a well-scrubbed, well-worn look, like an old table top perhaps, once painted nicely green, now warped, faded to a patina, chips of paint remaining only in the cracks. This worn flowing surface has been smoothed by different types of frost action, all of which work to level high mountain surfaces. The high alpine ridges surrounded but not covered by glaciers were especially subject to frost actions of the colder and wetter climate of the Pleistocene. (Today, when it is warmer and drier, these forces operate on only a very small scale.)

Permanent moisture, along with a certain temperature pattern, both depends upon and creates permafrost, the subsurface soil which has been solidly frozen for thousands of years. The combination of permafrost overlaid by saturated soil provides optimum conditions for the freeze-and-thaw phenomena that are common in both arctic and alpine regions. Rocks are heaved out of the ground, falling into polygonal patterns; soil, thawed and saturated, creeps downslope over a firm underlayer of either bedrock or permafrost or both, in a process known as solifluction, forming solifluction terraces; frost hummocks are raised, forming alternating mounds and depressions across the landscape.

The continual freezing and thawing of water eventually fractures all bare rock surfaces that it assaults. As rock fragments fall away, new layers are unsealed and opened to weathering. Over the millennia bedrock is splintered into boulders, boulders into fist-sized rocks called talus, talus into scree and gravel, and gravel into sand.

Gently curved solifluction terraces, lightly shadowed by the low sunlight, lie across the slopes on which they were molded by solifluction. Such wet soils are extremely unstable since their soil particles tend to separate rather than cohere. Solifluction is a very slow process, but over the centuries it moves enough soil downward to round off the uneven landscape. The presence of old, no longer active solifluction terraces is revealed in the subtle undulations beneath the vegetation that are characteristic of many cold regions. In small areas, where solifluction is still active in places, such as below melting snowbanks,

SOLIFLUCTION

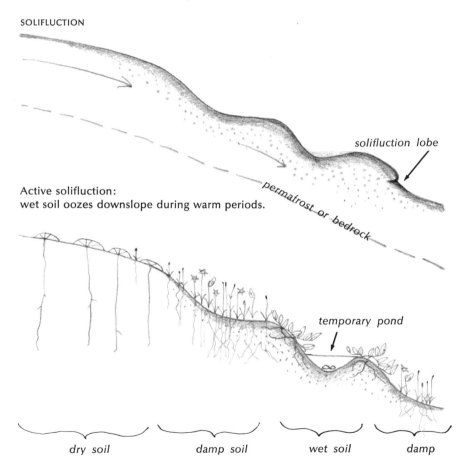

solifluction lobe

Active solifluction:
wet soil oozes downslope during warm periods.

permafrost or bedrock

temporary pond

dry soil   damp soil   wet soil   damp

Stabilized: vegetation stabilizes soil movement, taking up soil water; plant roots interweave and keep soil from slipping.

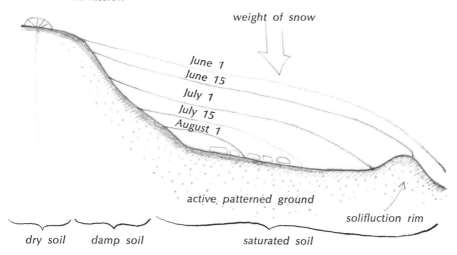

weight of snow

June 1
June 15
July 1
July 15
August 1

active patterned ground

solifluction rim

dry soil   damp soil   saturated soil

the soil is wet and crumbling, tiny chunks separating and slipping downslope even as one watches.

Old snow patches left over from winter, firmer in outline than the smaller scattered remnants of summer storms, lie in nivation depressions. A cross-section of such a depression shows a gentle backslope that drops more sharply just as it contacts the almost level floor. The weight of the snow operates like a thumb on a toothpaste tube, pressing the wet lubricated soil out from beneath; one or several solifluction terraces may rim the front edge. A nivation depression has erosive effect in proportion to the depth and duration of the snowcover and the degree of slope on which it lies.

Freezing and thawing also force buried rocks to the surface where they roll into depressions, forming the "patterned ground" observed in nearly all tundra areas. As ice forms in the soil, the soil's volume increases, creating pressure on the solid rocks and expelling them. Often "patterned ground" has amorphous arrangements of rock in undefined heaps and piles, like the sea of huge rocks forming a felsenmeer, or the scattered patches of smaller stones pock-marking the turfs. Sometimes the patterning is as precise and clear as if drawn for a textbook illustration. Long rock streams flow downslope or drape across slope, pulling into garlands where the slope steepens. Sometimes huge polygons are formed, often with smaller patterns netted within. Where patterned ground occurs in regions other than tundra, it

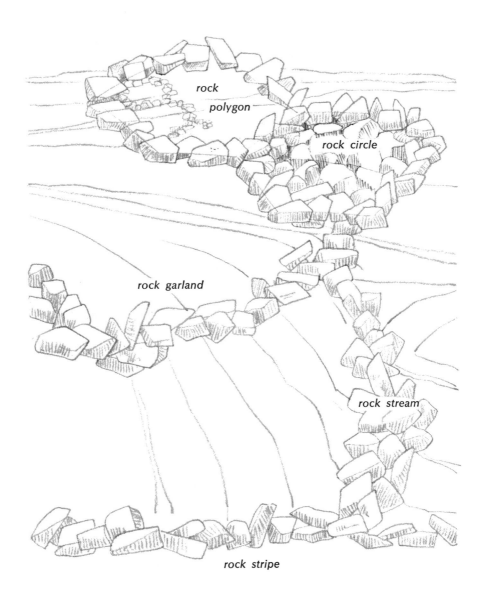

rock
polygon

rock circle

rock garland

rock stream

rock stripe

PATTERNED GROUND

The degree of slope determines the rock patterns which form patterned ground. Polygons and circles form on level surfaces; smaller patterns may appear within these. Rock streams flow downhill. If rocks are extruded across the fall line of the slope, they create rock stripes; where the slope steepens, gravity pulls them into stone garlands.

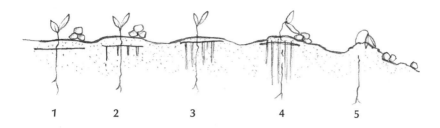

NEEDLE ICE FORMATION
1. A thin layer of ice forms near the soil surface.
2. Water is pulled up from saturated soil to form needles perpendicular to this thin layer.
3. Ice continues to form; its increased volume raises the soil surface.
4. As the mound elevates, seedling roots tear and small rocks are displaced.
5. Warming and/or drying stop needle ice formation, leaving dead plants and a granulated soil surface open to erosion.

is a clue to previous climatic conditions. Old patterns are often buried in alpine meadows by the build-up of soil and thick growth of meadow grasses and sedges.

Needle ice forms at all elevations, usually in the spring or fall, but is a more marked phenomenon at high altitudes where freezing temperatures are common even in summer. It has two prerequisites: very wet soil and temperatures that drop slowly below the freezing point. Needle ice is most visible when ice crystals raise the soil and are revealed like bundles of glass threads. It is most commonly seen in hummocks of damp granulated earth near streams or in other sites with ample moisture, fine soil, and little or no plant cover. Needle ice formation is exceedingly common in bare alpine soils where it can form throughout the summer.

Ice congeals first parallel to the surface of the soil; freezing proceeds slowly downwards. The freezing water attracts free water from deeper in the wet soil, sucking it through soil pores to freeze into long ice needles perpendicular to the soil surface. Needles can continue solidifying for long periods without being melted by daytime warmth, and ice formation for each day shows in the needles' stratification. As they grow in length, the rapidity of the ice formation decreases as water from below is used up, and needles seldom grow longer than five inches.

When needle ice forms on inclined slopes, the dirt and pebbles it raises often roll downslope, causing a considerable amount of soil movement and instability. The crumbly soil lifted by needle ice is porous, dries quickly, and is easily windblown; it has a distinctive granular appearance. Seedlings which invade the bare ground are wrenched up. Both the heaving action of the ice, breaking plant roots and stems, and exposure to wind drying prevent plants from becoming established where needle ice is active. Conversely, needle ice is seldom formed where there is good plant cover.

Present-day frost action is most marked in wet areas. Tiny patterns of pebbles and small rocks tile seep areas. Hummocks, from teacup size to that of a large pillow, are raised across an alpine bog. Some of the hummocks are low, while others have been elevated by the frost heaving that lifts their plant cover out of the thin winter snow blanket of the marsh into the murderous environment of an alpine winter. Small snow drifts form between the hummocks in early fall, but leave the higher tops free of snow and exposed to wind, freezing and drying. Several dead and desiccated plants hold to the soil by a root thread, ready to fall away with the first tug.

When plant cover is finally torn away, needle ice crumbles the soil, and it is soon vacuumed away by winter winds. When the insulating layer of soil on top is reduced and removed by wind erosion, the permafrost beneath the hummock retreats. Surface water penetrates deeper and frost heaving begins, creating a frost scar. Buried rocks are pushed up and out through the scar at the top of the hummock. As the stones are extruded they tumble down the sides of the convex frost-heaved center. Eventually the center of the hummock is lowered and leveled, leaving a center of fine materials ringed by the ejected rocks.

Plants insinuate themselves into the edges of the rock rings; these edges are more stable than the still-active centers of the frost boils where roots and rhizomes are continually torn. As soil begins to build up over the rocks, other plants are able to grow. As more vegetation begins to insulate the frost boil center, frost activity decreases and still

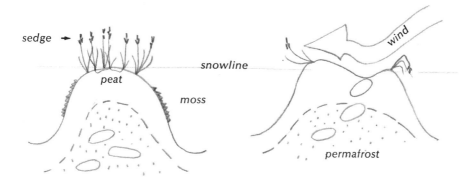

sedge →

snowline

peat

moss

wind

permafrost

1. A typical frost hummock is topped with sedges; mosses frost the sides. The peat soil overlies permafrost.
2. When the top of the hummock is raised above the snowline by expanding ice mass, winter winds remove the insulating layer of peat, and the permafrost retreats.

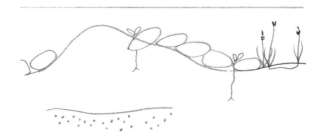

3. With permafrost deeper beneath ground, water penetrates the soil. Frost heaving pushes rocks out of the erosion scar at the top; they tumble down to form a ring around the deflated hummock.

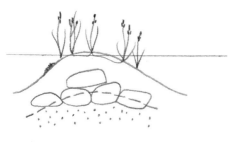

4. Small plants, followed by sedges, invade the rock rings. As the sedges flourish, they build up soil. The soil insulates the hummock and permafrost rises. When the top of the hummock is raised beyond the snowline, the cycle will begin anew.

more plants colonize the center of the boil. When heaving finally subsides altogether, plant cover becomes almost total. When the hummock is again raised to eroding winds, the cycle begins anew.

Wind is a constant presence at high altitude. Its average velocity increases with height above sea level and with height above ground. It erodes soil and nudges turfs until "wind scarps" are carved out. It dictates the shape of plants, scatters seeds, spores and pollen, distributes lichens that reproduce by fragmentation, and molds the snow surface into fanciful sculptures. It plucks at one's clothing and waters the eyes. It makes hiking tiring and exasperating. It increases the intensity of evaporation at high altitude; chapped lips and dehydration are two discomforts for which every experienced mountain hiker is prepared.

Wind distributes snow, the most important factor controlling plant communities in the alpine region. Under the snow, plants are protected from the wind; above it, they are pruned back. The prevailing westerly winds move clouds rapidly across the sky, constantly altering light values and bringing the afternoon storms and clouds that are frequent in alpine areas; the differential wind velocities above the ground move different layers of clouds at varying speeds, creating kaleidoscopic skies.

Wind further lowers high-altitude temperatures by the severity of the chill factor. A few drops of warm water on the back of the hand become cool when blown upon; on a cool day at high altitude, a thirty-mile wind can lower the temperature twenty degrees, a chill factor which makes high-altitude work extremely hazardous at lower temperatures, freezing exposed flesh in a matter of seconds. Wind velocities are the greatest in winter and spring. In the winter they make working conditions above treelimit nearly impossible, demanding special equipment and clothing, as well as extreme self-discipline and stamina. In the spring warm "chinook" winds often reach gale velocity, evaporating the snows of eastern mountain slopes like a blow torch.

Since wind speed and pressure increase with height above ground, the environment is colder and windier at a man's height than at plant height. The difference can be discerned by lying prone and becoming part of the plant world; indeed, sometimes this is the only place one can work comfortably. The wind still twitches and frets the grasses at eight inches, but scarcely nudges the small cushions and mats at two.

When the wind is strong, it carries sand and snow and has considerable abrasive effect at the ground surface, pitting and sculpting outcrops on the windward side, sand-blasting bark and twigs. If water is not available to plants at these times, either because the soil is frozen or because of lack of moisture, strong ground winds cause plants to wilt as if under severe drought. Wind desiccation is most lethal in the winter when it prunes all elevated growth.

Local upslope winds, caused by ground heating in the lowlands, begin about midmorning. The air at lower elevations absorbs ground warmth from the sun-heated soil; the air expands and rises, cooling about 3 degrees F for every thousand feet. If there is enough moisture in the air, this cooling often causes afternoon precipitation of either rain or snow. At sunset, when the soil on high mountain ridges cools rapidly, the thin air loses its heat quickly and becomes heavier, flowing downslope at night. Because of this cold air drainage, the tundra may often be warmer at night than the subalpine valleys below: campers have learned to pitch their tents anywhere but the bottom of a subalpine valley.

These continental and mountain wind patterns are further modified by very local variations in mountain terrain—the direction a steep slope faces, rock outcrops, steep valleys—which cause eddies, gusting and Venturi effects. In a Venturi, as the wind passes through a constriction, the air pressure drops and the wind accelerates. In one high valley that faces east, the high-water mark of the trees at its head is notched with a distinct "V." The relief of the landscape at this particular spot channels the wind, causing the Venturi effect. An eddy is created that drops a large amount of snow in the lee of the notch, snow which lasts long into the growing season. The increased velocity of the wind lowers temperature by several degrees; at treelimit, this can be the difference between freezing and nonfreezing, tree growth and no tree growth.

The alpine tundra is a place of infinite enchantment, causing a reluctance to go down at the end of the day, and one finds as many excuses as possible to prolong the descent. The next outcrop catches my attention: what small plants grow in its shelter? A glimmer of water across slope piques the curiosity. I walk to it and explore, finding tiny pink alpine willowherb and deep blue speedwell at its margin; I am pulled by an inexplicable curiosity and fascination.

The sun disappears as I poke around the outer edges of the little pond, and I take off my backpack to get out my down sweater. The wind is suddenly chill and sharp; I have foolishly miscalculated the alpine weather, forgetting in my concentration the caprice of its clouds and the swiftness of its tempers.

Towards the east the plains are still sun-bathed. To the west a mountain storm, like a hand across the sun, shreds across the peaks. As lightning flashes I automatically begin to count, "One-thousand-one, one-thousand-two, one-thousand-three, one-thousand-four," hoping to get to the seven that means the strike is a mile away. When thunder rolls down the valley below, the strike is less than half a mile away, too close for comfort. The thunder echoes from ahead and behind, as it must have sounded to Rip van Winkle.

This natural amphitheater gathers in the direct blast of the storm and piles it up against the surrounding slopes. The wind swirls like a dervish and snatches off my hood. The first raindrops hit with the force of hail. Then graupel—a kind of half-snow, half-hail common in the mountains—drives horizontally, stinging my face with the force of hurled gravel. It whitens the ground like handfuls of tapioca, and dances off the rocks like popcorn. My hands ache with the cold. I cannot see ten feet in front of me. The snow and sleet smoke all around. I wish I had my windbreaker. I have grim thoughts of death by exposure when body temperature drops to ninety-two degrees and body heat cannot replace it, and I think of things I wish I had told my children.

Lightning detonates again. A human on the treeless tundra is often the highest object and therefore a lightning attractor. Sighting the wall above me, I hope that I am within the forty-five-degree angle that deflects direct hits. To be safer, I crouch down on a narrow ridge of dirt within a cluster of rocks slightly higher than I. I shove my backpack under me for balance and insulation, and hunch to form the least possible lightning focus. My heart pounds against my knees.

Lightning and thunder seem to hit simultaneously—I hear the

lightning bang and feel the percussion of the thunder. I discipline myself to making a visual check of my surroundings to be sure I've avoided a damp gully that carries ground current, the discharge of lightning that travels through damp soil and is as fatal as a direct hit. I take care not to touch the rocks so that I do not conduct current from them. Ground currents can be strong enough to make rocks buzz and one's muscles twitch. It takes no imagination to feel the ominous presence of electrical emanations from the surrounding malevolent rocks.

Looking at the crevice plants within the few square inches of my vision, I try to reassure myself with the physical fact of their survival. The tiny furred cushion plant is adapted to take advantage of minimum warmth and moisture, and a growing season of less than three months, securely anchored by its deep taproot. A wolf spider hies to safety beneath it. I envy the pika, tucked safely behind his boulders, able to survive on the herbs and grasses of the tundra summer. Everything that lives here is adapted to survive here. Humans are not.

The hail and rain stop as suddenly as they began, and a shaft of sunlight fingers a distant peak. I stand up and brush myself off, drier than I expected to be, a little stiff but very much alive. Every flower and grass quivers in the wind and shakes itself free of the weight of the water drops. One by one the stems spring upright, shaken by the fresh breeze. The sunlight catches each drop of rain still pendant, and even the rocks glitter in the brilliant crystalline light. I feel a primitive sense of survival, a renewed and refreshed sense of living—and considerable relief that the storm is over. I feel like running across the slope, but one who dashes across this rocky terrain is both foolish and winded, and might miss something. I walk sensibly back, seeing in every windrow of graupel and every white parenthesis of hail that snow is eternally a part of the alpine world, and that winter is never more than six weeks away.

2 : Alpine Plant Adaptations

Life survives at these outer and upper extremes of the environment because it has been rigorously selected and adapted to the harsh conditions that surround it. The more severe the environmental conditions, the more pronounced are the adaptations for plant and animal survival. Adaptations generally involve characteristics that are immediately responsive to environmental conditions of temperature, light, moisture, etc. Most adaptations persist, retained by a plant even if moved to another habitat, where the same plant may or may not be adapted to survive; a dwarf alpine, for as long as it survives in a lowland garden, remains a dwarf.

Documentation of some of the physiological adaptations of plants that survive at high altitudes was provided by a series of transplant gardens maintained on a transect across California. Gardens were maintained at sea level, mid-altitude, and tree line: California is one of the few places in the world where vegetation changes so rapidly in such a short distance. The main purpose of the transplant experiments was to discover the extent to which changes in plant species are hereditary or environmental, and to explore the physiological mechanisms that help plants to adjust to changing climates and habitats, changes that eventually result in the creation of different plant species.

At the same time, the physical qualities of plants in specific environments were extracted and compiled. Alpine tundra plants as a group had shorter, slenderer, less branched and fewer flowering stems; fewer and smaller leaves; and fewer flowers. However, the size of the individual flowers remained the same in all plants, alpine or otherwise. This change in proportion between plant and flower gives many alpine plants the appearance of oversized flowers on dwarf plants.

The studies documented that a large proportion of alpine plants are marked with the distinctive red color of anthocyanin pigments in stems and leaves, the pigment which makes red apples red. Anthocyanin reds range from the red-purple of red cabbage and beets to the orange-red of poppies, the lavender of violets, and the blue of cornflowers, depending upon whether the plant's sap is acid (producing reds) or alkaline (producing blues). It is especially marked in the springtime, before photosynthesis is fully operative in the leaves. Colored pigments are present in all green leaves, but are usually masked by the greater amount of green chlorophyll, visible only when the chlorophyll is reduced or absent, or other pigments are in greater abundance.

Anthocyanins are a product of the carbohydrates stored in the roots from the previous growing season. When rapid growth begins in early spring, part of the carbohydrates is incorporated into new plant tissue and part into anthocyanins. The redness appears only in those cells exposed to light: the origami-folded leaves of an incipient alpine avens, if spread open, are green inside, but when released they assume their complex folding, and only the red shows. Anthocyanins are capable of converting incident light rays into heat to warm plant tissues, important in the chill temperatures of an alpine spring. Those plants which have an abundance of anthocyanins endure cold better than greener plants, and anthocyanin production is an important factor in cold-hardiness, an essential attribute at high altitudes. A great many plants on the tundra have red-tinged leaves and stems, giving a distinctive tonality at the beginning and end of the growing season.

In the California plant experiments, alpine plants at treelimit were able to flower earlier and set fruit earlier than lower mountain or lowland plants, giving them an advantage in an environment with an abbreviated growing season. Plants brought up to treelimit were severely injured by spring frosts and were seldom able to flower, let alone set seed, and most died the first season.

Nor did natives from high altitudes survive at sea level, and this led to the speculation that some alpine plants may be so physiologically adapted to the short cold growing season of the tundra that they are limited to it, unable to survive at lower altitudes because of increased rates of photosynthesis and respiration (burning the products of photosynthesis with oxygen for plant growth) that deplete an alpine plant in the higher temperatures of lower elevations. This is comparable to the runner who runs the hundred-yard dash in a brief concerted effort. A man running the mile measures himself over the course and could not complete the race with the all-out burst of speed possible for the shorter span.

A few plants live in the tundra by default, perhaps finding too much competition at lower altitudes; these flourished when taken down to mid-altitude gardens. But those taken all the way down to sea level were unsuccessful although they might survive a few years. It was determined that, other factors being equal, early blooming and frost resistance probably best fit a plant for survival at high altitude, and indeed, early flowering is one of the marked characteristics of alpine plants. The better a plant species can adapt to the short alpine growing season, the more quickly it can complete its life cycle, the more successful it is in the high mountains. Early flowering leaves the major part of the meagre summer warmth for ripening seeds, a process which requires heat that flowering does not.

Many alpine plants are able to begin growing, and their roots to absorb nutrients, just above 32 degrees F, and to grow very rapidly since they are also able to carry on photosynthesis at lower temperatures. Most lowland plants require temperatures in the 40's or 50's or above. Respiration rates are more rapid in alpine plants at low temperatures than in those growing in temperate regions. The initial burgeoning of growth is somewhat independent of alpine weather, and this is fortunate because few plants could even sprout in the kind of weather under which the alpine tundra congeals in the spring, or in the blankets of snow that may descend in the middle of summer.

Flower buds are often begun early in the previous year's growing season, sometimes even several years before, and are usually well-formed by the end of the summer so that they are safely protected before winter sets in. Studies on an alpine buttercup that grows in Norway pinpointed a cell which eventually gave rise to the yellow flower: it formed the first year, divided many times during the second growing season, formed bud during the third, and finally came to bloom in the fourth summer. The great advantage of this extended growth pattern is that stem growth and flowering can and do occur very quickly after snow melt. Flowering is more dependent upon the environmental conditions of the previous summer or summers than on the immediate icy spring of bloom. Setting and ripening seed, or reproducing vegetatively, do require summer heat which such preset flowering does not, and the reproductive structures have time to develop in the maximum warmth of the alpine summer.

Early growth is also made possible because of the large amount of starches and sugars stored as carbohydrates in below-ground parts during the last summer's growing season. When the plant is dormant during winter's forbiddingly low temperatures, these underground reserves are not reduced. As the temperature warms, growth resumes and the accumulated carbohydrates are converted for rapid sprouting. During this time growth may be so rapid that food is used up faster than it can be made, and the carbohydrates are to a large degree depleted. The plant may even grow at a deficit until its growth is about seventy-five to ninety percent completed for the season. Then expansion slows and the replenishment of carbohydrate reserves begins. By the onset of dormancy in the fall, the underground carbohydrate reserves are back to the highest level of the year.

In addition, alpine plants are all small plants, a size advantage that keeps them both snugged low to the ground and out of the worst of alpine weather, and requires less energy for the production of plant tissue. Dwarfing usually involves only the growth shoots, making the flowers *seem* larger in proportion. The fundamental form and growth pattern of the plant is already impressed at a very early stage of growth, when environmental influences are yet at a minimum; hence the flower size is relatively unaltered.

A large proportion of the flowering plants in the tundra are grasses and sedges (dwarf heath shrubs are prevalent in the eastern alpine). The narrow leaves and stems of grasses and sedges are not likely to be torn by alpine winds; their flowers are reduced to essentials—no bright petals or cupped sepals, just the reproductive parts enclosed in a simple protective envelope. They are extremely hardy, thriving in the cooler climates and alpine reaches. Of the more colorful flowering plants, most belong to the Rose, Pink, Buckwheat, Mustard and Saxifrage families, plant families also more prevalent in the temperate zone than in the tropics. Cold-hardiness seems to be a quality of many genera within these families. There are no outliers of tropical plant families at high altitude.

There are many nonflowering plants—lichens, mosses and clubmosses—with minimal requirements for survival. Lichens are formed from a fungus and an alga; fungus forms the tough outer layers while the inner layers contain algal cells enmeshed in fungal threads. This association produces a more elaborate and durable plant than either fungus or alga achieves alone. Specific species of fungus and alga form specific species of lichen. Lichens, crusted on rocks or clinging to soil, have the ability to absorb more than their own weight of water after a spell of dry weather. They can carry on food production at any temperature above 32 degrees F. If temporary liquid is available, such as dew, it can be taken almost directly into the algal cells of the lichen and does not need to enter a complicated conducting system by way of soil and roots, upon which vascular plants primarily depend.

Mosses too are spongelike, greening and fruiting in minimal warmth. Mosses curl their leaves tightly against the stem when dry, unfolding them to absorb moisture through the whole leaf surface during a rain or heavy dew.

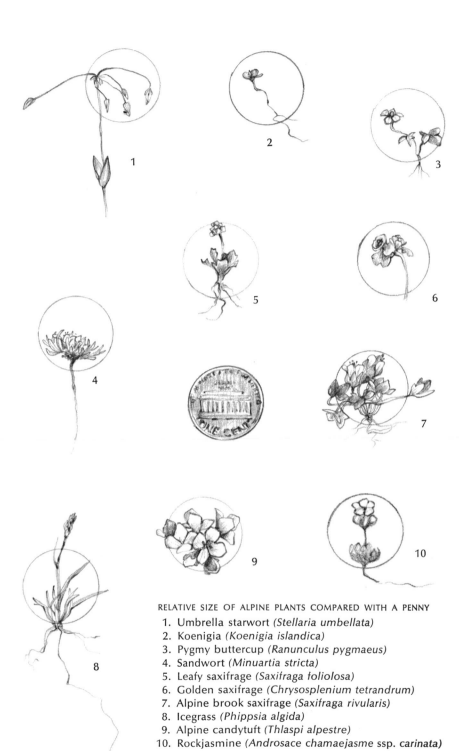

RELATIVE SIZE OF ALPINE PLANTS COMPARED WITH A PENNY

1. Umbrella starwort (Stellaria umbellata)
2. Koenigia (Koenigia islandica)
3. Pygmy buttercup (Ranunculus pygmaeus)
4. Sandwort (Minuartia stricta)
5. Leafy saxifrage (Saxifraga foliolosa)
6. Golden saxifrage (Chrysosplenium tetrandrum)
7. Alpine brook saxifrage (Saxifraga rivularis)
8. Icegrass (Phippsia algida)
9. Alpine candytuft (Thlaspi alpestre)
10. Rockjasmine (Androsace chamaejasme ssp. carinata)

Most alpine plants are perennials; they do not have to expend the energy necessary in producing stems, leaves, flowers and fruit all in one short growing season as an annual does. Instead they add to what is already established, depending upon a stable root system, able to survive without flower if either the season is bad or the plant is not yet large enough to have energy for both leafing and flowering. In the alpine tundra some plants may be ten to fifteen years old or more before they flower. Alpine perennials have winter buds protected just below or at or just above the soil surface; plants with winter buds well above the soil, like trees, cannot survive here.

In most alpine tundra there are few or no annuals; in the Colorado Rockies there is only one, a minute buckwheat called koenigia. This is out of a total list of well over three hundred Colorado alpine species. The White Mountains in California have about half that number of flowering plants, and the East Coast alpine areas contain about a third. Since there are some 100,000 species of plants recorded for the tropics alone, the number of alpine plants in itself is telling: only a few can survive the stringent requirements of an alpine climate.

Cushion plants give a distinctive low-growing aspect to the alpine tundra. They dot the ground and espalier over the rocks in a growth habit peculiar to other cold and dry regions; some of these high dry rock fields have even been called "alpine deserts." Cushion plants are the ideal pioneers in windy areas. Their low-growing streamlined shape allows the wind to flow over them as over an airplane wing. At the same time, there is maximum exposed leaf surface for photosynthesis with minimum exposure to the elements. Temperatures may be several degrees higher inside a cushion plant than outside; the colder it is outside, the greater the difference. The outer part of the cushion slows the impact of the wind on the inner part and reduces its drying effect. The hemispherical shape is caused by short dense branching; the inter-

CUSHION GROWTH PATTERN

Branches of a moss campion *(Silene acaulis* ssp. *acaulescens)* form a tightly interwoven cushion, connecting to a central taproot. The cushion traps wind-blown debris and dead leaves, slowly raising the level of soil within its periphery.

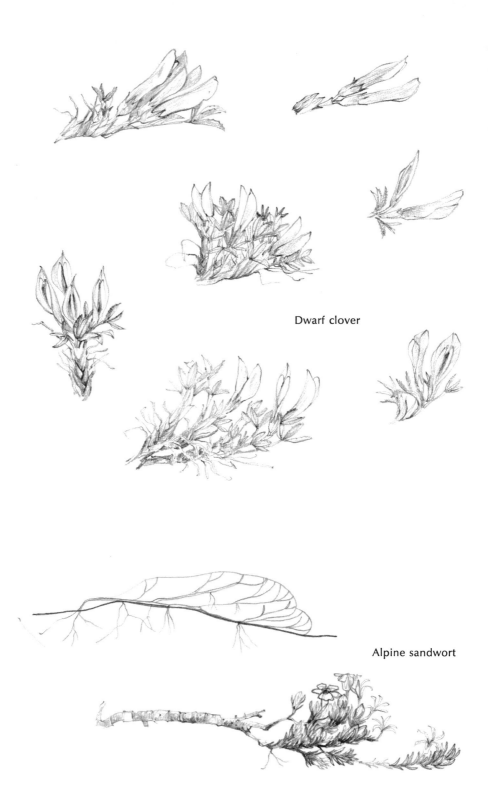

Dwarf clover

Alpine sandwort

action of the plant with drying wind and sun and abrading snow have resulted in an even thickly branched cushion.

Moss campion, a circumpolar plant, is the prototype cushion. The stubby branches catch and hold blown-in dirt which, together with old leaves, absorbs moisture, contributing to soil building and stabilization and giving each plant an extra tablespoon of moisture. The wind is so reduced within the cushion that not even the dried bits move. Even after a plant is dead, the dry tussock remains anchored, the stems closed together and interlocked with dead leaves. When the wind finally sands them off, the bare cushion has a distinctive pattern of close-packed circles, each a separate ring of leaf stubs around the clipped stems.

In a community of slow-growing plants, moss campion grows fairly rapidly. It may reach half an inch in five years, and requires about twenty-five years to reach seven inches if it has no competition from other plants. It may be ten years old before flowering, and twenty-before it flowers profusely. Most of the early growth energy goes into establishing a good root system; a cushion the size of a salad plate may have a four- to five-foot taproot that probes for deep water and anchors the plant against the constant wind.

Mat plants are also specially adapted to alpine conditions but are more spreading instead of tightly cushioned. Where the spreading branches of alpine sandwort or dwarf clover touch the ground, they are able to root, attaching the mat over a wider area than the cushion, which tends to grow from a single rootstalk. Mats are less compact in growth than a cushion, but are equally tenacious. A dwarf clover roots so often and so tightly to the ground that it is almost impossible to separate the branches to discern its growing pattern.

MAT GROWTH
Dwarf clover (Trifolium nanum) may root so frequently that it is almost continuously attached to the ground in a growth pattern that may equal the tenacity of a cushion.
Alpine sandwort (Minuartia obtusiloba), still bearing last year's dried seedpods, reveals the more open but still low mat growth form.

ROSETTE GROWTH

The radial symmetry of a rosette of a tundra dandelion *(Taraxacum cerato-phorum)*, although limited in expansion, exposes a maximum amount of leaf surface to light.

An alpine rosette resembles, in perennial form, the first year's growth of a lowland biennial such as mullein. A rosette may be even less exposed to desiccating winds than a cushion since it may be flatter to the ground. It grows in the warmer air at the soil's surface, receiving direct sunlight as well as reflected heat from beneath. There is little or no vertical separation between the leaves, thus a happy balance is attained between the greatest exposure to light and the least exposure to cold, wind damage and drying. Water coming from the roots has the shortest possible distance to travel to the leaf tip.

Radial symmetry is especially efficient for plants whose moisture, light and nutrients come from all directions, as is the case with many alpine plants that have no trees or large shrubs either to shade them or to usurp soil moisture. But the rosette is a confined form, never able to achieve the extension of a cushion, and expansion is only accomplished by the addition of new rosettes.

Snowball saxifrage *(Saxifraga rhomboidea)*

Big-rooted springbeauty *(Claytonia megarhiza)*

Succulence, combined with a rosette form, provides even greater protection against high-altitude desiccation. A perfect rosette of big-rooted springbeauty, the size of a saucer, is ruffled beneath with pale pink flowers. The fleshy leaves are succulent, a shiny dark green, often fine-lined with red on the edge. They are coated with a waxy surface that prevents evaporation of precious moisture. The taproot, often as thick as a thumb or thicker, may go down six feet or more into the soil, growing downward where the ground is cooled by a rock above. Snowball saxifrages with similar rosettes stud the fellfields and turfs.

Yellow stonecrop *(Sedum lanceolatum)*

Succulence, also common in desert plants, is another adaptation for water retention. Stonecrop rosettes, the size of marbles, are reminiscent of desert plants. Not only are the leaves protected with a cutinized surface, but they also retain water because of a profusion of interior cells filled with a slightly mucilaginous sap, unlike the watery sap of most plants.

Many alpine plants look pale gray-green, a softness of color even more distinctive when the flowers are not in bloom. These plants are as green as lowland ones beneath their various coatings of all kinds of hairs: short and spiny, glandular, stellate, long and soft and crinkled, tangled, strigose, felty, attached in the middle, closely laid and scattered. Bladderpod leaves look like snakeskin, heavily covered with hairs as many-branched as a sun starfish. Leaves of oval-leafed buckwheat growing in the far western mountains seem covered with quilt batting, a heavy layer which can be peeled off intact to reveal the green beneath. The underside of a snow cinquefoil leaf is covered with crinkled hairs, looking like a wool ski sock under the microscope. Red-stemmed cinquefoil is furred with long silky hairs, and alpine cinquefoil has crinkled and straight hairs intermixed.

These hairs protect the plant's stomata, the pores through which a plant breathes. The hairs diffuse the strong alpine light, reducing both the intensity and directness of that reaching the leaf surface since light levels on a mountain top are so much more intense than at sea level. Although this is not sufficient to upset photosynthesis, it may cause cell damage if combined with high reflection from rock or snow sur-

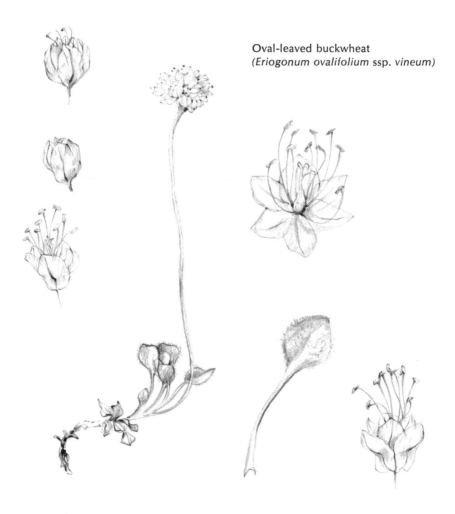

Oval-leaved buckwheat
(*Eriogonum ovalifolium* ssp. *vineum*)

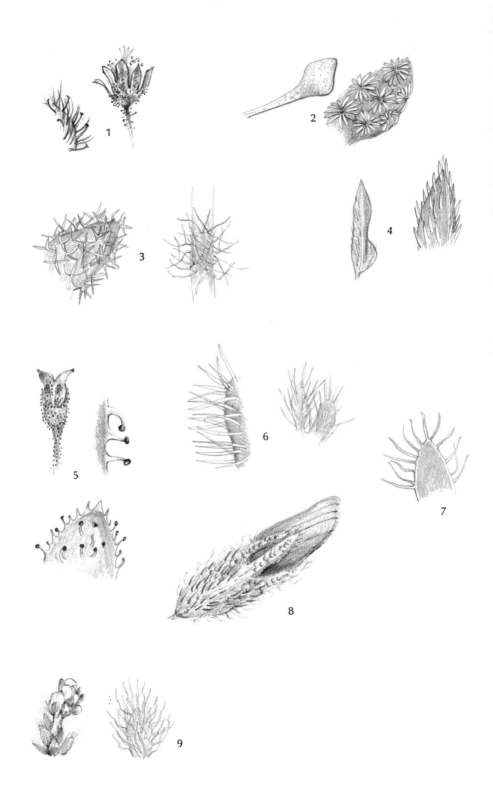

faces. The same insulating hairs can also measurably reduce water loss, of immense value in an area of sparse moisture and high winds.

While hairs reflect visible light rays they trap heat rays, warming the surface of the plant in a greenhouse effect. An alpine forget-me-not bud looks like an elfin fur muff. The dark brown hairs on an alpine poppy bud and the black hairs on the sepals of a black-headed snow buttercup absorb even more heat than white hairs, warming the nascent flower within. Some of the furriest species are the earliest flowering.

There are various means of vegetative reproduction that occur at lower altitudes but are proportionately more widespread at high altitudes. Plants which reproduce in this way are most prevalent in wet and moist areas where the growing season is so short as to make seed production unreliable; time-consuming reproductive processes are the first to be curtailed from lack of heat and time. Often a plant that produces seed at lower altitudes, as some bluegrasses, reproduces vegetatively at high altitudes. Vegetative reproduction also allows rapid colonization of areas of newly opened ground, since there is nourishment available from the parent plant, an advantage over the seedling which must seek its own nutrition from soil and water.

Rhizomes, bulblets, runners, layering, corms, and underground bulbs are all modifications of bud-bearing stems, and are all methods of vegetative reproduction. Many alpine lichens can become established

VARIOUS TYPES OF HAIRS ON ALPINE PLANTS
1. Alpine dryad (*Dryas octopetala* ssp. *hookeriana*): mixed nail-shaped and featherlike hairs.
2. Alpine bladderpod (*Lesquerella alpina*): stellate hairs.
3. Golden and twisted-pod draba (*Draba aurea* and *D. streptocarpa*): pilose, with branched and forked hairs.
4. Green-leaf chiming bells (*Mertensia viridis*): strigose hairs.
5. Whiplash saxifrage (*Saxifraga flagellaris*): glandular pubescent hairs.
6. Alpine cryptantha (*Cryptantha nubigena*): slender bristly hairs.
7. Rockjasmine (*Androsace chamaejasme* ssp. *carinata*): silky ciliate hairs.
8. Sticky locoweed (*Oxytropis viscida*): black and white hairs with sticky glandular pubescence.
9. Alpine forget-me-not (*Eritrichium aretioides*): villous, with long soft, somewhat wavy hairs.

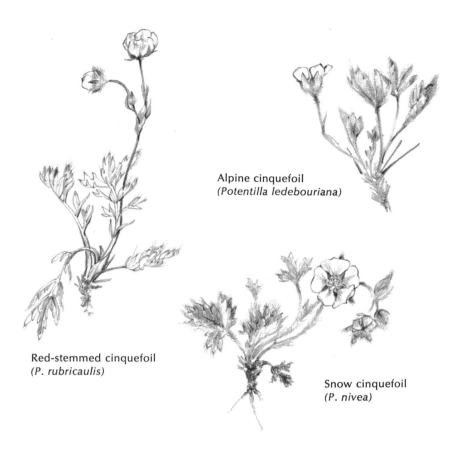

Alpine cinquefoil
(Potentilla ledebouriana)

Red-stemmed cinquefoil
(P. rubricaulis)

Snow cinquefoil
(P. nivea)

elsewhere from small bits broken off from the parent plant. The disadvantage of vegetative reproduction is that it is asexual, and there are none of the different combinations produced by the crossing of two different plants. The new plant produced by vegetative means is an exact reproduction of its parent.

Underground rhizomes are subterranean sprouting stems that are very common in both arctic and alpine plants, and particularly common in the Grass, Mint, Sedge, Rush and Iris families. Any gardener who has planted mint in his garden and attempted to control its wanderings is familiar with the tenacity of rhizomes; some of the most aggressive sea-level weeds, such as Canadian thistle, spread by this means.

In a cold climate this opportunistic assumption of new territory is of definite advantage. Rhizomes persist from year to year, forming new buds underground and carrying successive generations outward from the parent plant. Although rhizome spread is gradual in the alpine tundra, the new shoots have abundant food reserves from the parent plant that insures their establishment. The shorter the growing season, the greater the proportion of rhizomatous plants in the area. Whether or not new rhizomes are produced each year, the parent plant endures. The rhizomes spread out into the open soil, interconnecting in the muck like a giant disarticulated spider web.

New sedge *(Carex nova)* and Chestnut rush *(Juncus castaneus)* showing rhizomes

rhizomes

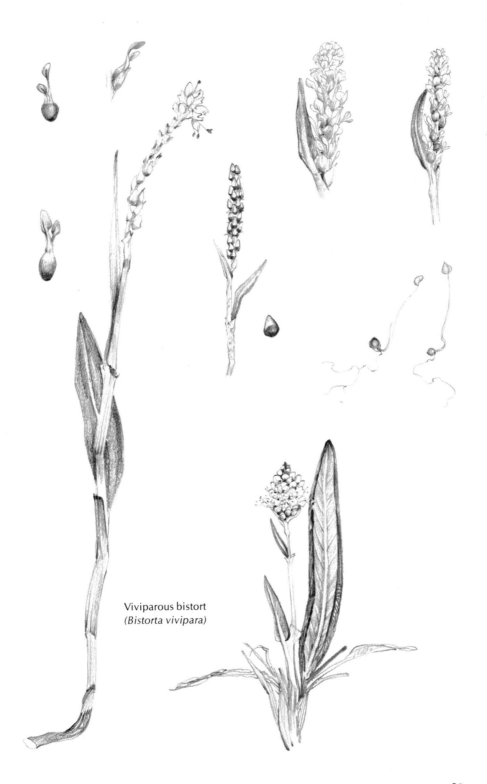

Viviparous bistort
(*Bistorta vivipara*)

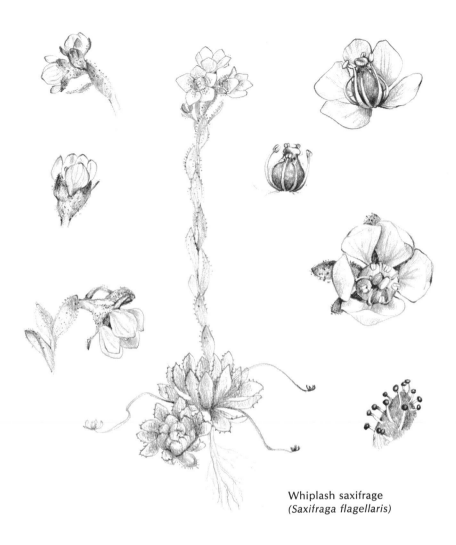

Whiplash saxifrage
(Saxifraga flagellaris)

One of the most prolific plants in the alpine tundra is viviparous bistort. It bears an insignificant-looking stalk of small white flowers with protruding rosy anthers at the top of the stalk, and bulblets beneath. Bulblets are tiny kernels of plants that fall from the parent stalk and are able to establish themselves during the same growing season as that in which they are produced, often sprouting before they separate from the parent plant. They are relatively large and heavy (compared to moss gentian seeds the size of a pepper grain, or the infinitesimal spore of a moss) and lack any apparent adaptation to wind transport. Yet the tiny red tops turn up by the dozen in almost every handful of soil.

Other plants send runners over the ground, strawberry-fashion. Whiplash saxifrage is able to invade bare areas by dropping the tiny rosette of a new plant up and over a pebble. The rosette draws nourishment from the mother plant until it has rooted and then the connection disintegrates.

The tiny alplily of the Alps and Rockies produces new buds from its green-onion-sized bulb. Most lilies expand in this manner, the bulbs developing clusters of new shoots depending upon the felicity of the growing conditions.

Despite the forbidding alpine climate—severe cold, cutting wind, sparse warmth—alpine plants have a vigor all out of proportion to their seeming delicacy of size. Every empty spot of soil, if it is not actively stirred by frost action, contains sprigs of new growth, infinitesimal plants that have survived the first summer. And although they may not survive the second, a few will endure and persist, maintaining the life patterns of the tundra.

3 : Alpine Animal Adaptations

Animals are also adapted to this harsh climate. Mobility allows many to spend the summer on the tundra, where days are long and cool, and to winter in the lowlands. Life cycles may be stretched out over several seasons, larval stages being accomplished over several summers instead of a month. The number of litters or broods produced in a summer is reduced, usually to one, and these usually mature at a quickened rate. Physiological adjustments may occur in metabolisms that make it possible for an animal to remain either part or all of the year in this rigorous environment.

The minute I put my orange notebook down, a dozen black flies land on it, finding it a somewhat unsatisfactory flower. A cinnamon brown cranefly, big as a silver dollar, stalks across a waffle of snow, awkward as a daddy-long-legs. It dodders, catching a hairlike leg in a snow crystal, leaving no footprints to mark its passage. Of the few insect families here, the most prevalent are the ubiquitous two-winged flies —black flies, mosquitoes, craneflies and various tiny flies.

Flies are extremely important as pollinators on the tundra. At lower altitudes, bees regularly visit specific plants and are therefore more efficient pollinators than flies, which tend to be irregular in their visits. But bees are immobilized below 50 degrees F, and need brighter light in which to work. Low summer temperatures restrict insect activities mainly to sunny daylight hours, limiting pollination activities and potentially limiting insect-pollinated plants. With their lower energy requirements and ability to work under restricted conditions, flies assume considerable importance in the alpine region. But even flies are stilled when the sun goes behind the clouds, centering the flowers with black. The sun comes out and they all pop up in a frenzy of flight.

Most alpine bumblebees are solitary. Early in the morning they fumble around on the ground, wing muscles not yet warmed enough to fly. There are also ants on the tundra, although only four species live on the Colorado tundra all year round. Small popping grasshoppers animate the summer and fall meadows. Large ladybugs cling to grass stems. Many small metallic beetles track the ground, and often a thick dusting of tiny white leaf hoppers salts the dark marsh soils. For someone not fond of spiders there seems to be a plethora of them in every rock pile: scurrying black wolf spiders, crab spiders and orb-weaving spiders, and others that disappear before one can identify them. Several butterflies lark across the tundra, but few lay their eggs above treelimit; if they do, the young may take several summers to develop into adults. Many species of mites occupy the soil.

Water courses have a variety of insects common to lower elevations: diving beetles, back-swimmers, whirlygig beetles, water striders and water mites, along with some insect larvae of mosquitoes, caddis flies and bloodworms. White threadworms animate the root clumps of sedges and rushes growing in and near the water. The adults of these insects are usually smaller than lowland counterparts; water striders are only about half as large. Stonefly and mayfly nymphs, planarian worms and tiny crustaceans have all been found in icy alpine streamlets, although not in great number.

Small pools, shallow and sun-warmed, contain murderous little communities, happily at work. Bloodworm and mosquito larvae twitch along the bottom. Water mites pulsate through the water. Aquatic beetles prowl the washtubs of water, darting diagonal bubbles. Ordinarily the hind legs of most diving beetles have a thick fringe of hairs on the edge as an adaptation for swimming; the legs of the alpine genus are very slender with only a few long hairs.

Fairy shrimp appear long after they have come and gone in lower ponds. Transparent, they scull across the ponds on their backs, ten pairs of beating feet needing only a coxswain to be a miniature crew shell. Eggs are produced both by parthenogenesis and fertilization, released in clusters at intervals to drop to the bottom. Winter eggs have a thick shell that enables them to withstand the cold and desiccation of the empty winter pool. If these pools dry up in an arid summer, the inhabitants have already seeded to the bottom, or hatched into marauding mosquitoes to bedevil an alpine hiker. But next spring the pool that forms anew will be just as animated with snippets of life as this summer's pool.

Recent research has discovered several insects active at night, contrary to previous belief. Moth millers have been caught flying towards the summit house on Mount Evans, and ground beetles, dwarf spiders and millipedes are mobile in the low temperatures of alpine nights.

A boreal chorus frog has been found living in protected ponds above treelimit in the southwestern Rockies, but in very limited populations. A mountain salamander lays eggs in high mountain ponds in Colorado. But no small snakes wind through the sedges and no lizards skitter across the rocks.

The number of birds on the western alpine tundra is also small. Only one bird, the ptarmigan, lives on the tundra all year. It is a large pullet-sized bird that demonstrates Bergmann's rule: animals of cold climates tend to be larger, having a better ratio of volume to exposed area, and making it easier to maintain body heat. Adult ptarmigan sit out a storm in relative security, since once nestled in the snow in a group, an individual loses little of its body heat. In a tight circle, they expose even less surface in proportion to their mass. In addition, a ptarmigan's legs and feet are so heavily feathered in the winter that they look like pantaloons, giving both foot-warmth and snowshoes to cross the snow.

Less than half a dozen other birds nest and breed here: water pipits, horned larks, rosy finches and white-crowned sparrows frequent the Rocky Mountain tundra. Others regularly patrol the tundra although they live lower: ravens, hawks, eagles, falcons, gray and Stellar's jays, Clark's nutcrackers. Slate-colored juncos and white-throated sparrows are common on the East Coast tundra.

Most of the large mammals remain above treelimit in the winter only if forced to, since winter grazing is impoverished. Smaller animals can remain year round—pocket gophers, meadow voles, mice, shrews, marmots, pika and weasels—surviving the winter by storing food, hibernation or incessant hunting.

Pocket gophers spend their lives underground; they are the only totally burrowing animal on the tundra. Marmots may burrow but neither as extensively nor as exclusively for food. Burrowing is not a common activity in the alpine tundra because so much of the ground is too rocky. Not even earthworms tunnel here. Next to the duration of snow cover, gophers are the most influential factor on alpine vegetation patterns. This example of an ecosystem controlled by an animal rather than environment factors is a rather rare one in the natural world.

Underground burrowers recycle the minerals of the environment; they distribute seeds and aerate soil, and add their own excreta and organic remains when they die. They bring subsoil to the surface and bury plant parts that decompose and help to fertilize the soil. A zoological doodler estimated that a dense population of pocket gophers can move between four and eight tons of topsoil per acre per year. An animal that can dig a tunnel more than a hundred feet long in one night is an efficient one.

In the early summer, meandering pocket gopher eskers appear, like rough brown snakes, from beneath melting snowbanks, grading from firm two-inch-high humps just uncovered to flattened mounds that are sinking back into the soil. The term "esker" is a geological one, referring to the ridge of coarse gravel dropped by streams that flow from beneath glaciers or down narrow icebound valleys. The analogy is clear when one sees gopher eskers that remain on the soil surface for a week or so, much the same as true eskers would appear if seen from high altitude. Pocket gophers dig through and under the snow because the meadow soils that they commonly tunnel are solidly frozen. This winter activity allows pocket gophers to feed throughout the cold season, under the protection of the snow blanket, and to survive the winter without migrating or hibernating.

Pika, small members of the Rabbit family, look more like guinea pigs, long ears having diminished to small round ones that are not as likely to freeze. Tails, ears and other extremities subject to rapid heat loss are often reduced or missing on animals in extremely cold climates. In addition they have fur on the soles of their feet, a nonskid device aiding their purchase on precipitous rock surfaces.

Pika dens can often be discovered by the Lilliputian stacks of hay at the doorstep. Pika begin preparing food for the winter by mid-July, continuing until all available food is snowcovered, adding materials for storage gradually so that the stems become completely dry and do not mold beneath.

A pika's vegetarian diet is not high in calories, and a pika must fill its stomach almost hourly to meet its energy needs. The little meadow worked over by a pika looks like a newly mown miniature hay meadow cut by a diminutive scythe. In order to obtain maximum food value, pika, like rabbits, are able to reingest fecal matter, which is high in protein content and energy value. Pika also preserve body moisture in dry climates by depositing almost crystalline uric acids, leaving a white nitrogenous salt deposit on boulder surfaces.

Biologists have estimated that the energy cost of normal small mammal activity at sea level is about double their rest metabolism. Pika probably expend energy at a triple rate, easy to believe watching their faster-than-the-eye-can-see dashes across the rocks. Food consumption is also higher for warm-blooded animals in low temperatures, and greater if the animal must climb over rough terrain or travel long distances for food.

Pika have been observed to be active during every month of the year—even on nice days in the winter—and there is no evidence that they hibernate. For this reason they must rely on stored food for nine to ten months, since it is often July before fresh vegetation is well greened.

Like ptarmigan, marmots are comparatively large animals. Related to ground hogs and woodchucks at lower elevations, marmots eat themselves fat in the summer and hibernate all winter, body temperatures sinking almost to 32 degrees F. They emerge in late spring, sprawling on a warm rock surface in what seems to be blissful enjoyment of sunshine and warmth.

Just when marmots go into hibernation is not positively known; as with so many other alpine species, it is difficult to obtain concrete data after heavy snows set in. Marmots have been seen as late as mid-October and as early as mid-May, sunning themselves on warm rocks. They become quite rotund by late July when they are feeding most heavily, acquiring an accumulation of fat that is necessary to carry them through the winter.

Hibernation is a form of seasonal migration, a way to pass the unfavorable time of year, and is associated with low temperatures and inaccessible water. During hibernation, an animal's metabolism is considerably lowered and the reserves of food stored in its body are used very slowly, comparable in some ways to the manner in which a perennial plant passes the winter. The primary impetus for hibernation is probably the lowering of temperature; at the same time, food begins to be scarce and dry. As an animal spends more time inside its den, carbon dioxide begins to increase there, adding to the lethargy that culminates in the long winter sleep of hibernation.

Bull elk are known to remain above treelimit in the winter, moving across the tundra in search of open meadows upon which to graze. Mountain goats and bighorn sheep patrol the rocky ledges. But deer migrate downward with the coming of winter, as do mountain lions and coyotes who have hunted the summer tundra. There is not enough food available for large numbers of big animals. The gales of winter combined with low temperatures create a chill factor well below zero, and this combination of cold and wind that freezes exposed human flesh can also penetrate the thickest pelt. Survival for most is impossible without access to lower pastures.

4 : Alpine Ecosystems

The limited number of plants and animals in the alpine tundra, and the lack of trees, make for visual simplicity in the landscape. Above tree line, one can see all the major tundra plant communities from one vantage point, an impossibility in the lowlands. An oak forest in Indiana has acres and acres of trees, a rich understory of smaller trees and shrubs, and a ground layer of spring flowers over mosses and ferns, all blooming in sequence, and in all, multiple species of both plants and animals. Alpine communities can be seen superficially at a glance, almost as two-dimensional as a patchwork quilt. The oak forest is a vast interwoven tangle which requires more points of view than a human can have at one time. The alpine tundra, because of its simplicity, is a good place for a beginning ecology student to get his bearings in understanding the elegant relationships of a vast natural world.

However, alpine plant communities, at first glance, may seem a tangled, incoherent mixture of plant species. A slight rise, an area of disturbed earth, a boulder pulled out of a meadow turf, may make havoc of the homogeneous characteristics one usually associates with lowland plant communities of similar smallness. In the alpine region, one can sit in a gopher garden, rest one's feet in a fellfield and put a hand in a sedge meadow. Alpine plants, in varying degrees, are specific to single communities, but the smallness of these communities in some instances, and their proximity to each other, may cause a visual misinterpretation that can be corrected only by looking closely at the immediate site in question.

As seen from a high ridge, the high-water mark of trees stains the mountain slopes an inky green, the boundary between a lower familiar world and the open sweep of the tundra. The boulder field above it is a first step in breaking down the mountain. Here many plants lurk beneath protected overhangs, and the most primitive plant pioneers, lichens, encrust almost every rock surface. Small animals shelter and hunt here.

As the boulders fracture and disintegrate, they become talus and gravel and slide downslope, demanding of the plants that grow among them strong root systems and the ability to withstand drought. In flatter areas, where gravels have stabilized over a long period of time, rudimentary soils form into fellfields. *Fell* is the Gaelic word for stone, and fellfield communities are literally stone fields, with rocky ground and dry soils, less than half covered with plants. Most of these are cushion plants over which the wind flows easily, and which can hold both warmth and moisture in their intermeshed stems and leaves.

On a more protected level slope a meadow has begun to form. If enough soil is built up, the fellfield cushion plants will be invaded by taller sedges, grasses and flowering plants. In time, these erect plants will shade out the cushions and replace them. Most tundra turfs are dominated by sedges, grasslike plants growing in thick tussocks and mats. The soils beneath are deeper and more mature, just as the aboveground aspect is denser and more luxuriant.

The snowbank that summers in a protected hollow determines several concentric rings of communities. As the snow melts, the communities uncovered reflect the moisture available, the length of the growing season, and the soil temperature. Where the snowbank persists very late into summer, the ground is covered with only a few mosses, soil lichens, a few sedges and rushes. The center of the snowbed has the most limited growing season in the tundra. Plants often do not have time enough to flower and set seed, so they are adapted to extend their domain by vegetative means, able to survive a totally snow-covered season if necessary.

Emerging from the snow patch are serpentine brown ridges, made by pocket gophers, that extend over into the turf community where they have begun to disintegrate as they dry. The vegetation of an animal-disturbed community superficially resembles an alpine meadow, but in truth consists of a distinctive group of plants which will soon die and be succeeded by fellfield plants.

The one community not visible in the western mountains is the alpine heath community, for heaths flourish only where there is more moisture and humidity—in the northeastern and, somewhat less, in the north-western alpine tundras.

A wet marsh community dyes the bottom of a slope a richer, darker green. The thick sedge and shrubby willow cover tell of wet soils and permafrost even when the glimmer of water is hidden. Small catch-ment basins may dry out later in the summer, but areas fed by per-manent ice or snow remain constantly verdant.

Greens take on new meaning in the alpine tundra. The nuances and variety of greens are subtle, and no words exist for their precise hue, but they indicate with precision both the changes within the alpine world and those that separate it from the greener world below. The turfs and fellfields look like gray-green carpet stretched too thinly and tightly over the ground so that the rocks beneath poke through. Only the alpine marsh community bears the rich green that one associates with the verdure of a lowland sward.

One more ecosystem should be added: that damaged by man's trampling and removal of rocks. This eroding and impoverished eco-system can be created in as few as ten days by concentrated walking across tundra fellfields, turfs and snowbeds, or within the time it takes to lean over and pick up a rock set in the turf or to kick it to one side. Restoration to the original vegetation may take one to five hundred years or more. There is no natural destruction of the tundra that com-pares with man's. In lowland communities, recovery time is roughly equal to the time it takes to disturb the area; on the tundra, recovery may require ten to a thousand times longer.

From barren rock to alpine turf requires a mental walk through centuries. Succession in the alpine tundra is painfully slow, but it progresses from infinitesimal lichen hanging by a thread on a weathering boulder to plump clumps of blowing grasses and sedges; from the sparest to the richest community; from raw gravels and sands to humus-enriched soil.

One cannot cross a boulder field and not be aware that lichens are the supreme plants here, for only they can grow on these wind-abraded bare rock surfaces. Light and dark gray, dark brown and black, red-orange, apple green and chartreuse, some encrust the surface so tightly that they cannot be pried off with a knife. They survive in an environment that no green-leafed plant can endure. All they need is a sufficient supply of moisture at some time during the year; often this comes from the half-inch of air immediately above the rock surface that is just warm enough to melt a grain of snow. They can carry on photosynthesis at any temperature above 32 degrees F, remaining dormant for long periods and resuming normal growth when thawed or wetted.

As in lowland communities, mosses are also the earliest plants in succession, contributing their remains to make a thimbleful of soil while the lichens nibble away at the rock's surface. Tiny seedlings become established in the rudimentary soil, roots probing for water and nourishment, the remains of each successive plant contributing to the humus enrichment of the ground beneath until a true soil is formed and the largest plants that are capable of growing under these climatic conditions take root and flourish.

Succession may detour, or may be so slow in this cold climate that a lifetime of observation satisfies few questions, but succession is irrevocable, given a stability of climate and other factors. Because succession in the alpine tundra is such an imperceptible progression, much of it must be conjectured and built out of evidence of past and present plant growth. Plants must be sampled and studied, and the evidence fitted together until it all makes sense: patterned ground buried under a foot of soil in an alpine turf, telling of a wetter, colder climate; depleted cushion plants in a thick turf, telling of former fellfield vegetation; plants that grow only in specific areas appearing in others, suggesting shifts from one community to another.

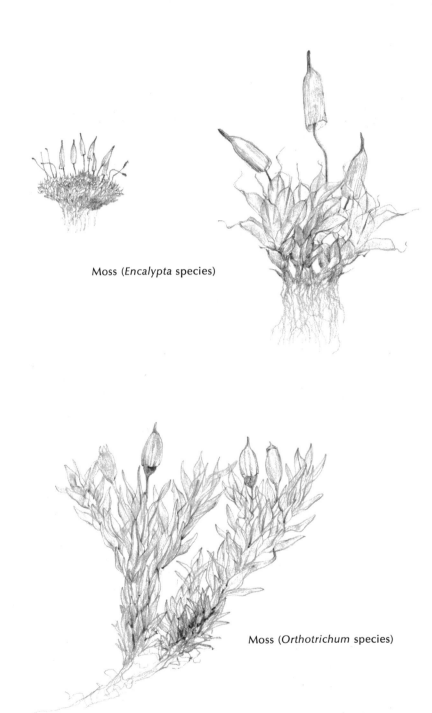

Moss (*Encalypta* species)

Moss (*Orthotrichum* species)

The alpine tundra, despite its surface simplicity, is not a unified whole, not a simple development in which every piece fits neatly into a linear progression. There are some plant communities which stand apart from the succession from boulder field to fellfield to turf. Because of placement or unusual physical influences, they have their own integrity and stability.

Two of these communities are determined by environmental situations: the first, the snowbed community, by the persistence of snow late into the summer, year after year, and the presence of ample water most or all of the year. This community is dependent upon winter snow protection and the adaptation of its plants to tolerate prolonged snow cover and to grow and reproduce quickly in the shortened growing season. The snowbed exerts the greatest effect on the patterns of plant and animal life in the tundra.

Wet marsh communities may be temporary, fed by transient snowbanks or springs, often drying out late in the summer. Or they may be permanent, lying beneath large snowfields or continual seeps, over permafrost or near alpine tarns. These are individual entities, depending upon no previous development, changing into no more complex ecosystem. An alpine marsh, like a sedge turf, is a stable community. But unlike the turf, which is the result of a long build-up of soil and succession of plants, the alpine marsh has no plant communities leading into it or beyond it. It depends primarily on a generous supply of water.

The third community, a "gopher garden," consists of short-lived plants that come in after animal damage, whether it be pocket gopher, meadow vole, sheep or man. When these plants die out the bare ground will be invaded by cushion plants, and the interminable succession from fellfield to turf will begin again as long as it is uninterrupted by disturbance.

The simplicity of alpine ecosystems has its price. The food chains are short: alpine clover—meadow vole—weasel or hawk. When food chains are complex and elaborate, as in a lowland community, a shift in any one component is less felt, the change is easily absorbed in the interwoven web, and the community retains its essential stability. When the food chains are short, the alteration of a single member results in a prompt and drastic change in the rest of the chain. Arctic trappers for years have noted wide cyclical changes in snowshoe hare populations, followed soon after by comparable shifts in predator populations. Where there is insufficient predation, lemmings, small volelike rodents, breed to a density that affects the whole population. They make a headlong rush out of their living area, most perishing in blind self-destruction that decimates the population and returns it to a more equitable number that can be supported by the environment. Similar population variations, although less dramatic, occur in alpine tundra meadow vole populations.

Lowland food chains are like an orb spider's web, a pattern of many very small segments: often one or more strands can be broken or removed without destroying the fabric of the whole web. But a break in the single line first thrown is disastrous for the whole construction, and so too is the alteration in a tundra food chain. Because of the cold climate and short growing season, if tundra plants are regularly trampled, overbrowsed or overgrazed, the tundra is slow to begin again and to regain its equilibrium. When vegetation cover is deleted from whole areas and opened to the action of needle ice, wind and soil movement, it may remain barren for many decades.

Plant production at best is minimal on the tundra, about three percent of that in a good lowland meadow. There are few consumers to feed upon this meagre production. Some of the consumers live on the tundra and will return their bodies and wastes to the soil; many are visitors from lower elevations and will not. In order to have a complete ecosystem, there must be decomposition, which proceeds very slowly in the short cool summers. The beat of the tundra is slow indeed, like the sliding weight of the metronome pushed to the absolute end of the pendulum.

5 : Treelimit and Krummholz

The boundaries between most major life zones are blurred, inter-fingered in a broad band that may be many miles wide, in which plants and animals from both regions intermix in a combined wealth not found in the life zones on either side. Although intermixing also occurs be-tween the subalpine and alpine regions, it is a narrower, sharper differ-entiation between areas than exists elsewhere. It is also the demarcation of two major climate regions, the Temperate and the Arctic. One can literally stand with a foot in each. The difference is that between trees and no trees, a sharp vegetational line with psychological overtones: above a band of dwarf trees the alpine tundra is sharp and bare and open, brightly lighted, a land of few shadows.

Treelimit is the highest elevation (or latitude) at which trees grow. Timberline is the more common term, a colorful word preserved more for its romantic connotations than its accuracy. Timberline refers to the marketable quality of the wood, which diminishes drastically at high altitude, a more commercial term that has a different meaning from "treelimit," which denotes a dynamic shifting line between two major life zones.

The alpine tundra has five months of temperatures below freezing and summers when temperatures never rise above 63 degrees F. It has measurably lower soil temperatures, less protective snow cover and less moisture, half as long a growing season, and twice as much wind as the subalpine zone—but the contrast between tall flowers and dwarf flowers, between trees and no trees, makes an unmistakable comment on growing conditions with more impact than any statistics. Subalpine forests are thick and dark and somber—dead branches snagging at clothes, blocked vistas, deep shadows. After walking through a closed subalpine forest, the tundra seems free and expansive, like leaving the city for the country. After being enveloped in shadow, intimidated by invasions of one's own three-dimensional space, the tundra seems such an open vacuum that one is physically drawn towards it.

It is the landscape of ultimate freedom.

Climate is by no means the only factor determining where treelimit may fall, although over the Northern Hemisphere it closely follows a line drawn where mean summer temperatures average 50 degrees F. Microclimate, competition, soil, wind and dryness are all involved. Probably the most important single factor is wind that desiccates trees in winter when no replacement water is available from frozen soils, and abrades upright branches with blowing snow and ice. At the highest altitudes, plant cells are killed by the cold. Where plants are able to grow in tiny pockets of warmer air or greater protection, microclimatic changes become important: where snow lies too late, trees are smothered. Where there is cold air drainage, trees may retreat; on sun-warmed open ridges they can advance. They remain stunted where avalanche paths delete tall growth. If the soil is too cold or too wet, trees cannot grow well. If soil is absent, as it is on precipitous rocky slopes, trees have nothing from which to gain nourishment. As if living conditions weren't difficult enough, there are also parasites and molds that are active only at low temperatures.

Treelimit trees are not drastically affected by cold during the winter because they are in a dormant cold-hardened state. When day temperatures are relatively high in the summer, photosynthesis proceeds at a good pace, to the tree's advantage; low summer night temperatures help to conserve the results of this production since they minimize respiration. These factors become crucial at treelimit in a way which they are not at lower elevations. At treelimit there is only enough heat to meet the tree's yearly requirements for respiration, the renewal of needles, and the production of a minuscule band of wood. There is almost no energy remaining for expansion, and little for the maintenance of a large root and stem system with considerable amounts of nonproductive cells as in lowland trees. Treelimit trees become progressively smaller, bearing more dead wood, as altitude increases. They usually do not even set seed or have cones.

Trees that are more adapted to growing in a cold climate survive less cold-hardy species; evergreen trees endure where deciduous trees cannot. Treelimit trees are all outliers of subalpine species. Evergreen trees are able to break dormancy somewhat later than deciduous trees, avoiding late freeze damage because old needles are already carrying on photosynthesis. But there is often heavy winterkill of exposed needles by drying winter winds, and snow blast damage where branches and trunks are not snowcovered.

Where the climate is dry and continental, treelimit is raised: in the southern Rockies it lies around 11,500 to 12,000 feet, lowering to 9500 feet in the central Rockies in Wyoming and to 7500 feet in the Montana Rockies. In the Rockies, as in continental climates in general, daily and seasonal temperature ranges are relatively large, and moisture tends to be distributed across the year.

In coastal areas, the nearby oceans tend to stabilize temperatures so that there is neither as much rapid cooling at night nor warming in the daytime. In California, most of the year's moisture comes as snow in winter, which, together with more open rock, depresses treelimit. Treelimit in the Sierra Nevada lies around 10,500 feet, diminishing 1000 feet in northern California, to as low as 6500 feet at Mount Rainier and the Olympics. The severe climatic conditions of Mount Washington in New Hampshire, which lies along the major west-east storm path that pulls in moisture from the Atlantic, depress treelimit to between 4200 and 5700 feet. The wide range is allowed by the many microsites in which trees may extend higher.

Since treelimit trees exist at the outer perimeters of tree growth, they are sensitive to the slightest changes in climate. Shifts in treelimit are also evidence of general climatic trends: it is advancing on Mount

Saint Helen's in the Cascades and in Alaska, but seems to be stable in the southern and central Rockies. There is some evidence of retreat in the northeastern mountains.

Beyond treelimit, trees are so stunted that they are no longer trees but shrubs. They are called *krummholz,* a descriptive German word which means "elfin timber" or "crooked wood." They look as if they had been cultivated by overly ambitious bonsai gardeners. Krummholz growth habit is shrubby and dense, becoming more prostrate, more twisted and contorted, with altitude. Treetops are flat or flagged or both; trunks are gnarled. Basal branches form impenetrable masses of long intertwined serpentines, impossible to walk through.

Any of the evergreen tree species of the subalpine forest may be represented in the krummholz, but they are the antithesis of those trees which at lower altitudes grow fifty to one hundred and fifty feet high and dangle hundreds of cones from clear spires. In the lee side of some obstruction to the wind, seeds are able to germinate and become established. Since krummholz trees rarely produce seed, most seedlings sprout from seeds blown up from lower altitudes. As they grow, they fill the tiny sheltered microsite. As they enlarge, they themselves offer protection from the wind on their lee, into which they continue to grow, into a self-contained and self-created microclimate. Krummholz trees constantly migrate into their own protection, rooting by layering where their branches make contact with the soil. The connections can be traced back to the original spot of protection where the seed first sprouted.

In forest soils, tree roots spread out in the finer soils near the surface in more or less even fashion, but the roots of cushion krummholz are asymmetrical, reflecting the accumulation of soil blown under and to the leeward side of the tree, diagramming the placement of the moisture-producing winter snowpack. The erratic topiary shapes of krummholz represent the outer boundaries of a favorable microclimate that is circumscribed by cold temperatures and abrasive drying winds.

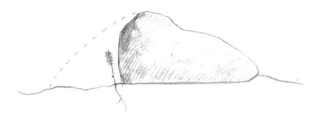

1. A seedling from a subalpine tree becomes established in the lee of a rock; the dotted line indicates the protected microclimate.

2. As the krummholz fills the protected area, it projects more protection in its own lee into which it may grow.

3. Branches root where they touch the ground, and the shrub migrates by layering into its own projected protection. The original part dies out.

Some krummholz forms flagged trees, clustered together in tree islands, like children waiting for the school bus on an icy morning. Only the part of the krummholz covered by the snowpack escapes winter damage; the upper perimeter of the sprawling lower branches corresponds precisely to the depth of winter snow cover. If the snow is too deep, it suffocates growth. If it is too shallow, the top branches are pruned back by the desiccating effect of winter wind. Branches and sprouts above the snow's protection are shorn off, and ice blasts their bark. Wintering animals nibble exposed branch tips. Only the leeward branches remain on the upper part of the trunk, semiprotected by its mass, looking like arboreal windsocks.

Often the contrast between the greener needles on the leeward branches and the browned needles of the windward stubs is visible from a distance. These needles were dried out in fall and winter and turned brown in the spring and will soon drop. The brown needles lower on the windward side were probably damaged before they were buried in snow, turning brown as soon as they were exposed to air.

The oldest needles can withstand the lowest temperatures that exist in the alpine region, but new needles may be frostbitten and dried as they enter the first winter. Conifer needles are elegantly engineered for survival in a cold, dry climate. They are shaped with less surface from which moisture can be evaporated than the leaves of deciduous trees, and are covered with a waxy coating. Evergreen sap does not freeze until very low temperatures are reached. Needles remain green throughout the winter on subalpine evergreens, in spite of repeated freezing and thawing, and can remain on the trees for years. But climatic conditions on the tundra are so severe that many needles of the exposed flags are bleached, and some of the small ones may dry out and fall while they are still green. At the end of a damaged branch, new needle clusters are flaccid and lifeless.

The wind is especially lethal to shoots that elongated too quickly in a spurt of growth the previous summer. Such shoots tend to grow later in the summer than older shoots, and probably have a higher water content when fall freeze comes so that ice forms inside them, making them less winter-hardy than shoots that completed their growth early and dried out at summer's end.

Single krummholz trees seldom exceed six to eight feet in height, and are more likely to be one to three feet. They may be several hundred to over a thousand years old. A tree in Rocky Mountain National Park, in a favorable subalpine site, measured thirty-seven inches in diameter and was well over 390 years old. A three-inch one at 11,500 feet cored out to be 328 years old.

Krummholz patches may die out but there are usually new islands beginning, so that although the interior pattern changes, a krummholz area is more or less stable. When krummholz does become established, it is a true dominant species: the largest plant of the area, outcompeting all other plants that can grow here. Many tundra creatures shelter here, and many lower-altitude plants are able to extend upward within its protection.

But in contrast to the sturdy ranks of trees below, krummholz is flung across the surface of the slope, battlescarred heroes in a kind of sylvan Valhalla.

6 : Boulder Fields

Whenever I look across an expanse of boulder that has to be crossed, my heart sinks. I have crossed too many not to be wary, but sometimes they are between here and there, or are preferable to beating through a willow thicket, and one goes. I fasten my backpack snugly around my waist and check to be sure that all the pockets are closed. I look to see if my bootlaces are well tied; I search for all loose objects in my pockets such as a hand lens to be sure that they are firmly pocketed and sealed in. A small object that falls into the depths of a boulder pile is usually gone forever.

A boulder pile looks like a tumble of blocks left by a giant's child just called in to lunch. In some places the blocks have fallen and wedged together in a stable interlocking Chinese puzzle which one can cross with a lot of stretch and scramble, but at least with relative safety. But more often there are some that teeter when stepped on; turned ankles and barked shins are par for the course. One must be both sure-footed and agile, and a little foolhardy, to navigate a boulder field with any speed or aplomb.

It seems obvious to say that mountains are rocky, but rock is so prevalent, either so close to or lying loose on the surface, that rockiness is a basic determinant in the kind of habitats available for plants and animals. The kind of rock and the way in which it weathers defines the kind of plants and animals that live there. Sometimes sheer rocky cliffs support only a few lichens so plastered to their surfaces that they seem part of the rock.

Many lichens are so small and adhere so closely that there seems to be no room for variety in this restricted scale. But under the microscope they have a whole compendium of shapes and colors. One looks like a spread of brown coffee beans interspersed with black raisinlike fruits. Another is ashy olive gray, sprinkled with sugar. A third is pale gray studded with black pustules, and another has doughnut-shaped fruits. A black patch looks like burned marshmallow under the lens. Sometimes sharp quartz crystals protrude, and the lichens pack around them. Others meander over the surface, a pale gray-green and apricot one looking as limp as a Dali watch. Some of the lichens are thick and form a tightly packed covering; red-orange jewel lichen marks a pika or a marmot perch. Rock plus extra nitrate from animal urine equals this brilliant lichen that grows at all elevations around the world wherever rocks are frequently wet with urine.

The oldest part of these crustose lichens lies in the center; the youngest is the pioneering periphery. Apple green map lichen has been used for dating in the central Rockies because the growth rate has been established at about three-eighths of an inch in diameter for the first thousand years. Even though individual plants are small, the pale almost fluorescent green makes it visible many feet away.

The more conspicuous lichens are leafy, still attached to the rock but more foliose and three-dimensional—corrugated, pitted, wrinkled and puckered in infinite fungal variations. Shield lichen is pale gray-green with a black underside that shows at the turned-up edges. A rocktripe lichen splays upwards in a brown leathery cup that casts an infinitesimal shadow, creating a microecosystem in its lee. It is held to the rock at only one point, but so firmly that it must be wet and pliable to be removed without shattering. A dry one dropped into a dish of water to freshen for drawing absorbs water so quickly that it jumps and writhes. Salted rocktripe is smaller and more furrowed, dotted with black fruits, the thallus looking as if it had been wet by ocean spray and dried, leaving it encrusted with salt.

CRUSTOSE LICHENS (enlarged)

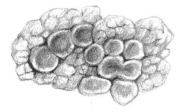

Candellaria sp.: yellow-orange.

Jewel lichen *(Caloplaca elegans):*
red-orange.

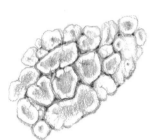

Granite lichen *(Lecanora rubina):*
gray-green, with olive or apricot.

Buellia sp.: dark gray.

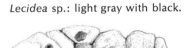

Lecidea sp.: light gray with black.

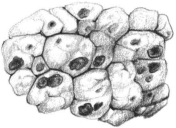

Button lichen *(Lecidea atrobrunnea):*
chocolate brown with black.

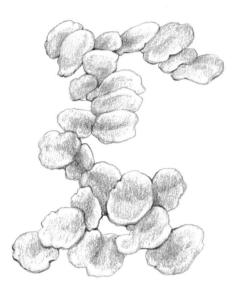

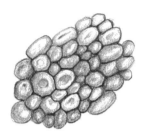

Stud lichen (*Buellia* sp.):
charcoal gray.

Lecanora sp.: fawn-colored.

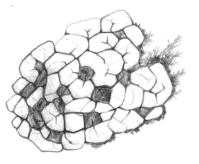

Two forms of a *Lecanora*,
illustrating differences of growth form.

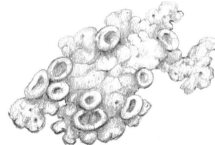
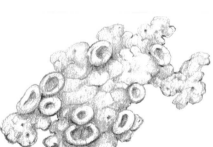

Map lichen (*Rhizocarpon geographicum*):
apple green with black.

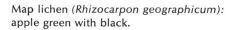

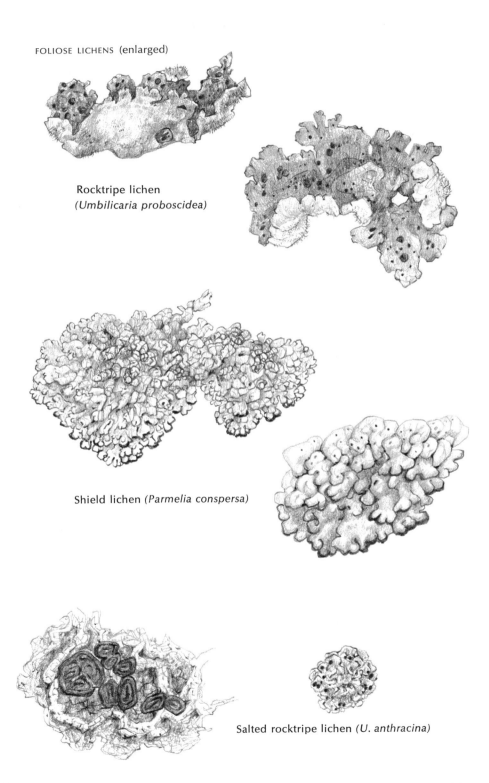

FOLIOSE LICHENS (enlarged)

Rocktripe lichen
(*Umbilicaria proboscidea*)

Shield lichen (*Parmelia conspersa*)

Salted rocktripe lichen (*U. anthracina*)

When weathering fractures rock masses into large boulders and they tumble downhill in untidy heaps, many habitats are created which are distinctive to the alpine world. The web of an orb-weaving spider glistens in the sunlight as a breeze sifts across the slope. When the female, sitting in the center, drops to the ground and vanishes into the rock, it seems a lifeless field. But in truth there is probably more varied animal life here than elsewhere in the alpine world, especially when a meadow lies adjacent to the boulder field, and animals find both food and shelter within a short distance.

More often than not, when I find a warm pocket in a boulder field, sun-warmed and wind-protected, and wedge myself into a comfortable position to take notes or to draw, a slight movement in the corner of my vision alerts me to a pika. Precisely the same color and even mottled like the rock, a pika is almost completely camouflaged. Perched on a boulder that gives a good view of its realm, it seems to conform even in shape, its nose up in the air, little body round with concentrated alertness. Pika are sometimes erroneously called conies; conies are hoofed animals that live in the Himalayas, bearing little resemblance to the little handful of fur scampering across the boulders. Pika live only in rock piles at and above treelimit in the United States, ranging down to sea level only in the far North.

Pika have three distinctive traits that endear them to alpine climbers: their distinctive piping squeak, their innocent childlike expression and their industriously gathered haypiles. Their best-known call is a single short querulous note, often with a question mark at the end. But following a pika's calls is no way to find one—either the animal itself, or the echoes bouncing off boulder surfaces, make it an accomplished ventriloquist. A better way to locate its perch, which may be feet or yards from its den, is to look for red-orange jewel lichen.

A pika soon decides that the watcher is merely an exotic rock and goes about its business of storing food. After a few moments I realize that there are three pika all engaged in the same activity. One twinkles across the rocks to a small patch of meadow, tugs and nibbles at the plants, turns, and scurries back to its den, a sprig of bistort and alpine avens poking out of either side of its mouth, its upper lip pushed up with the mouthful. Forty-five seconds pass, it appears again where it disappeared, and heads for the meadow at a dead run, having remained out of sight just long enough to deposit its load. It dashes back, this time with a yellow Indian paintbrush like a señorita with a rose between her teeth. A pika has catholic tastes and gathers what is available; among the identifiable plant parts are sprigs of chiming bells, snow buttercup, alpine clover, alpine avens, moss and a predominance of grasses and sedges. Occasionally last year's haystack turns up after spring melt, and one wonders what happened to the pika who stacked it: Was it merely absent-minded? Were its eyes bigger than its stomach? Or is it now inside a weasel or eagle?

Pika appear in numbers as soon as their rock slide is exposed in the spring, and oftentimes before there is any new growth of vegetation. When most of the snow is gone toward the beginning of July, activity increases to its peak, lasting for the two or three summer months. Pika live singly until mating sometime in early spring, raise their families together in the summer, and then resume single status in the winter. That as much is known about pika as there is is a triumph of scientific endurance aided by the fact that they are prevalent in nearly every alpine area of the United States. It is difficult to obtain much exact information about alpine animals since most alpine areas are inaccessible from October through May, and often part of June. The risk of transporting delicate scientific equipment by pack horse, the frequency of severe storms, the lack of physiological adjustment and the exhaustion of work at high altitudes, all make year-round data gathering a difficult if not impossible task.

Navigating across a boulder pile, one often finds pockets where dirt has blown in and caught in the interstices between rocks. There are many small plots that have been invaded by plants, varying in size from a nickel to a notebook. Overhanging boulders protect seedlings from the wind and reflect heat off their sun-warmed surfaces. Protective snow catches here in the winter. There is no competition from other plants as there is in an established plant community. Minerals for nourishment dissolve out of the rocks or come from animal droppings. Many of the more tender alpine plants, as well as the most energetic colonizers, grow in these stations. Many plants from lower elevations extend upwards under the rocks' protection.

The warmer microhabitats of boulder fields and rock slides make them favorable habitats for marmots. I admit to a romantic view of these alpine woodchucks although I know they can drive researchers to distraction by devouring plastic markers. But I happen to feel about marmots the way a six-year-old feels about his favorite teddy bear, combined with the affection I have for our baggy basset hound. Marmots are simply Everyman's stuffed animal, fifteen pounds of bone and muscle set adrift in a fur pouch that could easily hold twenty-five pounds.

My first encounter with a yellow-bellied marmot set the tone for my subsequent sentiments about marmots. There is a marmot colony in Rocky Mountain National Park that is a virtual welfare state, supported by peanut-dispensing tourists. Herman had climbed down into the boulder pile, cameras in hand, very cautious and quiet, to photograph a dozing marmot. As soon as the shutter clicked, the marmot opened its eyes, sat up, and posed, showing first one profile and then the other, raising its nose so that its double chin didn't show. When Herman took a new roll of film from his pocket, the paper crackled, and the marmot waddled over to see if there were any peanuts in the offing. By this time it was obvious that the problem was not caution but how to get the marmot out of Herman's lap.

The marmot finally gave up and shambled away, resumed its rock, put its head on one paw and surveyed the photographer with considerable disappointment. Having given up on being fed, it slowly and with considerable deliberation lowered its stomach onto the sunwarmed rock with a sybaritic indolence and fell sound asleep.

In North America marmots are known to have existed throughout the Pleistocene in lowland forms. They probably originated in the vast alpine recesses of the Himalayas. Today the hoary marmot with its grizzled muzzle lives in northern Idaho to Alaska; the yellow-bellied marmot occupies the Rockies, Cascades and Sierra Nevada; the Olympic marmot lives in the Olympics; and a fourth lives above treelimit in the Presidential Range.

7 : Talus and Scree Slopes

At the edges of bedrock cliffs the rocks are more exposed and likely to be more fractured and fragmented. They disintegrate slowly and stubbornly, doomed to eventual reduction by all the elements. As lichens encrust their surfaces, lichenic acids nibble away. As soil builds up between and around them, more plants move in, insistent roots prying into every crack. As water freezes in the interstices, it pressures the rock into ever smaller pieces.

Where boulders have been reduced to gravels they cascade down the slope in a slide, smallest pebbles nearest the cliff, larger rocks and boulders at the base. Walking across a scree or talus slope is at best tedious and dirty, at worst dangerous. Talus slopes are composed of rocks the size of a fist or larger, usually sharp and loose. Scree is smaller, down to gravel size, and also offers little in the way of secure footing, especially when the gravels are ankle deep. Often the slope is so steep that one has to dig at an angle, the outside of one boot and then the inside of the other, feeling as if one has extra knees in which to get tangled. With each step a cascade of gravel showers downhill and the walker slips down a few inches from where he intends to be. There is no use putting a hand in the scree; there's nothing to hold on to. One simply goes as slowly and carefully and as quietly as possible. When I want to go downhill, I sometimes give up and sit down. It's hard on the clothes but much less exhausting than trying to keep one's feet in order.

At the bottom, where the sun has warmed the slope, is a big cluster of alpine candytuft. It blooms here in the dry soils before it blooms in the alpine fellfields or meadows. There it grows in single rosettes; here there is no competition whatsoever and it spreads in luxuriant reiterated splendor, rosette after rosette topped with flowers, the top ones in full bloom, those at the base in bud. Spreading the gravel away reveals very damp soil about an inch beneath the surface. The stems of all the rosettes meet in one woody root that seems to extend down to China. All around, just under the surface, are smaller rosettes, studded with pinpoints of white buds, ready to break ground in a few more warm days.

The most successful plant in stabilizing scree slopes and soil building is alpine dryad, named after the mythical tree-nymph supposedly because of the resemblance of its foliage to that of some species of oak. Its thick evergreen leaves have leaf pores protected under a felt of shaggy hairs on the lower leaf surface, enabling it to survive in these surface-heated gravels and wind-burred slopes.

It is a circumpolar plant, occurring in the same habitats around the world, in both arctic and alpine situations. Wherever it grows, dryad thrives in the most severely buffeted above-treelimit sites, often on the shaded north-facing ridge where the wind is most biting. Its great usefulness in stabilizing soils is even more marked on very steep slopes where soil slippage is a constant factor that disrupts the growth of other plants, tearing their roots or inundating them with gravel. As the soil slips gradually downward on steep slopes, the mats of dryad are gradually tilted on edge, forming the "riser" of a step. In areas of high soil movement, the plants may even become inrolled. The "treads" are devoid of vegetation. Since no other plant is this tenacious, dryad

Alpine candytuft *(Thlaspi alpestre)*

is a pioneer that dominates wherever it grows. Its woody branches spread over the ground, its elaborated root system interwoven just below the surface, in the ideal growth pattern for soil stabilization.

Dryad also contributes nitrogen to these sterile well-drained gravels. Some nitrogen-fixing bacteria are free-living in the soil; others form prominent nodules on the roots of legumes, alders and dryad. Where dryad grows it enriches the soil with nitrogen, an element usually in scarce supply in the alpine tundra. Its branches also catch and hold dirt and debris which eventually form into humus; a dryad mat may have from two to five inches of humus under it, while the terrace treads have only mineral soil.

Alpine dryad *(Dryas octopetala* ssp. *hookeriana)*

While drawing, I have the uneasy sensation of slowly slipping down-slope. Looking up, I see the dryad mat illuminated by backlighting. The flowers form a pattern of ivory petals, stamped with molten gold stamens, like some beautifully worked medieval psalter cover.

Only a few other sturdy plants are able to root in these shifting gravels—Easter-daisies, alpine milkvetches, buckwheats, collomia, phlox, a few others—all either have long shallow root and rhizome systems which form an underground mesh, or massive taproots that seem to lock into the matrix of the mountain itself. Animals as well as plants are sparse here too, for there is little food and footing is precarious.

One tends to think of mountains as rocky blocks, permanent and immutable. But they are also as transient as the pellets which skip and bound down the slope, arching in diminishing scallops, restless as an alpine wind.

8 : Fellfields

From a distance a fellfield looks barren, especially early in the year. Almost nothing seems to be in bloom. It is faded, subdued, washed out, a dead carpet of last year's leftover debris scrubbed lifeless by the brutal winds of winter.

Although winter storms may blanket a fellfield, the snow is scoured off almost as quickly as it accumulates. I remember a winter skiing trip where there was a view of 14,000-foot mountains out our windows. For two days there had been a "whiteout" with blowing horizontal snow which obscured the view in a swirling icy cocoon. Not until the third day did the mountains appear. The snow lay thick in the sub-alpine forests, but the high flanks and ridges of the alpine tundra were straw-colored, swept clean of snow. Snow seethed and smoked off the peaks in plumes and banners. Snowbanks lay in depressions and sheltered terraces; they had been there since last fall and would persist into summer. But the fellfields were blown bare, as dry as an old crust of bread.

Only in the alpine spring are these rock fields covered for any length of time with protective snow. After a June snow has come and gone, the residual heat of the rocks bares them, leaving an irregular tan and white checkerboard pattern that, more clearly than at any other time of the year, diagrams that a fellfield is half rock.

The soil of a fellfield is rudimentary. In spite of a recent snow, soil from an open patch feels dusty in the hand, and very gritty. Only the crescent beside a rock, beneath a scrubby plant, has the extra chill of dampness.

The soil is so full of gravel, pale and clearly still unaltered from the basic composition of the rocks on the surface, that it can barely be called soil. Except that it lies on a flatter, more stable slope, it is reminiscent of the fine particles in scree and talus slopes: dusty to the fingers, unenriched by rotting organic matter that transforms sands and gravels into true soil. While fellfields have enough fine materials within their gravels to have developed a beginning soil, the environmental conditions of rapid drainage, summer drought and exposure to wind make them impoverished habitats for plants.

Well-developed soils contain four layers or horizons, separated by color and composition, often with several variations within each. The uppermost horizon is topsoil, rich in organic matter with considerable chemical alteration to rock particles, often the most productive. The horizon beneath receives the chemicals and some finer particles washed down from above. Beneath is the weathered broken bedrock or other soil-parent material which has not been altered chemically. The basal horizon is the unweathered and unaltered bedrock from which the soil is formed.

Immature soils, like those of a fellfield, have almost imperceptible horizons. If one scratches down only an inch with a knife the blade grates on the rock embedded within it. The top two horizons are mostly gravel and sand with meagre humus, a faint color alteration betraying some chemical change. Below it blends into parent rock with scarcely any differentiation, the grains of gravel matching the granular rock surface beneath.

It has been estimated that one hundred years are needed to form a single inch of soil on the plains. But in the cold dry climate of the alpine heights soil formation is many, many times slower.

The primary factor dictating the sparse character of a fellfield is wind: wind that worries out finer soil particles and whisks them away; wind that chews and gnaws at plant stems and leaves; wind that desiccates the soil and the plants in it. Wind keeps the air near the ground in constant circulation so that except for small hollows, the protective warmth at ground level is stirred away. Wind scourges fellfields free of snow in the winter, exposing the plants to the severest environmental stress on the tundra. During the summer wind blasts across the open surface and the fellfields broil under the intense solar radiation of high altitudes. The drought is relieved only by summer rain and snow showers, but even then the soil drains so rapidly and retains so little moisture that fellfield plants must be specifically adapted for survival.

It is no surprise, then, to find the fellfield plants cushioned or matted, frequently succulent, flat to the ground in rosettes and often densely haired and thickly cutinized: moss campion and phlox, sandwort and forget-me-nots, buckwheat and pussypaws, dwarf lupines and dwarf clovers.

Once a true fellfield has developed, it remains stable for hundreds, maybe thousands, of years until the slow process of soil building in a cold dry climate proceeds far enough for the invasion of taller meadow plants, or until it is disturbed or destroyed by animals. By default, the fellfield has an aspect of stability and permanence. Even with the streaming wind, it is a strangely quiet place, perhaps because there are few animals here. There is too little nourishment and too little protection. Only small insects wind among the leaves or cling to vertiginously swaying stems, while butterflies cavort undaunted by capricious updrafts.

Invasion does take place, however. In a phlox cushion a grass has rooted, slender sprigs vibrating two inches above the tight pad, fibrous

Alpine phlox *(Phlox condensata)* invaded by a bluegrass; the sturdy rootstock of the cushion plant contrasts with the fine fibrous roots of the grass.

root system in contrast to the taproot of the phlox. As more erect plants invade the fellfield, they will compete for light and water with the cushions. The cushions and mats will lose vitality and die out, and the fellfield will be succeeded by an alpine turf. With the strength with which the wind bears across this ridge, it seems an impossible achievement for these erect plants to grow rapidly enough to defeat the tenacious cushions. Yet in some areas, soil humus will build up, increasing the soil's water-holding capacity, and so increasing the ability of erect shallow-rooted plants to invade and outcompete the cushions, but only centuries—or millennia—from now.

And in other areas, the wind, like a nagging insistent child, will have its way, arresting the fellfield forever in an eternal frozen springtime of alpine development.

In spite of its barren appearance, a spring fellfield is bejeweled with many small and brilliant early-blooming flowers. One has to get down

Alpine fescue *(Festuca brachyphylla)*

on hands and knees, out of the bitter wind, to find them. By summer the aspect has dulled. The spring-blooming flowers are largely gone, and grasses, sedges, sages and rushes come into bloom. Although not as colorful, they are more important in soil-building than their predecessors. Bluegrasses shake exquisite apple green and white florets on hairlike stems; alpine fescues, thin and wiry, shiver in the breeze.

By the end of summer a fellfield has a dry and withdrawn aspect. One feels the water deficit as well as sees it. Heat vibrates upwards from the soil. The wind is dry. The ground is hard and unyielding. Looking for flowers one finds seedheads. Dry seeds rattle in almost empty pods, or tiny plumed seeds float away, leaving dry involucres like clusters of minute tan daisies. Tiny, wingless grasshoppers spurt out from under every footstep.

It is then that one remembers the confetti patterns of blue and pink, yellow and white, that brighten the gravel soils, sturdy witness to the cold-hardiness of alpine plants that bloom in the late May to early July tundra "spring." The ground then is as embellished as one of Fabergé's Easter eggs: exquisitely patterned, magnificently encrusted with jewels and enamel, precise, intricate, superb.

9 : Alpine Meadows and Turfs

High summer is a glorious time on the alpine tundra, and enjoyment of it is intensified because it is so brief. Often the sunlit days of July and August in the Rocky Mountains end around noon with a rain or snow storm, but there are occasional rare days when the sky is clear all day, the wind is light, the tundra is cool and fresh and bright and delights the senses. High summer is the time of the storybook meadows of alpine turf, forming green cut-velvet swards, gentling the rugged landscape. The sparse fellfields with their closely laid flowers are the spring gardens of the tundra; the turfs and meadows, with their larger later-flowering plants, are the summer gardens.

By beginning the day on a ridgetop fellfield, one can walk down into a turf, ending the afternoon ankle-deep in thick grasses and sedges and flowers. Each footstep is a perceptible progression from a sparse plant community to a fully developed plant-rich one. From a thin layer of plants, measured in millimeters of height from lichen to cushion plant, one proceeds to plants high enough to have a visible vertical layering. From an insect-only community, one enters areas labyrinthed

81

with meadow vole runways, humming with bumblebees, sometimes disturbed by pocket gopher dirt mounds and tunnels. At the top of the ridge, one's boots crunch on the gravel; at the bottom, they sink into thick tussocks of sedge and grass.

Walking across a sedge turf is like walking on a carpet. Most walking on the tundra can be described as scrambling one's way through tilting boulder piles or scuffling across unyielding gravel soils and stumbling over rocks. But sedge turfs are like a well-designed rug. They mask the rugged nature of the underlying rocks, covering the ground so completely that bare soil has to be looked for in gutters between the plants.

The change from fellfield to turf is gradual but perceptible: among the cushion plants are more and more taller plants which whip and shake in the breeze. There is less exposed rock and soil although in many ways the emptiness of the fellfield lingers far downslope. Fair amounts of gravel and sand remain in the soil although there is also more humus and more horizon development.

Finally, in the meadow, the cushion plants have nearly disappeared; those that remain are mere sprigs and wisps. A profusion of bright flowering plants, blue and yellow and white, rich in number and species, tesselate the ground. Below the flickering grasses and sedges are multitudes of lower plants, all astir in the afternoon breeze. On the ground, lichens insinuate themselves between tussocks, some leafy lichens with elaborate forms, some merely scabbing the soil. Mosses grow in the protection of larger plants. Tiny flowers bloom almost hidden in the wealth of overgrowth. An alpine turf is a fifteenth-century manuscript illumination, munificent and multiplied in detail, rich in life and faith in a natural world.

Most alpine turf plants bloom at midsummer. In the spring one must look for new growth in the thick thatching of old turf. By May, tiny leaves are up a quarter of an inch, lavender-mauve or red, tightly folded against the cold. Sedges begin growing from the bottom of last year's leaves instead of abandoning them to dry and expending precious growth energy to send up completely new shoots. From a distance the prevalence of red and violet pigments combining with some new green and the dried brown from last season blurs visually into a mauve slope.

By high summer the reds of early leaves and stems are replaced by green chlorophyll. The minute plants of May have risen to six or eight inches. Grasses and sedges grow in tight tussocks or slender fringes above the lower plants. The summer turf is a delightful place to draw. When it is hot and sticky in the foothills, one can count on a cool breeze and pleasant temperatures in the low sixties above treelimit. The turf is a comfortable place, the tussocks of sedge or grass making a greensward softer to sit on than the hard gravels of the fellfield or the shifting gravels of the scree slope.

I head for a comfortable-looking patch of turf, and a water pipit almost explodes out of the ground. Her nest is totally camouflaged in the thick green growth. An overhanging chunk of sedge protects and shadows the three-inch opening. Inside are five shiny light brown eggs. Pipits summer throughout the western alpine area, wintering as far south as South America. They belong to one of the original species that colonized during the Ice Age, and closely related species exist in the Himalayas still.

Water pipits arrive on tundra breeding grounds as early as nesting sites are available, usually the latter part of June. Nesting begins immediately. The incubation period is about two weeks, and the young are hatched by mid-July. They remain in the nest about three weeks longer before they are full-fledged. Like the alpine plants whose growth cycle is accelerated, alpine birds nest, produce and mature at a quickened rate.

By early August the young are able to fly well, and water pipits form into restless flocks, rising and dipping in staccato undulating flight. They feed throughout the alpine area, preferring pond borders and wet marshes. They often feed on caddis fly larvae at the edge of small pools, and have been observed wading into shallow water to pick up the cases in which the larvae live, removing the occupants, and rinsing them off before gulping them down. Their diet is almost totally of insects: beetle larvae and adults, butterfly larvae, midges, grasshoppers, mosquitoes and tiny wasps. Their final move down to winter territory depends in large degree upon weather conditions, and one may still hear their cheery conversations on the tundra as late as the end of August, or well into September in a halcyon fall.

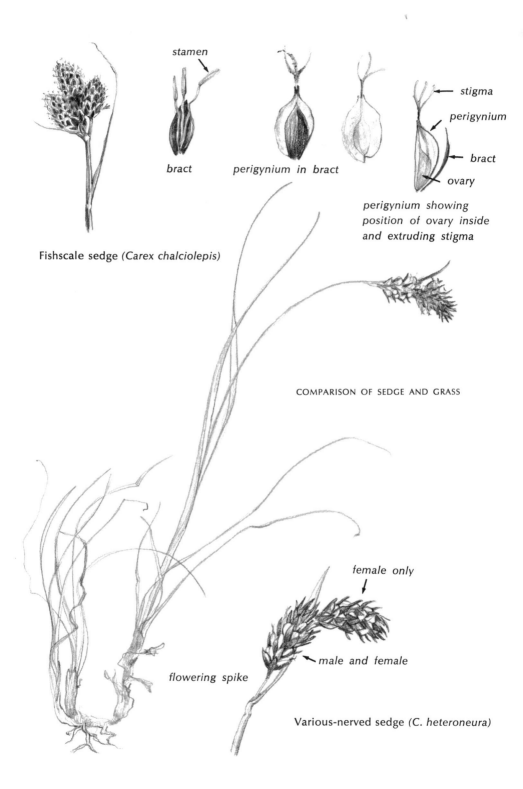

stamen

bract

perigynium in bract

stigma

perigynium

bract

ovary

perigynium showing
position of ovary inside
and extruding stigma

Fishscale sedge (Carex chalciolepis)

COMPARISON OF SEDGE AND GRASS

female only

male and female

flowering spike

Various-nerved sedge (C. heteroneura)

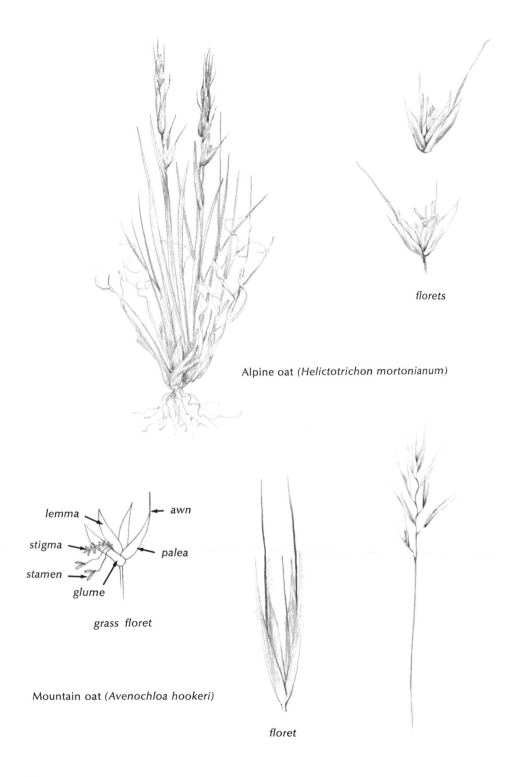

florets

Alpine oat *(Helictotrichon mortonianum)*

lemma → ← awn

stigma →

stamen →

← palea

glume

grass floret

Mountain oat *(Avenochloa hookeri)*

floret

I remember standing, enchanted, watching a pair of pipits. The female was feeding on insects on the ground, at the base of a large boulder, a slim gray-brown bird almost invisible in the shadows. The male, equally plain, made repeated flights, ten feet straight up and down, seldom higher or wider afield, landing on the rock, where his bobbing silhouette could be seen. His song was a sweet piercing trilling phrase which stirred some distant memory: was it what I had imagined, as a child, the nightingale's song to be as the rose thorn pierced its breast in the Hans Christian Andersen fairy tale?

The overall aspect of an alpine meadow is of a richly flowered and grassy turf. But sedges are more prevalent and dominant than grasses, except for hairgrass, and grow more densely in both meadows and marshes.

Superficially, sedges and grasses look alike: long narrow leaves, insignificant green, brown, or black flowers atop slender stems. The best way to tell the difference between the two is to hold one in each hand. Grasses have round hollow stems that roll easily in the fingers, solid only at the nodes where the leaves sheath outwards. Sedge stems are triangular and the angle is usually obvious to the touch. Seen from the top, grass leaves are arranged in ranks of two; sedge leaves in ranks of three. Both have flowers arranged in a head but grass flowers are "perfect," that is, they have both male and female parts included in each floret, and are often separated from each other by slender filamentous stems. Occasionally sedge flowers are perfect, but more often the flower head is segregated into part male and part female, or occasionally purely one or the other on separate plants. And the ovary in the female sedge flower is always enclosed in a minuscule vaselike membrane called a *perigynium*.

The identification of sedges is an acquired taste, a treat for someone who enjoys microscopic detail. Under the microscope they have an individuality of formal proportion and variation, all within a limited color range of green, pale yellow fading to ivory, and varying shades of purple, brown and black. When there is unlimited range of color and form, a plant has no excuse not to be beautiful. But when the limits of form and color are so stringently set, the wealth of subtle variations makes the chamber music of the plant world.

The long fine roots of grasses and sedges go a foot or more down into the most mature soils on the tundra. Beneath the tenacious roots, stones are distributed through the soil like raisins in a cake. The top horizon of the soil is dark with fine humus. The middle horizon, although rocky, is well-drained so that there is no puddling to kill plant roots. The lowest horizon is bedrock. Meadow plants chemically and physically alter the parent material beneath, building a deep soil (up to several feet thick) that supports the wealth of above-ground vegetation.

There is a rich vertical layering of plant cover from lichens crusting the soil to small plants and to the tall ones measuring the wind above. But when one thinks of a Washington rain forest, the environmental restrictions of an alpine world are dramatic. In the rain forest, trees reach to hundreds of feet, festooned with lichens and mosses, sheltering a rich understory of small trees, shrubs, and lower-growing herbs and ferns, with mosses blanketing the soil. But here no trees thunder to the ground; no waist-high bushes snag at one's passage. The inches of an alpine meadow's layering appear only when one partakes of Alice's bottle labeled DRINK ME and becomes eye-high to a hand-high forest, animated by a breeze that whispers secretly of other mountain tops and alpine meadows beyond one's horizon.

10 : Snowbed and Snow Communities

The atmosphere near the edge of a snowbank on a hot summer morning is contradictory and altogether pleasant. Summer sun glazes the top, the reflections superlighting the whole area. At the same time, cool vapors emanate from it. The bank melts with tiny gurgles and a steady trickle that sounds from beneath the bank like elusive distant church bells, echoing its retreat in the summer warmth.

Snow is always a part of the high alpine view, whether it hangs year round in high cirques or nestles in nivation depressions, melting out nearly every season. On the tundra, snow accumulates as a result of obstacles to the wind, from the triangular teaspoonful that remains behind a small rock to the acres of drifts which persist behind boulder piles or in nivation depressions or on leeward ridges.

A true snowbed community develops only when the snow lasts late into the summer, so late that the plants that have been free of snow all winter (or at least freed early in the summer) are in full bloom when the snowbed plants are just beginning to develop. The snowbed, as the most influential factor in alpine plant distribution, provides specialized conditions on the alpine tundra that result in specific ecosystems.

Snowbed communities develop in concentric rings or successive zones from the margin of the late-lasting snow inward to the center. The individual character of each community depends upon the endurance of the snow, which determines the length of the growing season, and the amount of moisture present. These are stable communities; any intermixing seems to be due to minute environmental variations. In spite of their proximity and intermeshing, there is no evidence of invasion of one group of plants into another ring, or of competition that signals the active changes that indicate succession. Each ring remains a more or less stable separate entity.

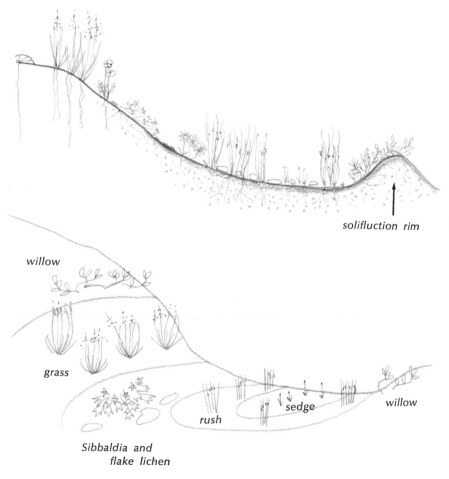

Snowbed zonation showing self-contained plant communities determined by the length of growing season; willows are snow-free longest; sedges, shortest.

Snow willow *(Salix nivalis)*

The snowbanks disappear like a visible clock tick, melting away to reveal a new ring of plants just greening while those first exposed are in full bloom. The range from sprout to flower to seed is contained within a few feet. In June one can watch an afternoon snow shower sift across dwarf willow catkins; in mid-July plants are so recently up that their shoots shine green against the dark wet muck. In late August the last rushes inscribe blue shadows on newly fallen snowpatches. And change goes on inside the snowbed even as one watches, from the momentary glitter of running water and the perceptible retreat of lacy snow ledges under summer sun to the slower pulse of solifluction taking wet earth slowly downward in a secret, silent slippage.

A snowbed provides more protected winter conditions for the plants which lie beneath it than they would have in a fellfield. Snow is protection on the tundra. Beneath the snow, the temperature is considerably higher than the air temperature throughout the winter, and it fluctuates little since the ground is not exposed to the contrasts of strong sunlight during the day and freezing at night. Temperatures beneath the snow cover remain around 26 degrees F, while those in fellfields may vary from -20 to $+15$ degrees F in the winter, with occasional lows of -35 degrees F. Plants beneath are sheltered from the wind; there is no chance of desiccation. On exposed snowbeds, dust lies in brown parentheses on the snow surface, melting down into the earth as the snow melts, adding fine materials to enrich the soil. Pollen grains from hundreds of miles away calligraph alpine snowbanks.

But snow also restricts plant growth. The weight of the snow compresses the plants beneath it. Summer soil temperatures are kept lower because of ice masses and permafrost in the soil, its high moisture content at the beginning of the season when the snow first melts, and the evaporation of the meltwater. Saturated soils tend to ooze downslope with solifluction, further disrupting plant growth, or are subject to active frost heaving or needle ice which wrenches seedlings and damages roots. Even in July and early August, there are pockets of brown on the tundra, areas held late under snow and not yet greened.

The persistence of snow may shorten the growing season to such an extent that there may not be time for the last exposed plant to flower;

in some years of heavy snowfall and cool summer some plants may not be uncovered at all. The plants that endure here are mostly mosses and lichens, and a few sedges and rushes with rhizomatous growth. Seed production, preceded by flowering, is often rendered impossible by insufficient heat and few days of warmth, and plants with vegetative means of reproduction are better equipped to survive under these conditions. The plants uncovered last have speeded-up growth compared with those uncovered earlier, and many manage to flower in the last breathless wisp of summer, although they may survive even if they are not uncovered at all during the growing season. When it exists in a snowbed habitat, a plant's ability to grow rapidly in the brief warm spell is more important than its ability to survive cold.

In the very center of long-lasting snowbeds, empty black-wet soil testifies that here is an area never open long enough for even the most tenacious sedge or moss or lichen to grow. The first snow of the fall may cover it before last year's snow is all melted, and by October the snowbed is already blocked in. Early fall snows melt quickly after a storm, leaving only scraped white patches across the slopes. But the snowbeds have an opaque whiteness and a depth of cover that mark them unmistakably as here to stay.

Many snowbed plants are "indicator plants." Such plants reveal the presence of precise environmental conditions because they can grow only under these conditions. Many snowbed plants are widespread, able to grow so widely because conditions are so nearly uniform beneath late-lying snowbeds. The tiniest such plant is an infinitesimal snow

Snow liverwort (Anthelia juratzkana)

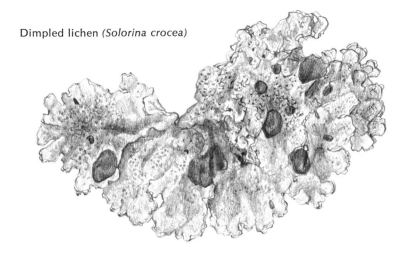

Dimpled lichen *(Solorina crocea)*

liverwort that looks like a gray ash in the hand because the green leafy plant is obscured by a parasitic charcoal gray fungus. Under a hand lens it looks like a miniature moldy clubmoss, but hints of emerald green turn out to be new growth not yet infected, the clear green cells forming blown-glass leaves. In spite of its minuteness it is an important soil binder in snowbed areas where soils tend to separate rather than cohere; the dissecting needle encounters surprising resistance in trying to divide the infinitesimal strands.

The blue-gray cast of flake lichen is visible from a considerable distance. While rocks are varied and mottled grays, flake lichen is a flat cold blue-gray that reflects light in an almost luminescent way on a dull day. On the tundra one's impression is often of greater plant cover than actually exists, crediting a meadow with a thick turf when in reality there is empty soil hidden beneath a crosshatching of taller plants. A snowbed community containing flake lichen looks quite barren, but is actually well-covered because of the amount of lichen that encrusts the ground. Flake lichen forms puffy polygonal patches over fine soil particles amassed beneath the lichen thallus; these are separated by narrow desiccation cracks which give the soil the appearance of a mosaic tile floor that no one has grouted.

Dimpled lichen, another worldwide snowbed species, is dull greenish gray-brown above with a brilliant orange underside; its specific name of *crocea* refers to this color of crocus anthers. It is able to grow at the highest elevations in the northern latitudes. When a corner is torn off, the layers appear: olive brown top covering an emerald green line of algae over a white cottony mass of fungus, underlined by the thin orange skin. The pioneer role of this liverwort and these lichens in soil holding, especially in areas where other plant growth is notably restricted, gives them an importance far out of proportion to their size.

Sibbaldia, named for the Scottish botanist Sibbald, is also a true snowbed indicator. It grows only where the snow melts out quite late, and is used in Scandinavian countries as an indicator of a poor place to build roads. Its bluish foliage with distinctive three-lobed tips looks much like clover and is easily mistaken for it.

Summer snow surface has quite uniform conditions: low air temperature, high intensity of reflected light and a great abundance of blown-in organic matter along with high humidity. Although the layer of air just above the surface may be dry, the prevailing low temperatures and evaporation from the snow lessen the risk of desiccation for insects that feed there, and most of these can absorb warmth from the direct sunshine without injury. There are usually various kinds of flies, several species of spiders and multitudes of mites and springtails. One of the most primitive of insects, springtails have a kind of tiddlywink arrangement on their abdomens that allows them to pop across the snow like water on a hot griddle. They browse for pollen, spores and debris, forming the basis of a food chain which culminates with the foraging birds that imprint three-tined tracks across the snow.

A remarkable variety of insects eventually turns up on top of the snow, many immobilized by the cold surface. Some are blown in by accident, others stalk the surface for available food. The interior areas of the snowbed also contain dirt and debris, providing ample food for insects. Because of the unusually rich hunting in an otherwise sparse area, a great number of small to diminutive carnivores, from insects to birds, hunt the snow surface. By the end of the summer, the snow begins to look like a well-washed quilt puckered from too many washings and in need of a good bleaching.

Brown-capped rosy finches tweezer insects off the snow's surface. These finches breed above treelimit in the west, and winter down to about 8500 feet. They are about a hand's length, soft brown, their

Sibbaldia *(Sibbaldia procumbens)*

breasts speckled with a rosy cast, making a graceful sight on the snow. Gray-crowned rosy finches also hunt the tundra; the light gray patch behind the eye gives a lighter tone to their heads. Brown-capped finches nest in small crannies in high inaccessible cliffs and craggy vertical rock walls. But in feeding habits they are gregarious, dipping and patterning the pink snow with moving blue shadows and trident footprints.

"Pink snow" is a mountain phenomenon. It is colored by a minute green alga that has resting cells encased in a tough gelatinous rose-red coat. Along with microscopic bacteria, fungi and protozoa, they form a microecosystem on a snowbank. This specialized community does not begin to develop until May or June, since some melting must occur so that there is water available for the alga's use. The temperature of the water within a snowbank is always 32 degrees F, since the heat energy entering the bank is used to melt more snow rather than to raise the temperature of that which is already melted, and the snow microorganisms are adapted to grow at the freezing point.

Pink is the most common color in the alpine region, but there are also orange and green snowbanks at lower elevations. The color usually depends upon the amount of sunlight received during the day. There is some evidence that the red pigments protect the algal plant cells from damage by radiation, and the ability to synthesize these red pigments may be one adaptation that permits the alga to exist in this extreme and transitory environment. These same cells also concentrate airborne radiation, a phenomenon discovered by a uranium prospector who inadvertently let his coffee pot go dry after melting snow in it and heard his Geiger counter nearby begin to click.

In the glistening snow the watermelon pink cells are visible even without a hand lens. They even smell faintly like watermelon, but too generous a sampling can have unexpected laxative effects on some of the unwary and thirsty.

11 : Animal-Disturbed Communities

It is almost impossible to spend a day on the Rocky Mountain tundra without coming across cone-shaped mounds of dry dirt that contrast with the denser meadow turf, the signs of pocket gopher activity. Bald spots are interspersed, some empty and flat, some bearing a few pioneer plants, some granulated with recent needle ice activity. They make the turf look like a somewhat moth-eaten fur coat. As the fresh mounds settle, and if needle ice is not too active, the erect, brilliant blue- and yellow-flowered plants characteristic of animal-disturbed areas form a "gopher garden."

But the gopher garden will be eroded and blown at and picked away at by the wind until it returns to a fellfield, and must undergo the whole long succession back to a meadow again. For some undiscovered reason, the taller plants die out after a few decades, and invading cushion plants expand vigorously, forming a typical fellfield vegetation. To develop into a well-established turf again takes many decades, even centuries. Succession may be continually interrupted; if gophers are more or less continuously active in an area they may maintain it as a gopher garden indefinitely. Although pocket gopher disturbance covers only a small segment of a total tundra area (one animal usually works only an acre or two at a time), several working close together can keep a meadow in a constant state of upheaval. In addition, marauding coyotes, bears or mountain lions may scratch open the tunnel to get at the occupant, further disrupting local vegetation.

The various turf and snowbed communities are the only ones that have a deep enough soil, enough drainage, and enough reward of succulent tasty roots to harbor gophers. The porous soil created by rodent burrowers allows rain to soak into the ground instead of running off, a boon to the dry alpine tundra. In the early spring, empty pocket gopher burrows often fill with water, spurting downhill in three- to six-inch fountains when runoff is heavy.

But pocket gophers destroy many peripheral plants while they burrow along underground, plants that are not directly involved in food or nesting. The dirt mounds thrown up smother small surface plants, doubling the impact of gopher digging on alpine meadows. Whole plant cushions can be chewed off below ground, left hanging by a single fiber like a six-year-old's front tooth. The mounds themselves are vulnerable to wind erosion which nudges the finer soil particles away, worrying the dead vegetative cover, eventually leaving a gravel mulch and a few plant sprigs. Sites that are severely wind-eroded may not be recolonized for years.

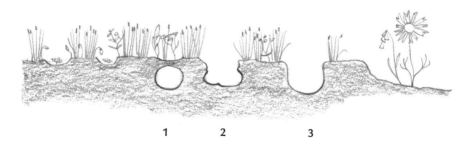

GOPHER TUNNELS
1. Fresh intact tunnel.
2. The roof has collapsed on an older tunnel; water erosion leaves rough irregular sides.
3. A tunnel used by meadow voles is smooth from the tamping of running feet.

A description of a pocket gopher sounds like a police wanted bulletin: slightly larger than a common white rat; broad blunt head, small ears, short legs, small beady eyes. Varies from brown to gray. Very well-muscled forelegs with greatly enlarged front claws for digging. Has a fur-lined pouch or "pocket" on each cheek which opens to the outside and is used for temporary storage and transport of food.

I wonder if one feels so negative about pocket gophers because they are virtually invisible. One sees pika and marmots, has glimpses of elk and bighorn sheep, hears pipits and finches and horned larks. But pocket gophers are eternally hidden and secretive, chomping roots and bulbs, unseen and unheard, tunneling about a foot or so beneath the surface in search of roots for food, reworking a single area over and over, and then venturing out into adjacent areas in long adventurous loops or haphazard crisscrosses, spending summer and winter, day after day, night after night, in a dark and driven search.

After pocket gopher holes are abandoned, they are sometimes taken over by meadow voles who use them as runways, small feet tamping the earth smooth until the roof caves in or they are flooded. Meadow voles are tiny mouselike animals with short tails and small close ears, related to lemmings. They feed mostly on grasses and sedges in wetter

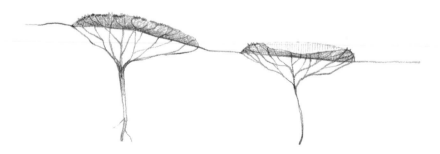

MEADOW VOLE DAMAGE
The center of the cushion plant on the right has been shredded by meadow voles; only the periphery survives. The plant may continue to grow as long as the taproot is not cut.

meadow areas, and also use the cuttings for nests. Their comings and goings make one- or two-inch runways among the grasses or sedges, scattered with tiny grass clippings. Although they often cut more than they eat or use, their impact is minimal except in times of population pressure, when they can effectively clip an area so that it looks as trimmed as a new-cut lawn. Population peaks occur in meadow vole populations every three to four years; they also have a more widely spaced and exceptionally high peak about every thirty years.

When winter comes they remain active beneath the snow. The home area of a single vole is only a few square feet, and where these few feet lie determines the amount and kind of grazing. If they nibble grasses and sedges, the damage to plants is slight as the leaves of these plants can keep on growing. If they work on cushion plants, the result is quite different. If there are many voles in one area, they also shred the center of some cushion plants, leaving only the perimeter alive, unless they have also cut the taproot. Quite possibly this is a reaction to overpopulation. Unlike gopher mounds, which dry and erode, the shredded cushions remain largely in place, retaining their outline for two to five years since decomposition is so slow and the shreddings lie close to the ground where the wind does not reach.

Although voles neither eat as many plants nor destroy the ground surface to the extent that pocket gophers do, in years of very heavy population they may destroy enough cushion plants to allow the invasion of the taller plants that often come in after pocket gopher disturbance. But the meadow voles, all in all, seem more in balance with the alpine ecosystem, peering with black beady eyes through picket fences of grass, dining on a moss campion cushion, and endlessly scurrying through tiny mazes, summer and winter.

Many alpine tundra areas have been used for summer sheep grazing. Although this has been largely terminated because of poor forage, heavily grazed areas still bear the imprint of damaged soil and impoverished plant communities. The same colorful plants come in as after pocket gopher disturbance, and the same bare spots occur in the plant cover. Grazing was most damaging where sheep crossed steep passes, for here the ground is open to wind erosion and downslope movement.

12 : Alpine Marsh and Lake Communities

My mental picture of an alpine marsh is of marsh-marigolds blooming in drifts among verdant mosses. The white flowers are mirrored in the pockets of water between clumps, as dazzling as the glints of sunlight shot off the moving water. A marsh-marigold's root system is tenacious, anchoring against the running water that would unseat a lesser plant. In August many of the marsh-marigolds are in stalky green seed while many more are still blooming in masses, white sepals streaked with lavender and green beneath, framed by dark glossy heart-shaped leaves. They remain in the mind like a reverse image through which one sees the ordinary world more clearly.

One usually sees an alpine marsh from the top of a slope, looking down to where the water is caught in terraces or threads its way across a flat. An alpine marsh from above is a darker green than the rest of the dusty-green tundra. The amount of water which comes from a melting snowbank or spring or permafrost that supports the marsh looks like rivers inked in blue on a map. Sometimes the rivulets cascade down precipitous slopes to feed a tarn below, and then they are drawn in white.

Marsh communities, no matter where they exist, have the same vertical greenness of plants that depends upon the constancy of the water supply. But marshes in the alpine zone do not flourish in the warm temperatures of a midwestern summer nor the year-round warmth of a southern flat. Here they form behind solifluction terraces underlaid by permafrost that holds water close to the surface through most of the summer and into the fall. Or they lie below melting snowbanks that provide a steady trickle of icy water twinkling swiftly downslope. Or they border the edge of a high rock-basined tarn.

Where the water runs swiftly it remains colder all summer than the temporary ponds, which are still and shallow and sun-warmed. The rivulets run in many ways, sometimes wide and shallow over gravel bottoms, sometimes through trenches three feet deep and a foot wide, heavily turfed over the edge of the low bank down to the water. It is hard to relate these mercurial streams to their source, often a dirty snowbank above, phlegmatic and dull.

Sometimes the snowmelt plaits and unravels across and among mossy tussocks. On top of the hummocks water-loving sedges form lush shiny swards, punctuated with their dark heads. They remain conspicuously bright green when the rest of the tundra is dry, especially striking in the fall when turf and fellfield moisture is low. Marshes have a malachite greenness, the different sedges making serpentine shades of green that ripple in the wind, a different texture from the low willow or the moss and lichens that pad the ground beneath. The combination of abundant mosses and lichens and low shrubs, together with permafrost, resembles the arctic tundra in a way that alpine fellfields and meadows do not.

An alpine marsh is enlivened by the musical sounds of water through sibilant sedges and wind fingering slender willow leaves. The soil in which these plants grow is cold and dark. Because of constant saturation and the predominantly sedge and moss cover on the hummocks, it is very high in organic matter and contains large deposits of peat.

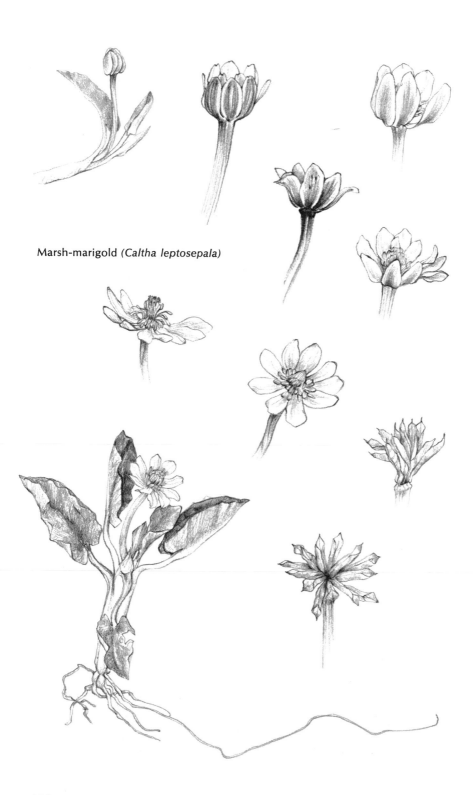

Marsh-marigold *(Caltha leptosepala)*

Peat acts as an effective insulation, preserving the permafrost beneath; permafrost occurs only in these wet soils and in those of snowbed communities on the alpine tundra, for only here is there enough consistent moisture.

The top layer of the soil is very black, very mucky, and tightly interwoven with roots. Contact between the top layer and the next horizon is irregular. The frost heaving of ice produces undulations in the soil, and prominent blue-gray, red or yellow iron stains or lenses of gray silt characteristic of waterlogged soils lie in the upper horizons.

Bog soils are very poor conductors of heat because of their high moisture and humus content, and because they are often underlaid by permafrost. They are always chill, the slowest of all tundra soils to heat up, and so growth begins later here. Even in August a marsh is just plain cold to walk on. The specific heat of water is about five times as great as that of the mineral particles of which dry soils are formed, so about five times as much heat is required to raise the temperature of an equivalent volume of wet soil as dry soil. Daytime warmth penetrates barely a hand's length below the surface. In addition, the peat works like a sponge, remaining springy and sodden. Earthworms cannot work it; there is almost no oxygen and the excess carbon dioxide and humic acids form a very acid soil.

No matter with what care one negotiates hummocks and tussocks, the soil spurts black mucky water over boot toes with every injudicious footstep. Often the alternative is balancing on rocks too small to hold one boot, let alone two, while considering which way to jump from a negative alternative to an impossible result.

High alpine lakes shine like strings of turquoise beads on far mountain slopes only in late summer, for many remain frozen well into July. Water fills basins dammed by a series of glacial moraines or especially resistant bedrock, dropped with the retreat of each succeeding glacier, one below the other. When lakes string down the high slopes they are called "pater noster lakes." These natural lakes are usually quite deep, kept full by water cascading from melting snow in the high rocky cirques above them. The water level remains extremely stable because there is ample run-in all summer and an outflow stream to channel off the excess.

None but the most hardy swims in an alpine lake. The waters remain around 40 degrees F most of the summer, reaching 50 degrees only in August, and then only on the sun-warmed surface. Algal populations remain rudimentary since, in addition to low temperatures, the rock and gravel basin surrounding the lake provides little organic nourishment. There are no rooted plants on the sides or bottom and scarcely any of the minute water animals or plants that animate lowland lakes. Fairy shrimp may appear but the populations are very small; water flea populations are minimal. Few fish live here naturally; such lakes must be stocked if heavily used for fishing.

Alpine lakes are truly clear. They are high in oxygen because there is so little plant or animal respiration, or bacterial action, to deplete them. Even though ice can cover the surface up to a yard thick in the winter and last into July, oxygen measurements remain high. Crossing a boulder pile high above the shore of an alpine lake gives one a certain uneasiness. There is an uncomfortable steely coldness below. One is able to see into a clear empty blackness, and the boulder pile seems to stretch further below the surface into a black maw deeper than one ever sees in lowland lakes.

Only in the late afternoon does an alpine lake seem gentle; then the boulders which ring its basin form a giant necklace around the blue-gray crushed velvet of the lake's wind-softened surface.

13 : Alpine Heath Communities

All major mountain ranges in the United States have heathers and heaths, to a greater or lesser extent, but the Southern Rockies have so few and in such isolated instances that for all intents and purposes they are missing from these alpine areas.

Heaths and heathers make up a large proportion of the plants in the East Coast tundra of Mount Washington and its environs. They are not as plentiful in the Western Cordillera although they extend through the Olympics and Cascades into the Sierra Nevada. They are widespread in the Northern Rockies. The answer to the hiatus in the southerly Rockies probably lies in local low desert topography across which these alpine plants could not migrate. Or, if heath species once existed in plenty, the present-day sunny, dry climate of the Southern Rockies might have eliminated these genera that require a colder, moister, less sunny environment. Heaths do proliferate in the Canadian Rockies so the proximity necessary for migration exists.

Heaths are low-growing shrubs. They are all Old World genera which grow in slightly acid soils that are moist but well-drained, usually where winter snow gives some protection but melts early. Blueberries and bilberries, bearberries, bell heathers, bog laurels, Labrador teas, alpine azaleas, cranberries, rhododendrons, mountain heaths, all belong to the Heath family. Crowberry, although not a heath, resembles it in its low growth and small leathery leaves. The composition of heath communities varies according to exposure and snow cover, and the thickness and height of their growth allows little room for other plants. Iceland lichen, insinuated between and under the shrubby

Bog bilberry *(Vaccinium uliginosum)*

plants, is a prominent member of heath communities. The combination of heath and thick lichen is characteristically arctic, the product of high atmospheric moisture and low light levels, and is well developed in the most arctic-like environment in the United States, that of the East Coast alpine tundra.

Many heaths and heath-type plants are evergreen; they can grow in exposed ill-favored sites above treelimit because they make fewer demands upon the environment than deciduous plants. Evergreen plants have lower photosynthesis and respiration rates than do deciduous plants, requiring less energy to survive. They do not have to expend food reserves on leafing out every spring. Heaths need not produce a large amount of new wood each summer because they scramble along the ground and do not need an extensive support system. Old leaves are capable of photosynthesis; though it may be minimal, it is enough to reduce the total energy needed during new leafing. Old leaves provide important storage of plant reserves, especially needed in these species because the roots of most heath shrubs are very limited in volume and therefore in storage capacity. Many heaths can remain alive and grow when one side of the stem is frozen or damaged.

A well-developed heath community is deceptive. Old bushes may proliferate over rocks, holes in the soil, wet sinks or dry pockets, totally obscuring the truths beneath. They have a thickness and density and sameness of color that is visually more arctic than alpine. They pour down slopes and spread up banks, the thick-leaved evergreen species providing color when the rest of the tundra is dead, and the deciduous species revealing a bird's nest of interwoven branches and stems. Although a few lichens, mosses, sedges, grasses and herbs may grow within the heath's shelter, a heath community is more homogeneous and single-familied than other alpine communities.

Most heath or heather flowers are small, often bell-like, ranging from pink to white, giving an effect of almost endless repetition with only minor variations. Heath communities lack the variety of both color and form that characterize western alpine meadows and fell-fields. But this is balanced by the charming profusion of small delicate flowers and a bonus of edible fruits. A heath community is like the continuous and elaborate interlacing design carved in wood, inlaid with pale and deep pink and white shells, of some primitive Oceanic artifact.

Part Two

ALPINE AREAS

Introduction

Alpine ecosystems are limited in number, and often small in area. Not all are found in every alpine situation, nor is there extensive overlapping of plant species in widely separated mountain ranges. Animal species are far less numerous and less variable. Pika and pocket gophers are widespread, and ground squirrels, meadow voles and birds are often of the same species across the western mountains.

The unique cold-hardy flora of the alpine tundra is composed of many strands of vegetation woven together. Part of this vegetation derives from the vast circumpolar reservoirs of plants that maintained their identity from middle and late Pliocene times throughout the glaciations of the Pleistocene. Some derive from local lowlands, plants with such amplitude that they can adapt to widely ranging environmental conditions, and have an extremely wide distribution, such as the buckwheats of California, some of the sedums and saxifrages of Colorado. Some alpine plant species, like rock jasmine, are true alpines, found only on mountain tops. Others, like spike trisetum, are worldwide, growing at altitude and high latitude in both hemispheres.

Spike trisetum; marmot-tail grass
(Trisetum spicatum)

Many lichens and mosses, with their simpler growing requirements, are almost cosmopolitan.

The circumpolar tundra plants of the present probably evolved first in the highlands of central Asia, some species reaching the Alps and Rockies during the late Pliocene. Some of these plants had already spread downslope during the cooling period that preceded the Pleistocene Age, when conditions on mountain summits became too rigorous for existence, and cooler and moister habitats were opened downslope and southward. They also migrated both east and west along the almost continuous mountain stepping-stones, west to the Alps and east to the Rockies across the then ice-free Bering land bridge. With more difficulty, they may also have traveled across the bridge from Norway to Jan Mayen Island, Iceland, Greenland, Baffin Island, into Labrador and south to the mountains of New England. The large continental glaciers at this time held enough water to lower ocean levels, allowing these land bridges to protrude.

During the periods of fullest reach, mountain glaciers covered some of what are now tundra areas. Alpine plants grew lower on mountain slopes, or on small mountain or ridge-top islands above the glaciers called "nunataks." The interglacial periods, in which plants and animals migrated upwards and outwards, were warm enough to decimate plant populations on the lower peaks and sever continuous arctic-alpine plant distribution.

The interglacial periods stranded many animals and plants. Birds were less affected because their aerial mobility made it easier for them to escape hostile habitats. The warmer periods, together with concurrent mountain building, which either erased or confined tundra plants, had their greatest effect in the European and western American mountains. The mountains of central Asia, higher, more extensive and closer to the Arctic, were able to maintain their populations relatively intact, forming a bank from which plants and animals repeatedly migrated outwards.

Some 8000 years ago, as the most recent major period of warming climate began to shrink the glaciers drop by icy drop, cold-loving plants began again to migrate northwards and upwards into the northern latitudes and high altitudes that provided the only environments cold enough for survival. But the total number of plant species had been depleted and reduced by the struggle to endure the swift climatic alternations of warm and dry periods with cold and wet glacial times, leaving a residue of circumpolar plants. In spite of this, alpine tundra, world over, shares more species than any other major vegetation region.

The flora of different mountain ranges developed under different climatic influences and physical factors. It consists of plants derived from different sources plus indigenous species developed in isolation. The flora of different mountain ranges has relatively little overlap. Other than some plant families consistently represented—Daisy, Buckwheat, Mustard, Pink, Rose, Sedge and Grass—there is a limited similarity between widely spaced mountain areas. The shared species tend to be extremely widespread and tolerant plants: alpine sorrel, spike trisetum, and many grasses, sedges, rushes, mosses and lichens.

With the onslaught of glaciation, many tundra plants and animals either moved ahead of the glaciers or remained stranded on isolated unglaciated peaks, such as some of the high plateaus of the Sierra Nevada or the high ridges of the Rocky Mountains. These mountain-top and ridge "nunataks" provided refuges where some plants and animals evolved distinctive forms separating them from other populations of the same species. Over the years species diverge so that they can no longer interbreed with the original parent species; some become endemic to their own limited mountain areas.

A plant species remains in a single place because, for one reason or another, it cannot migrate elsewhere. Plants may be immobile in the sense that they reproduce by underground offshoots and do not produce many, if any, viable seeds which can be carried by wind, water, or animals. Or they may be prevented from migrating by barriers of temperature or dryness, as mountain plants unable to cross the barrier of a hot dry valley between two mountain ranges. Or competition may be too intense at a lower altitude for them to penetrate the vegetation lying before the next alpine area.

Endemic plant species provide some of the most delightful discoveries of an alpine afternoon, and endow each mountain range with its unique and special character. The alpine flora has fewer unique plants than lowland floras, but plants that grow only in a single mountain area stand out more because of the smallness of the whole of alpine flora itself: Rocky Mountain snow buttercups, alpine primroses and Rydbergia; the bluets of Mount Washington; the alpine violets and Piper's harebell of the Olympics; the Muir primroses and Dana lupines of the Sierra Nevada.

The greatest common denominator between alpine floras is in their mode of parallel adaptation to similar environments. The furriness of a buckwheat in a Sierra Nevada fellfield resembles the hirsuteness of an alpine forget-me-not growing in a Rocky Mountain fellfield. Collomia, a scree plant of the Olympics, resembles the milkvetches and phloxes growing in screes in the Rockies. Rhizomatous sedges and rushes growing in a Rocky Mountain marsh strongly resemble those in a boggy area on Mount Washington. The heaths of the eastern coast resemble in habitat and growth patterns those of the Olympic Mountains.

Because of the great variation in place and plant, it is perhaps helpful for the reader to know what to look for where, and to this end a comprehensive list of plants is appended. Not all plants will occur in any one community, but those that are the most common are indicated, as well as those rare treasures that make a breathless alpine hike worthwhile. In order to protect individual areas, they are not specifically named although the descriptions themselves are specific.

A WARNING: *No alpine plant should be dug or picked.* Very few will survive over a season without the specific narrow conditions of the alpine tundra.

14 : The Southern Rocky Mountains

To the east are the high plains of Colorado, drawn in pastels, the horizon smudged as if with one long thumbstroke. Between them and this aerie where I sit lie the soft morning-blue foothills, as rough in outline as a torn blotter. A few dots of blue lakes flash in the early morning sun. Clouds still lie in the valleys, remnants of yesterday's storm, lost sheep left behind when the flock moved out. To the west the Continental Divide forms a choppy sea of jagged peaks, white-capped with snow, serrating the horizon as far as I can see. Clouds are already forming over it, a dotted white line marking the Divide just as a dotted black line marks it on a map of Colorado.

The Southern Rockies are underlaid by pre-Cambrian sediments into which granites later intruded, and are now exposed on the eastern flank, creating the pink, tan and gray characteristic of the eastern Rocky Mountain landscape. In other areas, the granites are grayer, intermixed with other rocks; farther west and north younger sediments and volcanics create vastly different landscapes and soils. The profile that is visible today is the result of massive folding and faulting and glacial sculpting during the Pleistocene.

The brilliant whiteness of the new snowfall covers the dusted older snow; it is so bright that it dazzles the eye, intensified by the deep blue of the sky. The clarity of this dry high-altitude atmosphere makes distant mountains seem closer than they really are, with a preciseness of detail that usually belongs only to nearby objects. In the winter snowbanners fume off these bony peaks, but this morning they seem enameled, unchanging, permanent. A raven caws overhead, breaking the vast silences of their summits.

A concatenation of cirques, the spawning beds of glaciers, chisels the sharply scalloped profile of the Divide. The cirques endure, huge silent amphitheaters labeled with snow. Glaciers blocked the valleys below four times, but many of the higher ridges and peaks to the east remained open, such as the one upon which I sit.

Most of the alpine plants of Colorado are found in the unglaciated eastern areas of the Rockies, in the easily accessible Trail Ridge, Mount Evans and Pikes Peak regions. But the high interior mountains contain other less prevalent plants. Many Rocky Mountain alpine plants are tolerant of a wide range of conditions; nearly every alpine hiker sees hundreds of white heads of bistort and plentiful clumps of alpine avens, no matter where he hikes. Other plants are more precise in their requirements, growing only in specific areas. Rocky Mountain columbine is seldom found growing any place except under an overhanging rock; koenigia thrives only in the most arctic environments of gravelled, peaty stream edges.

The richness of plant and animal life in the Central and Southern Rockies is largely due to there being a long uninterrupted series of ranges down which many plants have been able to migrate. North-south ranges also provide a change in climate offering more habitats, and many arctic plants reach their southernmost outpost here. Another reason lies in the fact that many of the high ridges and peaks were unglaciated. Soils were not scraped away and remained in place to develop and stabilize. The Rocky Mountains are old mountains. And they look older, with a softer landscape mantled with plants, than the rough-cut fresh contours of the far western mountains. One feels this most keenly flying over the high rolling Rockies in the morning and the jagged spires of the Sierran peaks or the isolated sharp cones of the Cascades in the afternoon.

The Southern Rocky Mountains have a multiplicity of both plant species and alpine ecosystems not found elsewhere in the United States. Colorado alone has more than three hundred alpine plant species, roughly double that of some of the West Coast tundras and triple that of the East Coast. Of these, about half are arctic-alpine in distribution, and more than a third are species shared with the Northern Hemisphere. The Southern Rockies contain boulder, scree and talus, fellfield, turf, snowbed, animal-disturbed and marsh communities, all with variations. Only the heath community is missing.

From across a high valley, treelimit rises higher on the sunny south-facing slopes than on the dark north-facing windswept side. The spruce, rising up to treelimit, are watercolored in dark black-green, dry-brushed on rough paper, leaving a sparkle of white snow showing through in a combination of sunlight and pristine whiteness that is dazzling in the early light. Although it is June, the snow still holds in patches and drops in little fat plops from the sturdy spruce branches, making feathered saucers on the white ground beneath.

Water drips off a rock wall behind me, its silvery dripping sounding like wind chimes or the sequacious tinkling of a slowly unwinding music box. The sunshine feels warm, the breeze light and pleasant. The air is saturated with birdsong. It is more of a springtime this summer morning than any spring I can ever remember: blowing flowers and grasses, the feeling of "morning's at seven," an early feeling that depends on neither time nor place: sharp, cool, clear and sparse. A brown-capped rosy finch lands on a gnarled tree branch, issues a soft "chip chip" and is off again. The tree is long dead, bare of bark. The grain spirals in shades of gray and buff to rust, soaked charcoal brown where snow holds in a branch crotch and seeps down into the wood. There is a brief high chittering in the trees downslope—someone is in someone else's territory.

An old forest burn on both sides of the valley resembles a scatter of matchsticks emphasized by the whiteness of the snow. Although this burn is well over a hundred years old, only a few new trees have become established, and these are only a few feet high. It will take centuries to replace the dense forest that once grew there. Plant life is slow to recover at this altitude.

Subalpine Jacob's ladder *(Polemonium delicatum)*

The contours of the Rocky Mountain alpine landscape succeed each other in flowing rhythms, like the stylized background of an old Chinese painting. This gentle summit surface is the result of frost action since there is no evidence of glaciation in most of these high-altitude areas. When the valley glaciers flowed below, the climate was wetter and colder; evidence of frost's massive action is still abundantly clear. Solifluction terraces lie across the slopes, deepened by the color of willows nestled in their hollows. Nivation depressions hold Jean Arp patterns of snow late into the summer. Rock streams ribbon many slopes, and concentrated clusters of heaved rocks pucker the turfs.

Where the underlying rock is exposed and weathered, large boulders

Mountain harebell (*Campanula rotundifolia*)

Wandlily or Death camas (*Zigadenus elegans*)

have fallen into haphazard heaps. Within their protected nooks and crannies are a few plants that grow more widely at lower elevations. Thin-leaved plants, like pale blue Jacob's ladder and wand lily, shelter here, for the rocks provide a screen against high-altitude winds. Plants that do not grow in closed communities grow here in solitary splendor; a big-rooted springbeauty seems to spring straight out of the rocks. Other plants are hardy pioneers—lichens and mosses—that grow where other plants cannot.

A boulder pile, appropriately enough, is prime territory for many of the alpine saxifrages, a name that means "rock-breaker." There are microhabitats made to order for everything from the sturdy colonizer

Snow alumroot (*Heuchera nivalis*)

to the shrinking violet. Snow alumroot grows in footholds gained from crevices, tufting out of vertical cracks far above my head, flowers pale and insignificant against the larger patterns of the rocks. But they come into their own in September when the leaves turn brilliant salmon-red. Mountain currant insinuates itself into a horizontal crack, leaves smaller than lowland plants but with thorns so lethal that it seems doubtful that any but the most cautious and dextrous animal could enjoy the fruits. The glandular hairs are tipped with red like the drops of blood on a Santos.

In tiny pockets of soil with plenty of sunshine, goldbloom saxifrage packs mats of miniature rosettes, each cluster no bigger than a dime;

serpyllifolia means thyme-leaved. The vibrant yellow petals are dotted with orange, giving an intensity of hue from a distance in the same way as an Impressionist painter, letting the eye mix dots of pure color, resulting in a resonance impossible with a single color alone. Dotted saxifrage, which grows more luxuriantly at lower elevations, stuffs a small crack with mosslike leaves and white flowers dotted with orange and magenta. Whiplash saxifrage is an efficient colonizer of bare ground, whether it be an empty teaspoonful in a boulder field or a bare frost boil. Only a few inches high, the mother plant sends out red thread runners which arch up and over small obstructions to drop new rosettes on the other side.

The thinner-leaved saxifrages find protection from both sun and wind under overhanging boulders: nodding saxifrage and weak-stemmed saxifrages grow on the shaded north side where water channels down rock faces. I get down on hands and knees to look at a minute tufted saxifrage. Cosseted under a slight east-facing overhang, it is less than an inch across, bearing seven quarter-inch flowers. As my shadow darkens the hollow, the sun is immediately searing on the back of my neck, and I realize that the saxifrage is growing in a reflector oven.

Mountain currant *(Ribes montigenúm)*

Dotted saxifrage *(Saxifraga bronchialis)*

Goldbloom saxifrage *(S. serpyllifolia)*

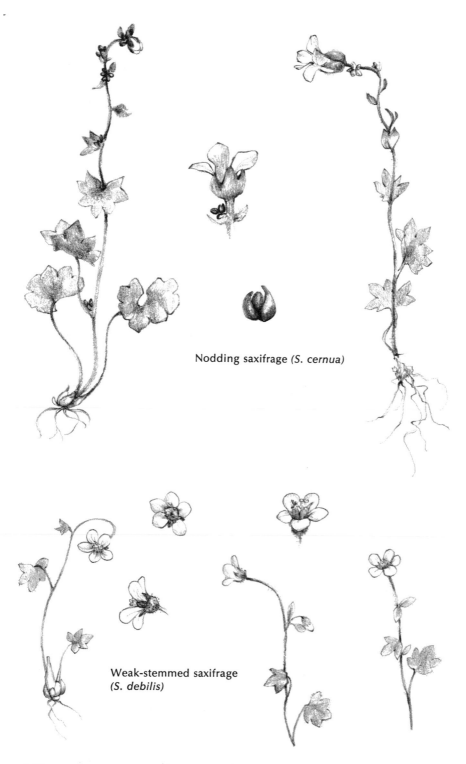

Nodding saxifrage *(S. cernua)*

Weak-stemmed saxifrage
(S. debilis)

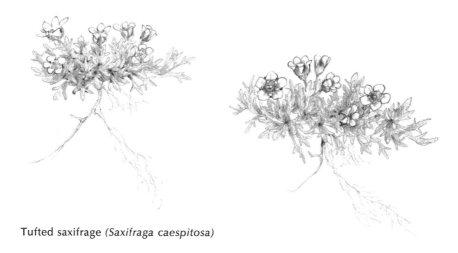

Tufted saxifrage *(Saxifraga caespitosa)*

One of the most widespread of all alpine plants is alpine sorrel, which grows from the Arctic southward around the Northern Hemisphere, from sea level in the north to high altitudes in the south. Its name is derived from the Middle High German word for "sour"; the leaves have a pleasant acid tang and are high in vitamin C. In the Arctic it is eaten regularly by Eskimos and relished by animals, and many a mountain climber has added flavor to a wild salad with its round leaves.

Extensive studies have been made on alpine sorrel, because it offers comparative material for arctic-alpine studies. Neither flowering nor new growth takes place until the carbohydrate level of the plant is sufficient for normal survival. It appears to be limited to high altitudes and latitudes because hot summer temperatures cause the plant to over-produce and deplete its reserves. It blooms every year, producing ample seeds which dangle from green thread stems like little Japanese lanterns, all shades from new green to ripe alizarin red. It is apparently wind-pollinated although it may be self-pollinated since it is not self-sterile. It must grow where there is some winter snowcover. The leaves die with the cold but the growing bud remains alive beneath the insulating snow. Seeds must have a mean average temperature of 59 degrees F or above to germinate, so the advantage of perennial growth is obvious.

The treasures of the Rocky Mountain boulder piles are the rare

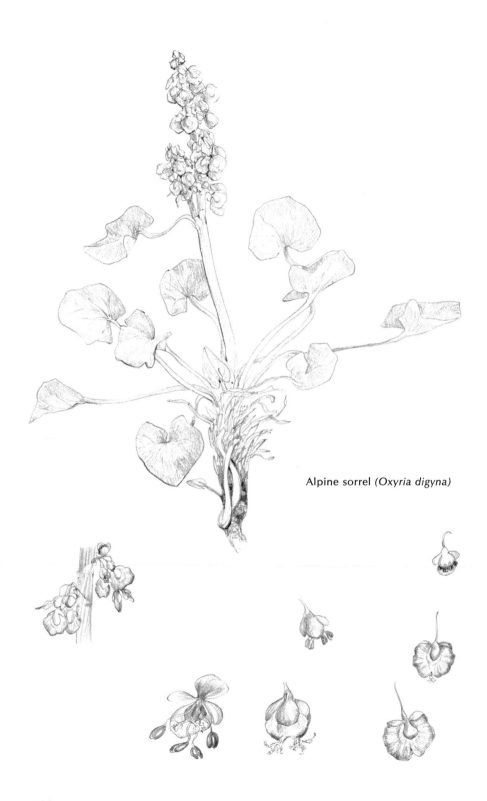

Alpine sorrel *(Oxyria digyna)*

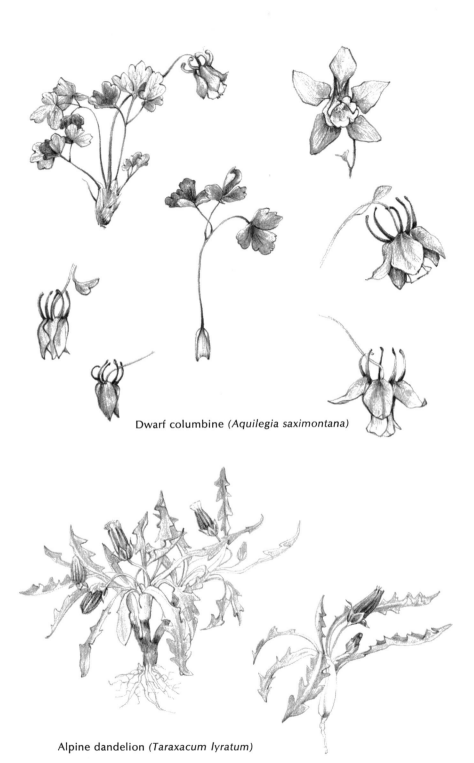

Dwarf columbine *(Aquilegia saximontana)*

Alpine dandelion *(Taraxacum lyratum)*

plants, such as the diminutive dwarf columbine, with a flower no wider than nickel, a Colorado endemic. An infrequent alpine dandelion plant measures little more than a silver dollar across, the leaves notched like the familiar lawn pest but the whole plant about a tenth as large. Behind it, in one of those frequent felicitous alpine juxtapositions, an alpine kittentail is in flower, fuzzed with a fringe of protruding stamens; a newly emerging plant looks like a lavender pinecone.

Seated alone in a boulder field one often has the uneasy feeling of being watched. About ten feet above, peering over a rock, is the feral face of a short-tailed weasel. Its triangular head on a long sinuous neck is almost snakelike, an impression intensified by the way in which it flows over the rocks. It is cinnamon brown above, sharply divided from the chamois hue below, surprisingly bright in color. It disappears, its back arching high, black tail tip clear, and appears again like a puppet bobbing up above a different rock. It is so close that its heart beat shows in its rib cage. Short-tailed weasels may hunt a thirty- to forty-acre area, and are found above treelimit where the habitat is suitable: rockpiles and available water. It disappears again only to pop up over another rock, seeming to stand almost on its hind legs to puzzle over my alien presence, a curious and exquisitely bright wild creature.

Two young water pipits upslope spot it and begin a nervous chattering. The weasel disappears. Soon the whole rockpile is full of warnings and staccato chirpings and squeakings.

At the crest of this boulder pile is a rocky ridge flanked on either side by turf, and from past excursions I know it to house a marmot colony. Usually marmots flump themselves across a rockpile in their flowing marmot shuffle but occasionally there is more action: a female appears downslope, hightailing it across the boulders, slightly smaller than the male who is in pursuit. Suddenly she turns and stands her ground and delivers an unmistakable comment. He retreats, looking somewhat like someone's old furpiece dragged on a string, a little motheaten and

Alpine kittentails *(Besseya alpina)*

unkempt. There isn't much green available yet and the marmots are not glossy coated as they are late in the summer. Marmots have catholic tastes, feeding on what is at hand, although they seem to prefer plants other than grasses and sedges.

And then, from beneath the rockpile, six baby marmots emerge, under the supervision of the vocal female and another adult. In contrast to the rather coarse grizzled coats of their elders, their coats are pale gray and soft with baby fur. They feed quietly, nuzzling along the grass, tumbling against each other. When one strays too far afield, an adult herds it back. And when danger appears, an older marmot gives a distinctive front-tooth-missing whistle of warning, and the young disappear back under the rocks.

The coarse-grained granites of the southern Rockies fragment into rough talus and scree, shifting down the steeper slopes in a constant barrage of dirt and gravel that inundates and destroys most plants. Those that are adapted are soil-stabilizers; very few are soil-builders. Perhaps for the former the struggle for survival goes only as far as clutching into these elusive gravels.

A network of long subsurface rhizomes underlies a minute milkvetch whose flowers are held in black-haired calyces, so tiny that they scarcely rise half an inch above the ground. Alpine Easter-daisies de-

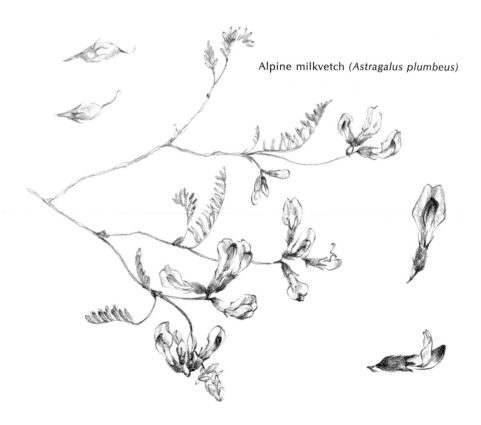

Alpine milkvetch (Astragalus plumbeus)

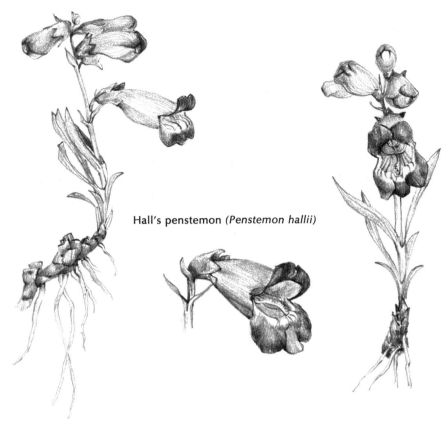

Hall's penstemon *(Penstemon hallii)*

pend from long loose-plaited root systems upslope that provide a mesh
from which the flowers spring. Hall's penstemon raises bright lavender
flowers. Alpine dusty maiden, pungent as yarrow and as furry, often
grows in scree sites. Yellow glows from the flowers of alpine bladderpod, the clusters of yellow draba and several sturdy bright yellow ragworts, their stems beet red at the cold end of summer.

One of the rare plants of the Southern Rockies is a tiny poppy that
exists in out-of-the-way banks in remote areas; it is so small that it
scarcely seems to belong in the same species; with its tenuous pale
yellow crinkled petals it seems almost too fragile to survive here. Beyond it, carpets of alpine dryad pave the slope with dozens of
white flowers and seed heads that look like the tousled pates of some
ancient elves.

Rocky Mountain Easter-daisy *(Townsendia rothrockii)*

Alpine Easter-daisy *(T. leptotes)*

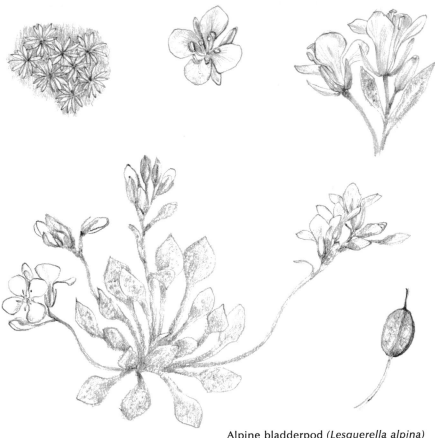

Alpine bladderpod (*Lesquerella alpina*)

A Rocky Mountain fellfield often has to be appreciated in a freezing gale because it blooms so early. I walk upslope, bent against the wind, sketch pad and notebook clutched tightly, needing three hands to hold my hood on and wipe the tears from my eyes. As usual, after any time on the tundra, my nose is running. If there is one complaint that recurs about being on the tundra, it is that everyone spends a great deal of time blotting watering eyes and dealing with a continually runny nose. There is enough bite to the June wind so that walking is exhausting. The wind beats against my jacket and makes it snap like a wet flag. I bend even lower, keeping a careful eye where I step.

When glaciers blocked the lower valleys, the bouldered mantle of this high unglaciated ridge was churned by freezing and thawing that thrust large rocks up on edge. This fellfield looks like an old abandoned

Thick draba *(Draba crassa)*

Clawless draba *(D. exunguiculata)*

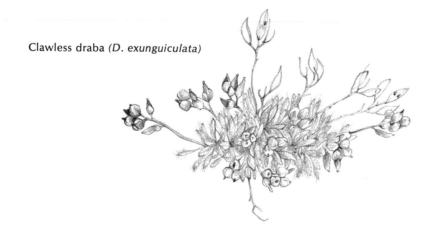

Ragwort *(Senecio werneriaefolius)*

Talus ragwort *(S. fremontii var. blitoides)*

Alpine poppy *(Papaver kluanense)*

cemetery, headstones toppled and tilted, weathered and rough, hiero-glyphed by lichens in unreadable inscriptions of what lies beneath.

When the wind is so strong and the air so cold, there is nothing to do but lie flat on the ground to rest, for within these few inches above the surface the wind is appreciably less, the air is slightly warmer, and it is here that one finds the flora of an alpine spring. Besides, rock-primroses are too small to see from a height of five feet.

The most profuse and the brightest are the clumps of yellow-eyed magenta alpine primroses. Their deep green leaves form narrow troughs that channel water down into the rosette. Their generic name of *primula* derives from the Latin for "first," an acknowledgment of their early blooming.

The flowers in a cushion of phlox shade from pure white to pale blue. Intensely blue alpine forget-me-not buds are so suffused with warming anthocyanins that they are nearly purple. The forget-me-nots and phlox are both sweetly fragrant, and the snow falling on their petals seems to be only crystallized fragrance. Alpine forget-me-nots are one of the special flowers of the Rocky Mountain tundra, not only

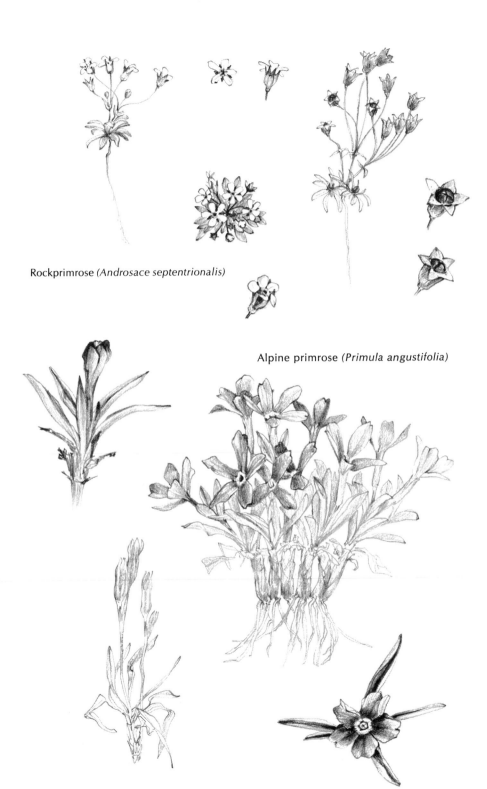

Rockprimrose *(Androsace septentrionalis)*

Alpine primrose *(Primula angustifolia)*

Alpine phlox
(*Phlox condensata*)

because of their fragrance but the special quality and deepness of their round blue color that is emphasized by their packed growth habit. Individually the open flowers are considerably smaller than a thumbtack; when a bumblebee lands on one, it more than covers the whole flower with its body.

Parsley flowers yellow the ground like drifted pollen. Infinitesimal drabas, less than half an inch high, flower in the protection of last year's dried stems which are bent like tiny krummholz. Alpine candy-tufts encrust the ground like pearls, stems so compressed that the flowers form flat nosegays scarcely an inch across. An alpine wallflower carries yellow pincushions of flowers just two inches high. Like the candytuft it too will lengthen its stem in summer's warmth, shaking long slender seedpods into the wind. A beginning cut-leaf daisy's petals are such pale lavender that they seem almost white. Alpine sandwort grows only in these snow-free sites and one is just coming into spangled bloom. In between all the plants clubmosses form almost unnoticed mats.

Dwarf clover insinuates itself into the edge of a sandwort mat. Its large tough root system makes it one of the most aggressive invaders of bare ground and other fellfield plant cushions. Typical lowland clovers have a mass of tiny flowers forming the familiar spherical heads; dwarf clover has only two or three, much enlarged. The mat is very slow growing, usually producing only two to four half-inch leaves annually; a cushion eight to ten inches across may be thirty to fifty years old or more.

Among the pink-flowered plants are a few with white flowers. In dwarf clover, the plant color may be controlled by a single gene. The mutation which causes the color change here, unlike most mutations, is neutral. When a plant is well suited to its immediate environment, any mutation is usually negative; it is possible for a mutation to be of positive value, usually, only when the environment is changing and the plant must change too.

Mutations range from the undetectable to the obviously disastrous. Small effects occur most often and are important in maintaining genetic flexibility in severe environments such as the tundra where plant populations are continuously being winnowed out. If the mutation is deleterious, the plant will not survive and the mutation will not be

Alpine forget-me-not *(Eritrichium aretioides)*

passed on; if it is of value, the plant will flourish and spread. In the case of the white clover, several more in the immediate area suggest that it has already reproduced successfully. Since bees are the only insects strong enough to pollinate clover blossoms, these white ones are evidently as attractive to them as the pink ones.

Once one's eyes become adjusted to the Lilliputian world a tough little mat of yellow-green alpine nailwort seems quite sensibly sized as it espaliers over a flat rock. The flowers, less than a quarter-inch, are wrapped in tissue paper bracts like a Christmas orange.

The prototype fellfield cushion, moss campion (named because the plant looks almost like a moss) filters among the rocks with a profu-

Alpine candytuft (*Thlaspi alpestre*)

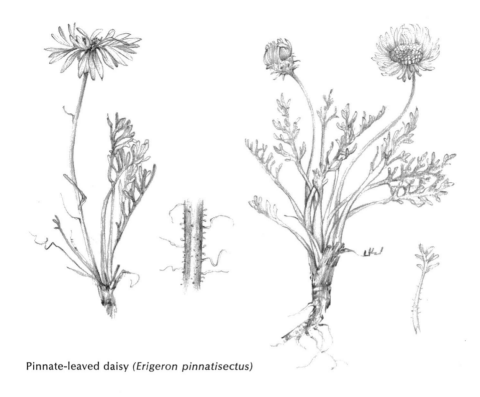

Pinnate-leaved daisy *(Erigeron pinnatisectus)*

sion of garnet buds that suggest it will be a mass of bloom in a few weeks. On another plant, a few peppermint pink flowers are open, fringing the south side of the cushion, the difference in microclimate a few inches can make in the tundra. Each blossom tapers into a very slender nectar-holding tube which can be pollinated only by butter-flies whose mouth parts have been adapted into coiled sucking tubes to siphon nectar. The stems and leaves of the moss campion are sticky and viscid to the touch, discouraging ant and beetle visitors that have to climb up from below. The base of the flowers is held by a calyx so firm and thick that not even a toothy bumblebee could bite through when frustrated at not being able to reach the deep nectar. I raise my head to see if any butterfly is foolish enough to be out in this weather. Of course there are none, but to my surprise I hear the whirr of a broadtailed hummingbird.

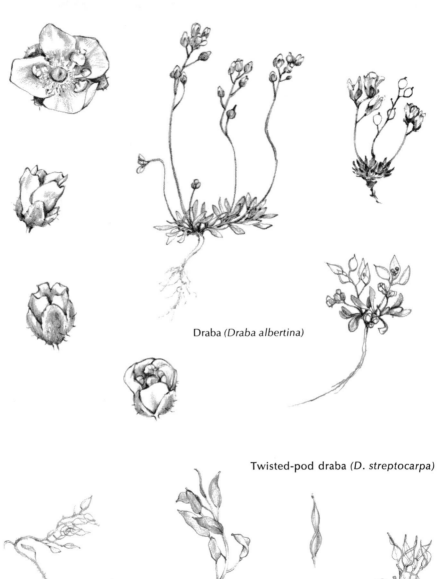

Draba *(Draba albertina)*

Twisted-pod draba *(D. streptocarpa)*

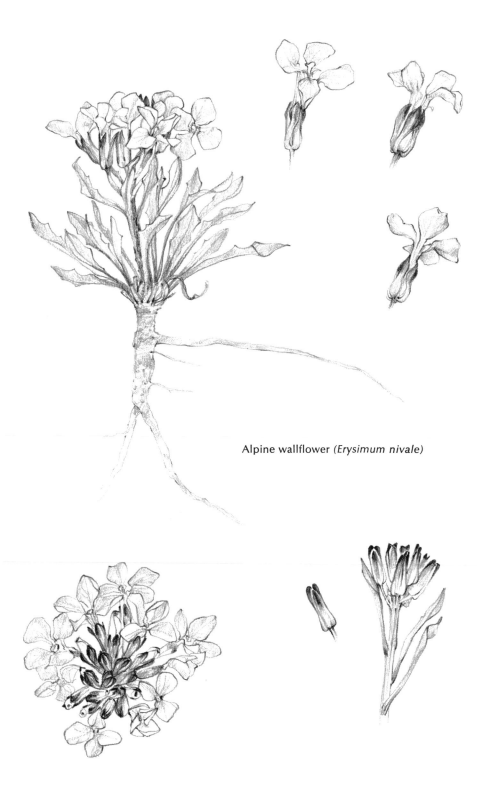

Alpine wallflower *(Erysimum nivale)*

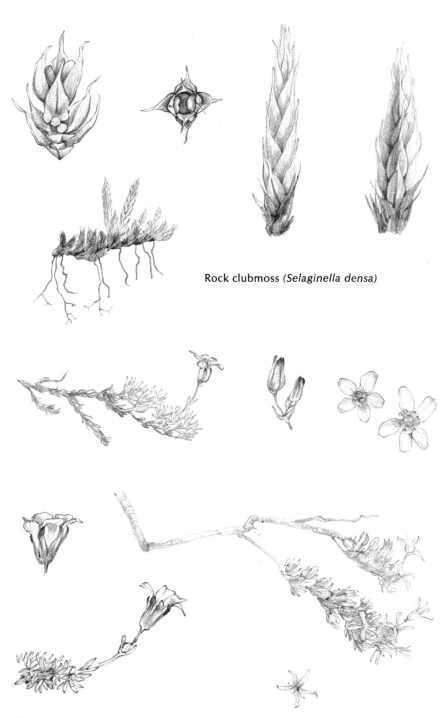

Rock clubmoss *(Selaginella densa)*

Alpine sandwort *(Minuartia obtusiloba)*

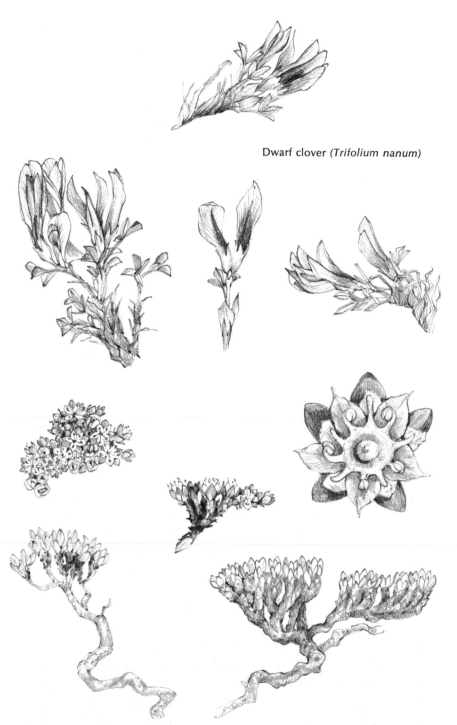

Dwarf clover (*Trifolium nanum*)

Alpine nailwort (*Paronychia pulvinata*)

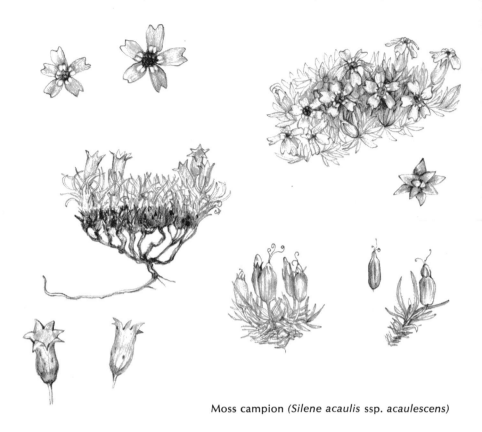

Moss campion *(Silene acaulis* ssp. *acaulescens)*

When I get up, it is almost a full minute before I discover that I am within a few yards of a white-tailed ptarmigan, and I realize it only when the bird moves. It is a large bird, almost the size of a small chicken, crouching at the edge of a snowy willow patch. Adult ptarmigan seem to know when they are changing color and remain on the periphery of snowbanks during the spring and fall moults, in a half-and-half environment that matches their neither-nor plumage. Half-moulted birds are piebald brown and white with flecks of black; the brown patches are often the size and shape and color of old willow leaves, and from a few feet away the birds remain invisible.

Ptarmigan winter in separate flocks: the females winter in willow thickets below treelimit while the males are the only birds to remain on the tundra. Mating time is triggered by the lengthening daylight of spring. Males return to their established territories on the tundra,

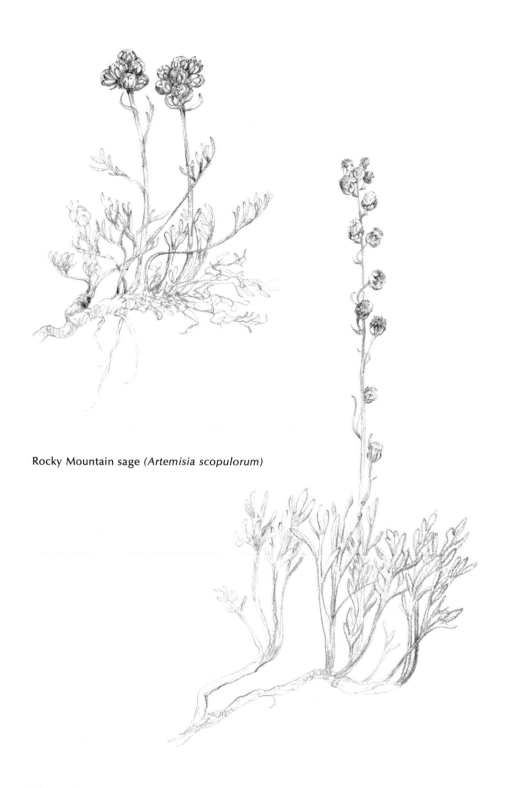

Rocky Mountain sage *(Artemisia scopulorum)*

followed soon after by the females. Breeding begins sometime in early May. Ptarmigan are monogamous during the breeding period, with a pair bond usually made for life. Once breeding is completed they have no further interest in each other until next year, and the females raise the chicks alone. But the following spring, incredibly, they find each other once more.

The females usually nest in July, and a heavy snow at this time of year can drive the mother off her nest, exposing the eggs to freezing. The nests are usually made in a depression on the open ground although well-hidden among plants. Weather causes the greatest egg mortality, although nutcrackers, falcons or weasels often find them when the mother is off the nest feeding. A mother ptarmigan will feign a broken wing to lead a predator or intruder away from the nest.

At this particular moment in time, ptarmigan resilience seems enviable to me. My eyes and nose are running and my ears are burning, and my fingers, when I take my gloves off to write, stiffen towards frostbite. Ptarmigan, in their down covering, can plump softly in a safe snowbank, their dark eyes looking like berries on a branch, feather patterns looking like dried willow leaves blown across the snow.

The millefleur pattern of the fellfield remains to some extent in the transition communities between the sparse high fellfields and the thick alpine turfs. Rock sedge is prominent in many of these interim communities, which often have a scraggly appearance because the sedges retain their dried leaves that curl in graceful Spencerian flourishes. Rock sedge thrives where there is no snow cover and soils are well-drained. These turfs are somewhere in succession between an easily recognized fellfield and an easily recognized mature meadow, partaking of some characteristics of each. The soil beneath is neither the skeletal soil of a fellfield nor yet that of a mature meadow. The organic horizon is not extensively developed and there remains a considerable amount of sand and gravel.

Some of the most striking plants of the Rocky Mountain tundra grow in these transitional communities. Big yellow daisylike Rydbergias shine out because of their size and color, all flower heads turned towards the east as supplicants towards Mecca. They are also called

Rock sedge (*Carex rupestris*)

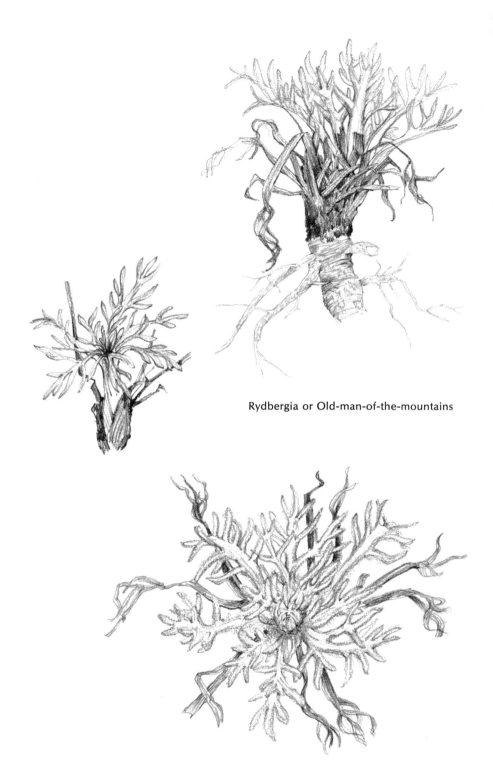

Rydbergia or Old-man-of-the-mountains

(Hymenoxys grandiflora)

"old-man-of-the-mountain" and alpine sunflower; Rydbergia commemorates Per Axel Rydberg, an early Rocky Mountain botanist. The two- to four-inch Rydbergia flowers, by far the largest in the alpine tundra, are achieved by a kind of modified annual growth pattern. Rydbergia makes only vegetative growth for several years until it stores enough food to produce flower and seed, and then it dies. No one knows exactly how many years are required from sprouting to flowering, but

Alplily (*Lloydia serotina*)

Alpine clover *(Trifolium dasyphyllum)*

some years on the tundra are marked by drifts of Rydbergia in bloom, suggesting that perhaps an unusually good previous summer or summers encourages mass flowering. The development of the head is not like a single bud opening, but rather a series of buds since the center is a cluster of disk flowers and the rim is formed by a series of ray flowers.

Tucked around the rocks of the turf are alplilies, tossing in the light air on three-inch stems, leaves so narrow that they are nearly invisible among the other plants. Their genus is named after a Welsh naturalist, Edward Lloyd, and their specific Latin name means "late-ripening." Alpine clover replaces dwarf clover in this community, the light magenta keel showing through a translucent white banner. Spike woodrush leaves, cottony with hairs and red-tipped, are attached to stems that shine like bronze wire in the sunshine. A bistort shafts six inches high, buds still ensheathed in copper. One-headed daisies and golden buckwheat, narcissus-flowered anemones and Parry's lousewort dot the meadow with yellow and ivory.

These intermediate turfs are carpets with a woof of yellows and a

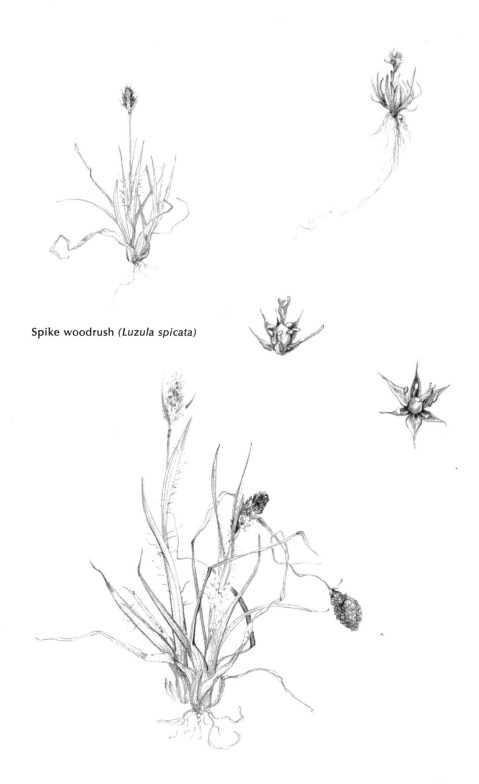

Spike woodrush *(Luzula spicata)*

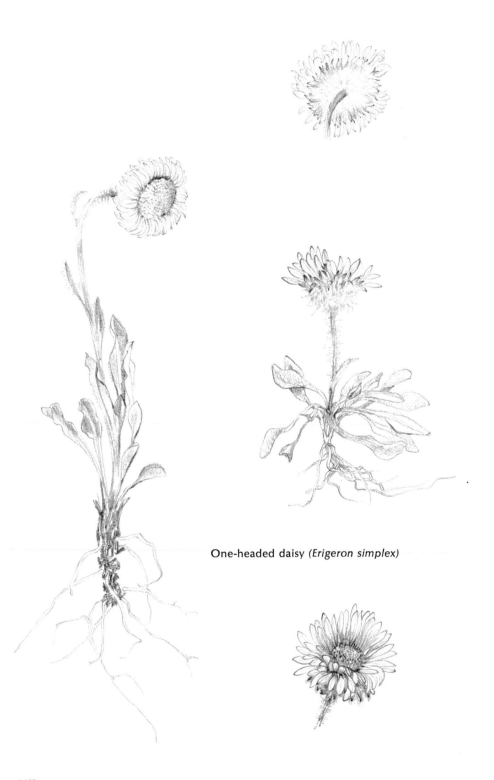

One-headed daisy *(Erigeron simplex)*

Alpine golden buckwheat *(Eriogonum flavum)*

warp of browns and whites: the yellows composed of Rydbergias, gold-flower, parsley, avens and paintbrush, and the whites of rockjasmine, one-headed daisies and phlox, and the browns of the dried sedge leaves. Where the vegetation is thickest and the clovers bloom pink and white, the ground resembles a Persian rug, well-worn, soft in color, close-woven in design, the pattern unified by the arabesques of the rock sedge leaves.

From a rock sedge meadow it may be only a few strides into a turf dominated by a small fine sedge called kobresia. Named for the early nineteenth-century naturalist Paul von Kobres, kobresia plants are small tussocks of resiliency and strength, no taller than my hand.

Within this community are more plant species than in any other tundra plant community.

In the summer it is easy to forget how cold it is at the end of May when the kobresia is just beginning to green. It wastes no shoots to drying and disintegration, but begins fresh green growth at the lower end of last year's now-brown leaf, the new green and the dried tip separated by a brown ring. Even in the chill spring it has a curious dry pliability, different from the rest of the wind-shattered, frost- and snow-sculptured tundra.

Kobresia grows only in sites blown free of snow throughout the winter. The lack of snow protection subjects this community to extremes of wind and minimum temperatures. Subzero temperatures are reached every winter. Winds of 130 to 140 miles per hour have been recorded two yards above the ground, and as high as 50 to 60 miles per hour in the plant tussock itself, an inch above the ground. Dead leaf tops can be abraded down to the sheaths which form a dense mat; these leaves normally hold little pads of snow within the tussock which are im-

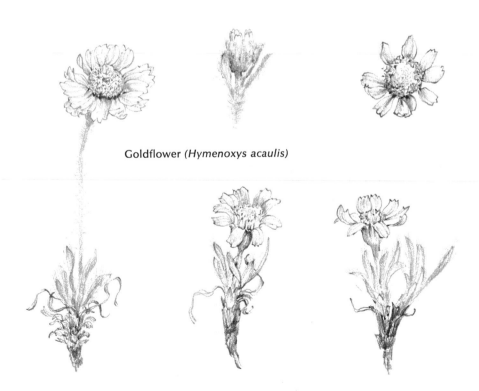

Goldflower (Hymenoxys acaulis)

portant in watering and insulating the soil beneath in this severe climate. It is physically possible for kobresia roots to absorb water vapor even when the temperature is below 32 degrees F, so that kobresia actually is able to grow in the winter. Major leaf growth begins in early spring, depending upon the site, and is normally finished in August and the leaves begin hardening to survive the winter, drying out so that water in the leaves will not freeze and kill plant cells.

Elk sedge, on shallower soils in the Southern Rockies and with a little more snow cover in the more Northern Rockies, forms the same kind of community as kobresia. Both sedges have efficient fibrous root systems which ramify through upper soil layers, providing for survival

Alpine pussytoes (*Antennaria media*)

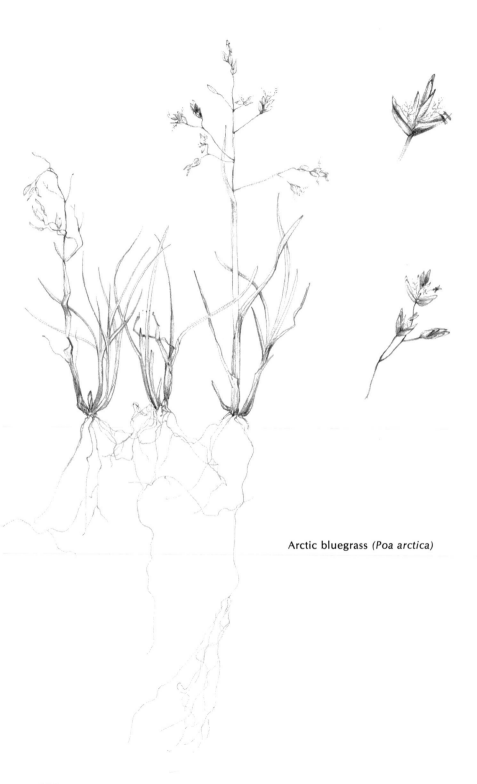

Arctic bluegrass *(Poa arctica)*

Narcissus-flowered anemone
(*Anemone narcissiflora* ssp. *zephyra*)

Parry's lousewort
(*Pedicularis parryi*)

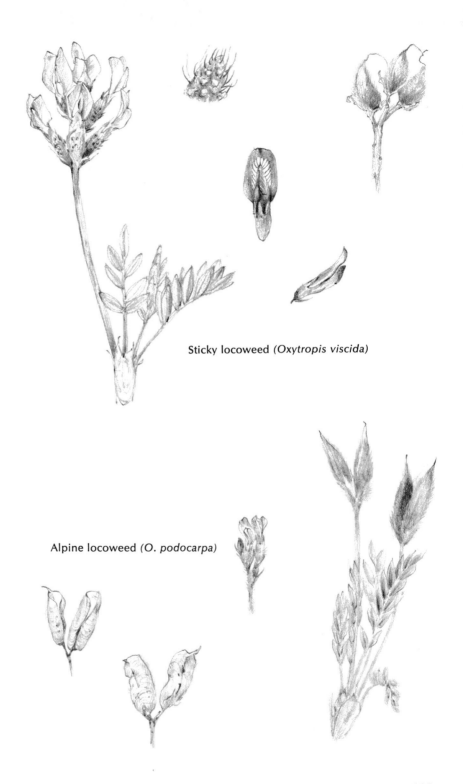

Sticky locoweed *(Oxytropis viscida)*

Alpine locoweed *(O. podocarpa)*

Many-rayed goldenrod *(Solidago multiradiata)*

on steep windswept slopes. These root systems so efficiently take up water that they can outcompete all other plants in snow-free sites: a single cubic foot of kobresia turf can absorb two to three gallons of water when arid, and the subsoil beneath remains dry.

Kobresia becomes established and flourishes only where the soil has developed four or more inches of humus. In many areas kobresia stands occupy areas of fossil patterned ground. Sometimes the patterns are still clearly visible because plants grow only on the concentrations of soil in the centers of the patterns. In others, vegetation completely overlies the rocks beneath. These patterns were formed during colder, wetter periods when frost heaving was active; they became plant covered only when they were no longer heaving.

The kobresia turf chemically and physically alters the parent material beneath it, a process crucial to soil maturing and characteristic of a highly developed climax vegetation. Beneath its tenacious intermeshed roots, stones are scattered through the soil, their undersides

Rockjasmine (*Androsace chamaejasme* ssp. *carinata*)

coated with a dark brown organic residue formed by the downward leaching of humic materials. The brown-coated rocks occur in rock sedge stands, but the coating is thinner and less extensive. The older and more mature the soil is, the more glaze adheres to the undersides of the rocks; under some kobresia turfs it may even lightly coat the upper side. Beneath this rocky middle layer, soil is dry most of the summer. Groundwater tables rarely occur beneath kobresia stands. The lowest horizon of weathered friable bedrock is quite acid.

Kobresia, hairgrass and many other grasses and sedges are highly nutritional. These form the best forage and are utilized by wild populations of elk, deer and mountain sheep. Native animals tend to space themselves and range widely, causing no perceptible damage to the tundra. The addition of domestic animals, or an overpopulation of native animals, causes considerable disturbance.

Kobresia, in the Southern Rockies, is a specialized plant, growing in tight clumps in snow-free areas, and on the most highly developed soils of the region. The dry stalks catch just enough snow to provide the limited moisture the plant needs; when the tussocks are grazed down to the ground, no snow holds and the plant dies. Kobresia plants have tenacious root systems and decomposition is slow on the tundra, but eventually the plant gives way, opening a spot to needle ice and erosion.

When heavy disturbance removes large numbers of plants, the bank of plants available to refurbish is depleted. Soil once lost on the tundra

Kobresia *(Kobresia myosuroides)*

Carex perigynium is entire,
contains only ovary.

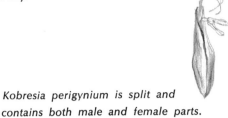

Kobresia perigynium is split and
contains both male and female parts.

Comparison of Carex sedges (Carex foenea) and kobresia (Kobresia sibirica)
showing difference in perigynia

cannot be replaced for hundreds of years. Once climax plants and animals are destroyed, it is almost impossible to replenish large areas. The recovery of most plants and animals under ordinary circumstances is relatively quick. Under severe environmental conditions, it is limited and slow. The estimate for revegetation of a kobresia meadow, assuming that it is totally protected after damage, is, at the minimum, five hundred years.

One needs to lie on one's stomach to appreciate the richness of a kobresia turf, the green stems and leaves fringing the brightness of the alpine view like eyelashes. One needs world enough and time to find the great variety of flowers and lichens crocheted among the sedge clumps. Some of the plants here are so fragile that even the sedge tussocks seem coarse by comparison.

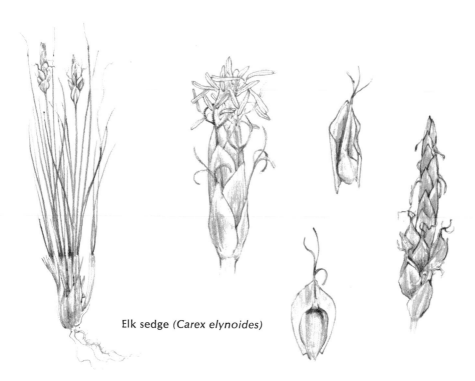

Elk sedge *(Carex elynoides)*

One-flowered harebell *(Campanula uniflora)*

A delicate one-flowered harebell has a solitary ultramarine flower, narrower than a pencil. Being insect pollinated, it offers a drop of nectar at its base. The flower is so small that even the tiniest insect would be touched with pollen. The tiny seed capsules are like elfin rattles with narrow openings, shaking out only a few seeds at a time.

A moss gentian, slightly lighter periwinkle blue, bears a single flower, its pointed lobes tucked into tiny pleated sepals. The gentian faces upward to the sky, and like many gentians it closes when the clouds come over or when breathed upon or touched, protecting its pollen from damage. Since pollinating insects are inactive during storms, there is no need to remain open and risk dampening precious pollen. Since one will close in forty-five seconds, not to open again for several hours, drawing one presents a problem.

An insect that crawls into a pendant harebell crawls upward toward the light to find nectar. An insect which enters the gentian must crawl downward, into darkness. Since many day insects have an aversion to darkness, such flowers as this gentian are often paler toward the base of the bell, making entrance more attractive to its diminutive pollinators. A minute black insect emerges from the throat of the flower, tentatively explores the convolutions of the petals, slips over the side and crawls down the stem. Its weight is insufficient to disturb and close the gentian.

At lower elevations meadowrue has male and female flowers on separate plants two or three feet high. Alpine meadowrue, in typical alpine economy, combines both on the same plant and grows just a few inches tall at best. This is a wind-pollinated plant; the pollen sifts down from well-exposed pale yellow anthers, and the lavender-red stigmas dangle like minute tassels. The tiny sepals drop off early, and there are no petals to disrupt the summer wind that sibilates its way between the kobresia tussocks.

It is easy to ignore the outside world and become totally immersed in a medieval tapestry of detail, each inch giving up a tiny treasure: a lapis lazuli gentian thumb-tall atop a green silk thread; a lichen curled like starched lace; two small round puffballs no bigger than milk glass marbles; a small onion that offers its flowers like a bunch of lavender tulips; the hatched run of a meadow vole forming a two-inch tunnel to somewhere; an alpine meadowrue with amethyst-rimmed leaves; a birdfoot buttercup pinched out of a pat of butter; a one-flowered harebell carved from ultramarine; a campion striped purple like a candy stick; an alpine oat grass with spun-glass florets; an arctic gentian forecasting winter in six weeks. The glandular leaves of alpine mouse-eared

Moss gentian (*Gentiana prostrata*)

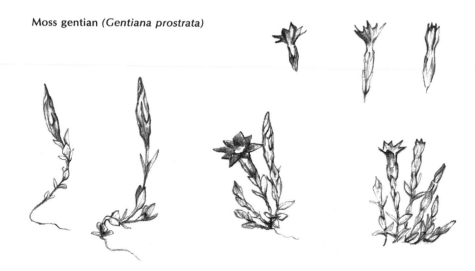

Alpine onion (*Allium geyeri*)

chickweed catch fine dust; its seeds show through translucent green pods that are as delicate as Tiffany glass. A tiny white draba has foliage so covered with hairs that it looks frosted.

Here and there a few snippets of fellfield plants barely survive: a single stem of moss campion, a furtive clover leaf, an impoverished rosette, all uneasy hangers-on in a populous community too crowded for their way of growth.

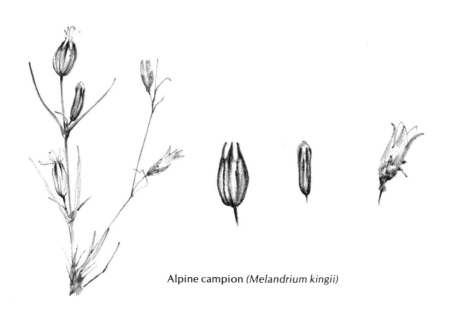

Alpine campion *(Melandrium kingii)*

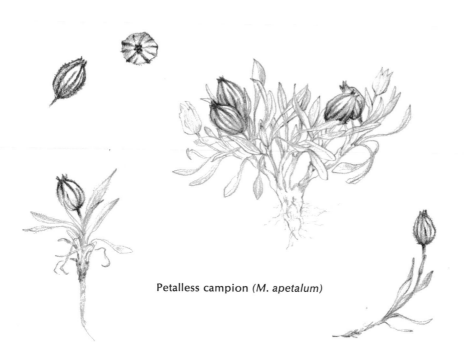

Petalless campion *(M. apetalum)*

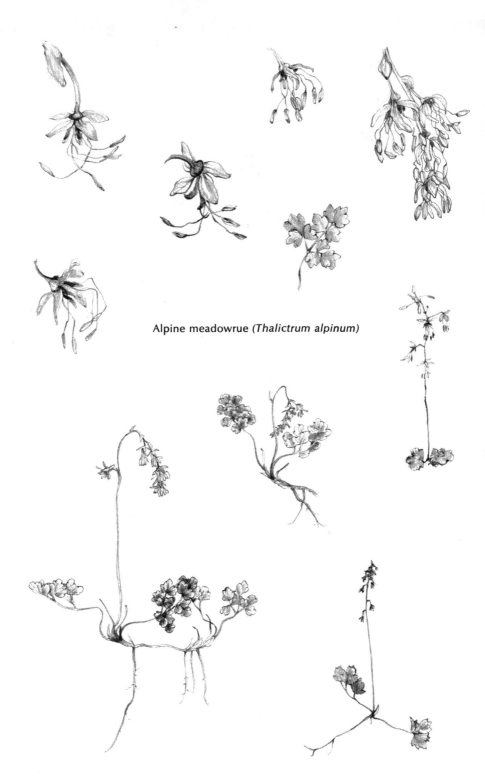

Alpine meadowrue *(Thalictrum alpinum)*

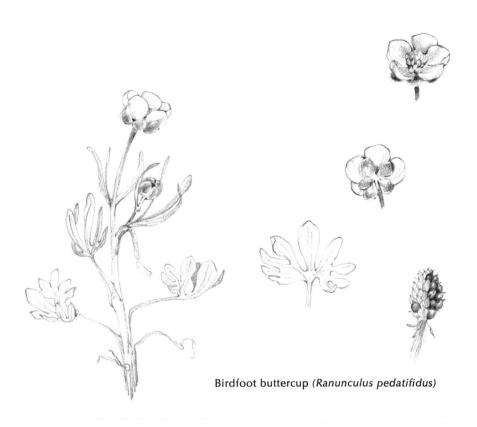

Birdfoot buttercup *(Ranunculus pedatifidus)*

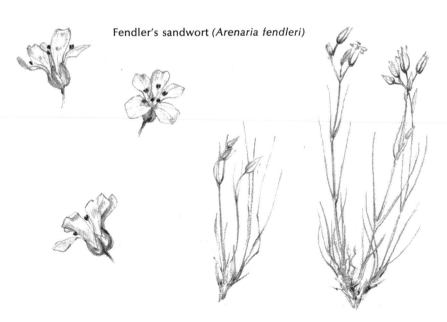

Fendler's sandwort *(Arenaria fendleri)*

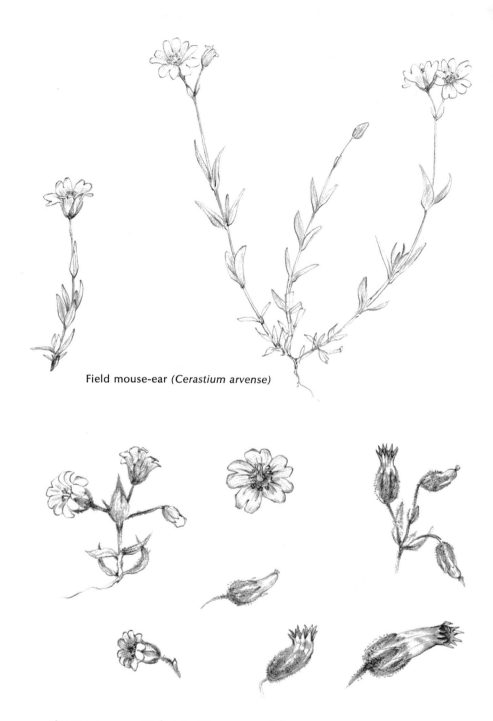

Field mouse-ear *(Cerastium arvense)*

Alpine mouse-ear *(C. beeringianum* ssp. *earlei)*

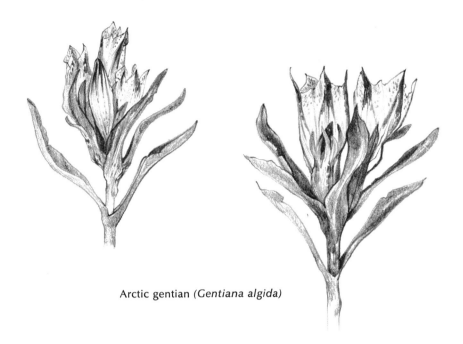

Arctic gentian *(Gentiana algida)*

Fingering through the turf makes one very aware of the profusion of even smaller plants: the crinkled lichens tatted on the soil between the tussocks or crusting the desiccated centers of dead kobresia tussocks. Over a fifth of the plants growing in this community are lichens. Some are able to grow on bare soils and do not even need to be attached, although they usually are in more stable communities.

The most abundant of the lichens is Iceland lichen, primarily an alpine species where it grows within the contiguous United States. It unfurls on soil across the northern latitudes in sites exposed to wind, and is very common, occurring from the New England mountains to the Olympic Range. Like kobresia it is intolerant of snow, and was probably isolated in these snow-free habitats during glacial periods. The paper-thin forking stalks are olive brown, changing to golden olive when wet, sometimes as full of holes as a Swiss cheese, and fringed with tiny spines—the only lichen with these features. Iceland lichen may be confused with another dark brown lichen which superficially resembles it, but *Cornicularia* has no spines, only seeming so because of its more slender branching.

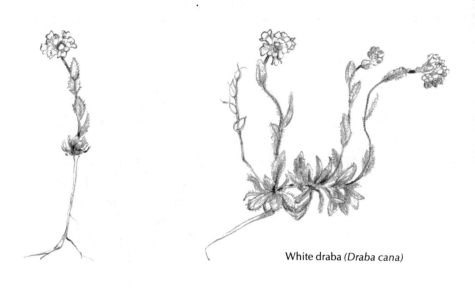

White draba *(Draba cana)*

Snow draba *(D. nivalis)*

Golden draba *(D. aurea)*

American bistort
(*Bistorta bistortoides*)

Snow lichen grows where a thimbleful of snow patches, a pale gray-green spineless version of Iceland lichen. Knob lichen is the same pale shade; its scientific name comes from the Greek word for finger. Worm lichen looks like hundreds of tiny chalky gray stalagmites or minute weathered antlers; *vermicularis* refers to its whitish wormlike shape. Most of these reproduce by fragmentation: pieces of lichen or algal cells enclosed in fungal threads drop to the ground and develop into identical lichens. Such devices must be of untold importance in maintaining lichen populations in frigid areas.

Wherever one goes in the Rocky Mountain tundra there are snow-banks—hanging on precipitous north-facing slopes that are so steep that, standing at the top, one looks down into nothingness below, or lying like limp ovals and ellipses in nivation depressions and hollows. Some remain far into the summer, some melt early, and some never melt.

Snow buttercups present a precise chronology of telescoped summer, marking the retreat of snow in snowbed communities. Although small, their pure brilliance of color is intensified by massed growth habit as they form great necklaces of plaited gold against the unredeemed brown of ungreened ground. While some of the first uncovered have already bloomed and are beginning to set seed, those nearer the snow-bed are progressively less developed. Within the crystalline perforated edges of the snow itself there are dozens, petals forming small pale green cups instead of tightly closed buds. Some open even beneath the snow, blooming though only an inch or so high, moonlike counter-parts of the brilliant yellow suns outside.

Their waxy buttercup petals gleam in the sunlight, made shiny by the combination of an oily substance in the outer epidermal cells, and a layer of cells beneath stuffed with pure white starch granules. Light shining through the outer surface and reflected by the starch beneath produces the peculiar brilliant sheen of buttercup petals. This glossy surface attracts inexperienced insect visitors, like flies, more effectively than a mat surface.

The generic name *Ranunculus* means "little frog" and describes the preference of nearly the entire Buttercup family for damp habitats. In

Iceland lichen *(Cetraria islandica)*

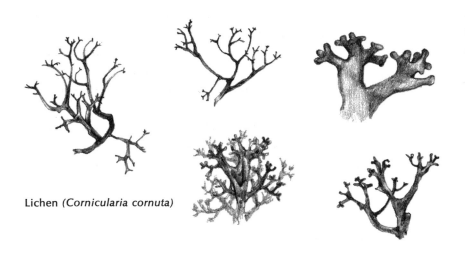

Lichen *(Cornicularia cornuta)*

Snow lichen *(Cetraria nivalis)*

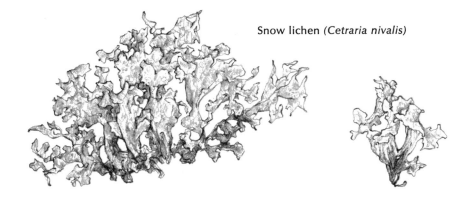

Knob lichen *(Dactylina madreporiformis)*

Worm lichen *(Thamnolia vermicularis)*

Snow buttercup *(Ranunculus adoneus)*

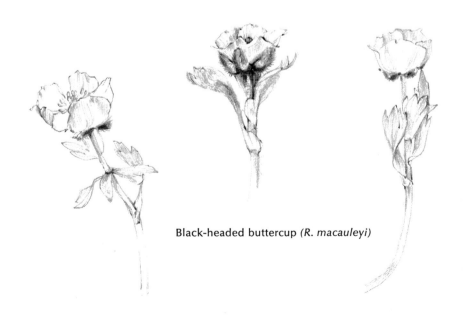

Black-headed buttercup *(R. macauleyi)*

the tundra, which dries out rather early in the summer, snow butter-cups find the necessary moisture near melting snowbanks, where they also have the protection of winter snow.

In late June, arctic willows form soft green patches across the large solifluction terrace at the outer edge of a snowbed. In years past, when wet soil slipped downslope, it formed a rim that held snow and mois-ture behind it. Now the willows hold it fast, and there is no longer enough water to instigate solifluction. Wisps of snow still cling in a few indentations, but for the most part the ground is clear.

This outer edge is protected by a shallow two- or three-foot snow blanket all winter, but is free early and will not begin to fill again until the snows of autumn, allowing a twelve- to eighteen-week growing season, as long as most on the tundra. The meltwater seeping into porous soil drips like miniature faucets. This depression will also catch rainwater and snow most of the summer, providing a more or less continual dampness, but good drainage prevents it from becoming waterlogged.

The yellow willow stems holding the catkins and leaves shine like snips of brass. The leaves are so tiny that the catkins seem enormous by comparison, male and female catkins growing on separate plants. Catkins have neither petals nor sepals, and therefore little color to attract pollinators, but they have well-developed nectaries to insure that they are at least in part insect pollinated. Later in the summer the patch is a spread of cotton as the ripened catkins burst open, loosing hundreds of brown seeds tipped with tiny brushes to catch the alpine winds.

The willow branches are like gnarled fingers, clawing into the soil for fingerhold. They interlace over and under the soil in as intricate a pattern as the illuminated letters in the *Book of Kells*, forever twisting, interwoven, interconnected and contorted, holding the soil like a steel net.

Within the month, the snow buttercups have faded to brown strings holding clusters of one-seeded fruits, lost in the burgeoning of a hair-grass meadow. Bright pink Parry's clover and yellow cinquefoil bloom in the thick grass. The big flower heads of Parry's clover are fat and deliciously fragrant, probed by hungry bees. Although insect pollination is responsible for most clover fertilization and seed production, Parry's clover also has long subterranean runners that help it to spread rapidly into new areas. Blueleaf cinquefoil is a typically fast-developing alpine plant, expanding embryonic flowering stems simultaneously with its leaves, yellow flowers appearing even when the season begins late. It produces its flowering stems at such a rapid rate because of the food reserves stored in its fleshy taproot from the previous summer.

Arctic willow *(Salix arctica)*

Parry's clover *(Trifolium parryi)*

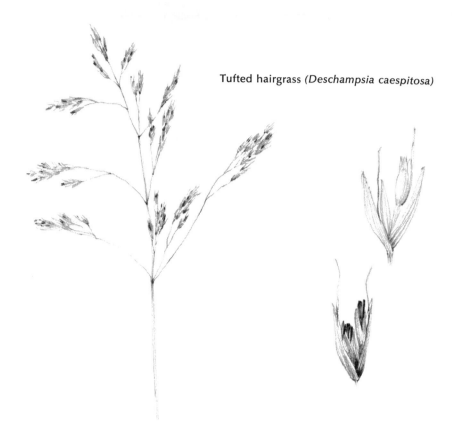

Tufted hairgrass *(Deschampsia caespitosa)*

Long-stalked stitchwort *(Stellaria longipes)*

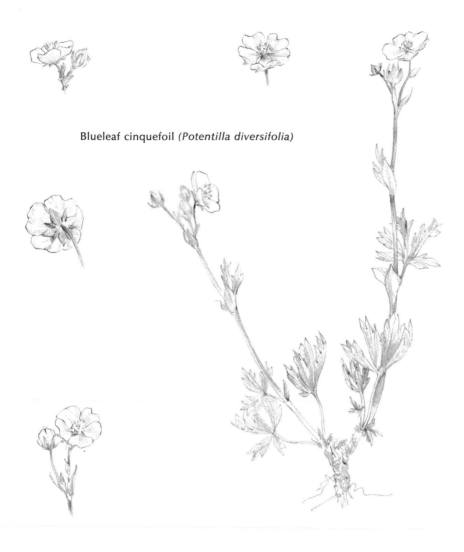

Blueleaf cinquefoil (*Potentilla diversifolia*)

The flower colors are stitched together by the big tussocks of hair-grass, forming the only true grass community in the Rocky Mountain tundra, and the most meadowlike one. The large dense clumps of hairgrass are difficult to walk through or on; individual tussocks are too small to hold a boot and give with one's weight, and the alleys between are too narrow. Hairgrass is one of the most widespread of all flowering plants, the same species growing in mountainous regions around the world. Its common name comes from the resemblance of the tussock to a head of shaggy hair.

The pinks and yellows of the clovers and the cinquefoils are punctuated by the bobbing white heads of bistort that beat the wind like metronomes. In furtive green shadows are clusters of pygmy bitterroot, sprigs of white chickweed, and nosegays of lavender violets. The grassy meadow has a certain medieval grace that speaks of lutes and mandolins and frivolous summers.

So precisely are snowbed plants adapted to the length of growing season that one can extrapolate the amount of time the snowbed has been melting by the plants that are growing there. With an open season of between seven and twelve weeks are gray flake lichen, the small rose called sibbaldia, and often white snowlover. Snowlover is a Rocky Mountain endemic first collected on Pikes Peak in 1821 by Edwin James. As its common as well as scientific name indicates, it is found only where there is winter snowcover.

Neither sibbaldia nor snowlover is especially noticeable in the summer; it is in the fall that they are most colorful: the sibbaldia turns a coppery crimson and the snowlover rosette a salmon red, strong warm colors against the cold blue-gray paving of the flake lichen.

Fresh patches of flake lichen and haircap moss often invade the snowbed's disintegrating gopher eskers. Haircap moss is a common moss, easily seen because of its size, and has a "missing link" status that provides a fascinating glimpse of the progression of simpler plants into a more complex vascular plant system. The moss plants resemble miniature juniper twigs, hence their specific name of *juniperinum*. Their generic name derives from the Greek words for "many" and "hair," referring to the shaggy capsule caps.

Mosses, by definition, do not have roots but simple-celled rhizoids, threadlike holdfasts into the soil. They have no vascular system to carry water from roots up through openings in the stem and out into leaf veins. Moss leaves usually have a single layer, or very few layers, of green cells making a paved leaf surface, lucidly green under the

Mountain blue violet *(Viola adunca* ssp. *bellidifolia)*

Snowlover *(Chionophila jamesii)*

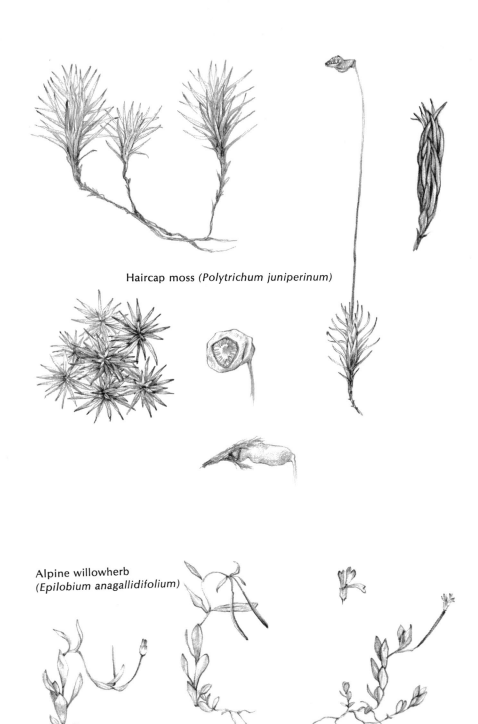

Haircap moss *(Polytrichum juniperinum)*

Alpine willowherb
(Epilobium anagallidifolium)

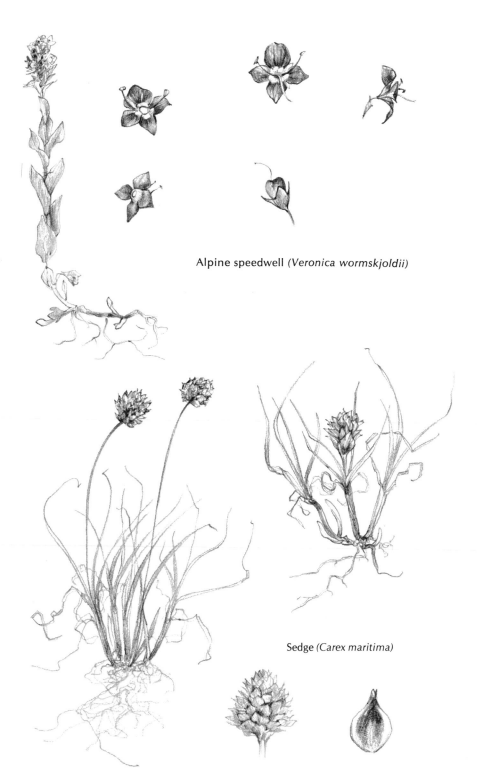

Alpine speedwell *(Veronica wormskjoldii)*

Sedge *(Carex maritima)*

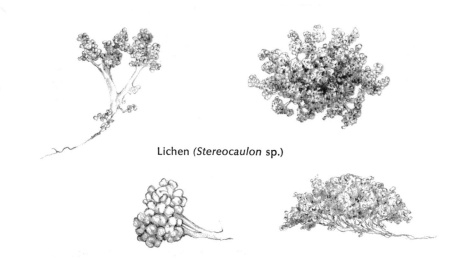

Lichen *(Stereocaulon* sp.)

Pixie-cup lichen *(Cladonia pyxidata)*

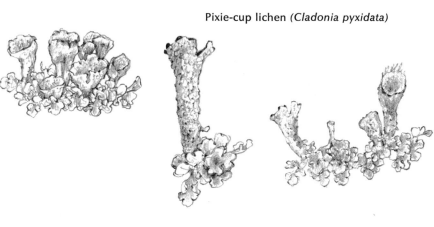

Green dog lichen *(Peltigera aphthosa)*

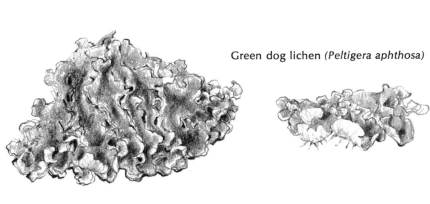

microscope. The leaves receive moisture over the entire surface, not from water fed from within by an interior vein system.

Haircap moss is anchored by several strands of rhizoids closely twisted together. Although not as efficient as true roots, the cable is still more effective than the primitive moss rhizoid alone. The leaves are also much more sophisticated. The midrib is thickened much like the water-conducting veins in higher plants, and only the edge of the leaf is single-layered. Most moss leaves are translucent to transparent, delicate and easily torn. Haircap moss leaves have the opacity that resembles a true leaf, and are firm and somewhat spiky to touch. Like many snowbed plants, haircap moss has a very low light requirement. The upper surface of the leaf is thin and easily damaged by excessive heat and dryness, not adapted to withstand tundra conditions. But when the air is dry the leaves roll inward with the tougher underside out, contracting against the stem.

Toward the end of July the snow in the bottom of the nivation depression is finally beginning to melt. In the center, saffron ragwort is still in bud while the orange-yellow flowers bloom a few feet out. Black-headed daisies are both in bud and blooming. At the most there is only a month to six weeks growing season for these plants. Uncovered late, they develop rapidly and, with ample sunshine and plenty of moisture, achieve a peak of production just after the snow withdraws.

The more showy daisies catch the eye, but this is a community dominated by Drummond's rush. Because the soil here is frequently at saturation point, frost action tiles it with rock patterns. Between them, Drummond's rush forms shining deep green clumps, rosy brown tipped in the summer light. There is no plant more impeccably and elegantly proportioned, drawn with a single perfect attenuated brush stroke, than these rushes.

Rushes are perennial grasslike herbs which flourish in wet places. Their generic name *Juncus* derives from the Latin "to bind"; their stems have been used for weaving time out of mind. The stems and leaves spring up from a rhizóme which sends one joint above the ground each year. The wind-pollinated flowers are rosy brown, glint-

Saffron ragwort *(Senecio crocatus)*

ing with copper, splendid in their lilylike symmetry and delicacy: feathery watermelon pink stigmas, pale yellow stamens, and shiny brown ovaries.

Signs of pocket gophers are conspicuous at the beginning of summer or just after an early autumn storm has whitewashed the tundra. When the snow melts back in the warm sunshine, gopher eskers lie exposed and fresh, serpentines and volutes crossing and entwining in gopher calligraphy.

Parry's rush (*Juncus parryi*)

Black-headed daisy
(*Erigeron melanocephalus*)

Even without the cone-shaped mounds of the summer turf, there are plants which unmistakably point to animal disturbance: lavender-blue sky pilots, yellow cinquefoils and alpine avens, blended with deep blue chiming bells or fernleaf candytuft. Rydbergia, Rocky Mountain and arctic sages, bistort and sleek grasses flourish in the open rocky soils. These meadows are blue and yellow, pink and white, sunshine and shadow, against far blue-gray mountain ridges velveted with tundra, all animated by droning bees and a dozen butterflies sky-writing "glory!"

A gopher garden is likely to be a very active place for another reason. Because the plants that come in after gopher disturbance are, for the tundra, fairly large and brightly colored, there are many flies and bees about. Even with a constant wind, the air may be heavy with the droning of bees working the sky pilots and chiming bells, and flies sampling the alpine avens.

Both sky pilots and chiming bells have bell-shaped flowers, and larger bees have a hard time hanging on in order to crawl up into the blossom. One portly bee systematically forages from sky pilot to sky pilot, the brilliant orange pollen on its legs standing a good chance of being transferred before it has been in the air long enough to lose its viability. Anyone who has been close to a sky pilot is aware of a very pungent characteristic: the small round leaflets smell like an unhappy skunk. Although the spherical blue flower head, composed of close-packed blossoms, is the primary attraction, odor may be one of the close-up recognition signs to insect pollinators. The stamens are very full of bright orange pollen which contrasts vividly with the royal blue of the flower, forming a "honey-guide."

Bright flowers are of no advantage to a plant other than as a device to attract insects and insure cross-fertilization. The diversity of flower shapes and colors can only be explained by the hypothesis that such variety encourages insect visits; these same plants also produce nectar to entice visiting insects.

Two opulent clumps of alpine avens grow near the sky pilots, their bright yellow flowers raised upward to the sun on rose-red stems. When the sun goes behind a cloud I count twelve black flies in one plant and seven in the other, sharp against the vivid yellow. Flowers

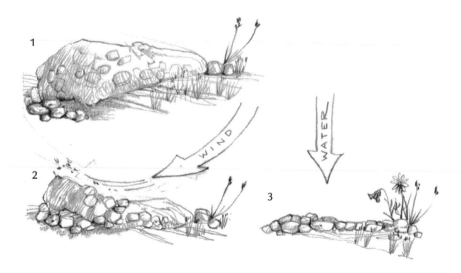

POCKET GOPHER MOUNDS
1. Pocket gopher mounds may cover a square foot or more, smothering plants beneath.
2. Wind blows out topsoil particles.
3. Water washes away soil; erosive action of both wind and water leaves a gravel surface that is invaded by short-lived "gopher garden" plants.

Sticky sky pilot *(Polemonium viscosum)*

Alpine avens (*Acomastylis rossii*)

Drummond's rush (*Juncus drummondii*)

preferred by flies are usually regular, simple, often flat open like the avens. Nectar guides are often present, and nectar is easily available. Unlike bee flowers, fly flowers commonly have little odor. Stamens and pistils are numerous and well exposed so that the pollen rubs off readily as the fly crawls across the flower. Flies are so prevalent in buttercups and avens and parsleys that one becomes accustomed to seeing the yellow flowers punctuated with black.

Parsleys, whose minute yellow flowers cluster together in a flat umbrellalike head, are fly favorites. They are low growing so a fly approaches easily from above. The flower has two widespread stamens which bend upward and inward with the fly's weight, powdering its underside with pollen.

Beetles are also flower pollinators, but are spoken of with contempt by most entomologists as "mess and soil pollinators." They are shambling creatures; after the gyrating flies, the poor creatures look like scrubwomen coming home in the morning, weary and sore of foot.

The perpendicular position of a beetle's mouth parts in relation to its body axis is a primitive one. Beetles can only lap up nectar from flat open flowers, getting pollen on their bodies by accident, and only by chance transferring it to a compatible stigma. In addition, in this cold environment many are flightless and so cannot make the rapid transfer of pollen necessary if the pollen is to remain viable.

Alpine parsley *(Oreoxis alpina)*

Green-leaf chiming bells *(Mertensia viridis)*

Entomologists are even more derisive about ants, who are the scoundrels in the pollination drama because they are so notoriously fond of the sugar in the sweet-tasting nectar. They rear broods and so, like bees, need the protein concentrated in pollen. They are so small that they can sneak in and out of a flower without rubbing against either anther or stigma, and pollen does not cling to their smooth shiny bodies. They are gregarious and often aggressive and drive other pollinators away. It is too bad that the fiddle-playing grasshopper, after being filled with homilies on antly virtues, didn't know about antly vices.

Mosquitoes also crave sugar, and both male and female are frequent flower visitors. Their effectiveness as pollinators is not yet well studied but at least one entomologist feels that they have been underrated. The myth about there being no mosquitoes at high altitudes is just that; the females are voracious, perhaps because the season is so short and there are so few humans to feed on.

Like sky pilots, chiming bells and avens, some grasses and Rocky Mountain sage are also prime pioneers in gopher-disturbed areas.

These tall, slender plants of reedgrass and bluegrass, wheatgrass and timothy give a fringed aspect, a lightness and litheness of line, to the community. Being wind-pollinated, grasses produce neither colorful petals nor nectar or volatile oils for aroma, but instead produce pollen in superabundance.

For wind pollination to be efficient, there must be many individuals of one kind, preferably massed close to each other. Even so, pecks of pollen are cast to the winds and wasted. Great amounts of precious plant protein must be produced in order to make up for the odds of one infinitesimal pollen grain finding the proper minute receptive stigma. Wind pollination is most effective in open windy areas—a perfect description of alpine tundra.

Fernleaf candytuft (Smelowskia calycina)

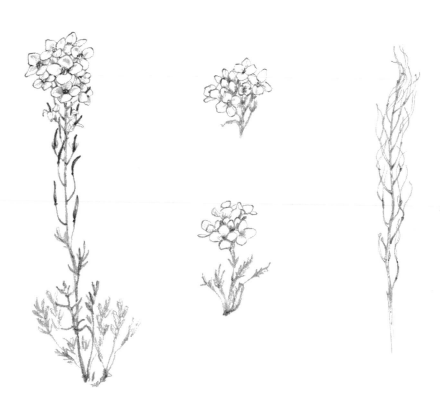

Alpine bluegrass (*Poa alpina*)

Scribner's wheatgrass *(Agropyron scribneri)*

Rocky Mountain sedge *(Carex scopulorum)*

Man-hater sedge *(Carex misandra)*

Rock bluegrass (*Poa glauca*)

A Rocky Mountain marsh is deeply green and thickly growing in the summer, touched with rose and pink and yellow. Bright green mosses pad the wet ground. Dusty rose paintbrush or pink queen's crown jewel the sward; king's crown has deep Victorian rose flowers, replete with yellow pollen when in full bloom, the whole plant turning salmon-maroon in the fall. The leaves of the sedums are succulent—usually an adaptation for plants growing in dry situations. In a sense this wet bog is desertlike because these shallow-rooted plants have difficulty taking up water from the acid unaerated cold soils.

Because of the saturated soils and cold temperatures, there is considerable frost action in alpine marshes, from the tiny pavings of pebbles to the hummocks of sedge heaved a foot high. In the frost boils tiny tendrils of plants invade at the outer rim, gradually inching toward the center as frost action subsides. Pearlwort and umbrella starwort, tiny as they are, are tenacious colonizers. Whiplash saxifrage

Alpine timothy *(Phleum alpinum)*

drops rosettes in an open crack and viviparous bistort sprinkles the loose soil with red bulblets. Goldbloom saxifrage and snowlover insinuate their shoots. Arctic saxifrage, yellow petals dotted with orange, are arrayed in tight drifts among the sedges. Tiny blue grasses send down fibrous roots.

Rocky Mountain sedge mantles much of the ground, forming a shiny turf punctuated with jet-black heads. Growing widely throughout the Rockies, it is conspicuously thick and bright green here, especially in the fall when soil moisture is low on the rest of the tundra. It is able to outcompete all other plants as long as it has adequate soil moisture, thriving where water is close to the soil surface nearly all summer. Tucked among its tussocks are other moisture-loving sedges—delicate capillary sedge, water sedge, sturdy Nelson's sedge.

Rocky mountain lousewort is found only in this ecosystem; its fernlike basal leaves are like those of little red elephant, to which it is

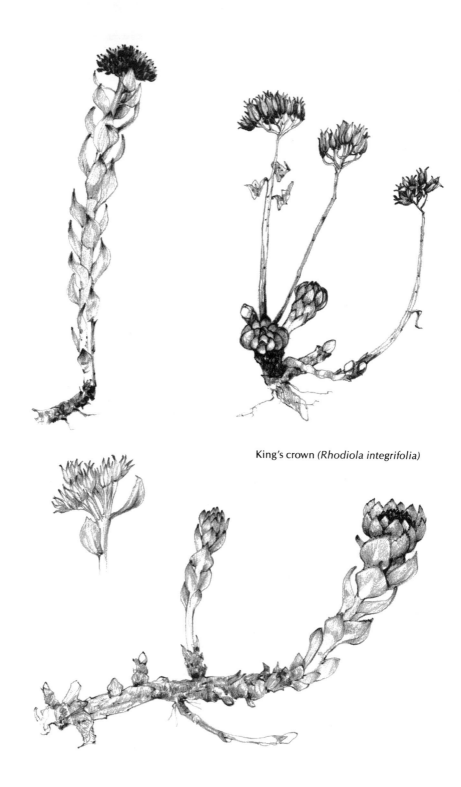

King's crown (*Rhodiola integrifolia*)

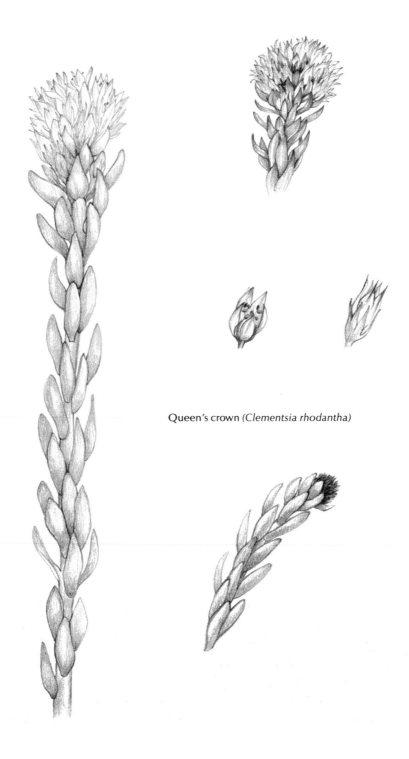

Queen's crown *(Clementsia rhodantha)*

Arctic sage (*Artemisia arctica* ssp. *saxicola*)

closely related. The latter is aptly named for the long curved flower beak that descends and curves like an elephant's trunk, and side petals which protrude to form the ears, and a top lobe which forms the characteristic elephantine domelike head.

The lousewort flowers are pollinated by bumblebees that are precisely shaped to fit into the blossom. When the bee alights, the flower head bends slightly forward from the bee's weight. When the bee

Parry's primrose *(Primula parryi)*

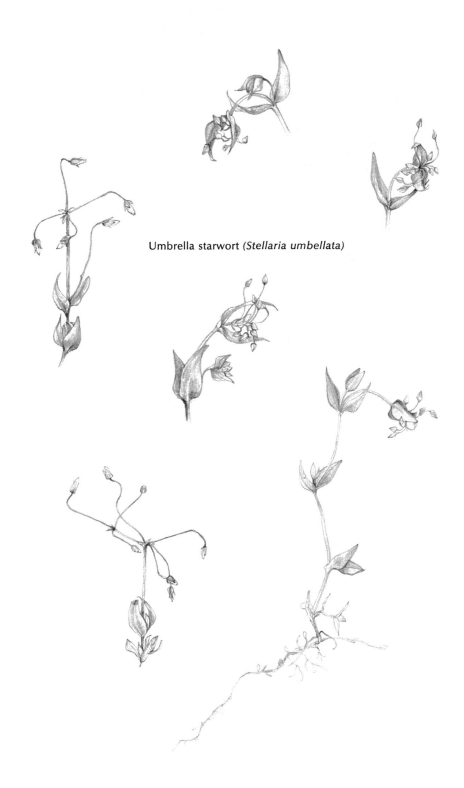

Umbrella starwort *(Stellaria umbellata)*

Siberian sandwort *(Minuartia biflora)*

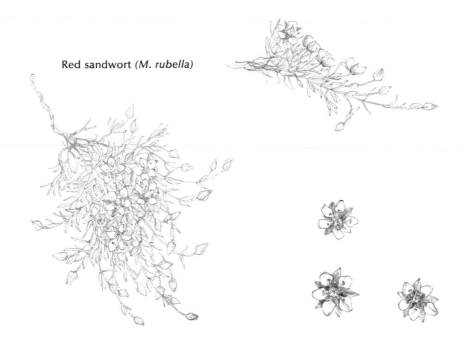

Red sandwort *(M. rubella)*

crawls inside for nectar, the various flower parts fit closely around it, pollen sifting over its hairy body and the flower's stigma arching forward and down to touch its back. This precise adaptation is especially true for little red elephant flowers; the "trunk" enclosing the style is just the right length to touch the spot between the bee's abdomen and thorax where the pollen from another flower is carried.

The marsh provides food and protection for white-crowned sparrows who summer in the high western mountains, nesting within the cradles of willow stems. They come from the south, as far as Mexico, following an internal physiological rhythm that drives them northward for mating and nesting. The nests, secreted beneath the willow branches, are protected from the cooler air above them; this difference of a few degrees in temperature is a crucial factor in warming small speckled eggs to hatching in the cool tundra summer. The parents feed on midges and tiny insects around the water, darting back into the willows for shadowed safety, speckled brown wings and dark-streaked white heads lost in the crosshatched patterns of leaves and twigs.

One follows me for half an hour, perching on top of each succeeding willow along the way. Its black and white crown is sharp as is its short clacking warning. I walk beyond its territory and it flies home. Only the sound of the waning wind of late afternoon remains.

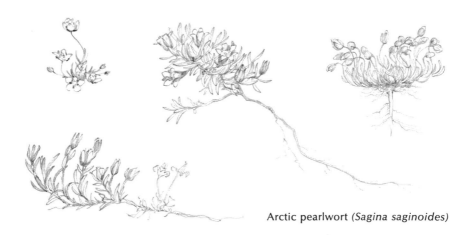

Arctic pearlwort (*Sagina saginoides*)

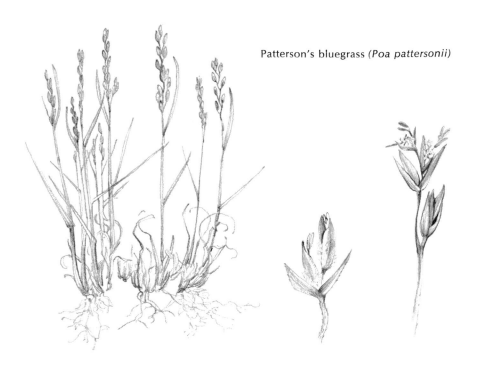

Patterson's bluegrass *(Poa pattersonii)*

Capillary sedge *(Carex capillaris)*

Nelson's sedge *(Carex nelsonii)*

Many of the rare and special flowers of the Rocky Mountains are to be found in the marsh: pygmy buttercup, leafy saxifrage, arctic and golden saxifrage. Only in this environment can one find koenigia and its companions: icegrass, a fine dark green moss and two tiny rushes.

Koenigia grows in the gravel frost scars of shallow streams and within mats of moss which make dime-sized drifts or huge pillows that sieve the running water. It nearly always grows with running water twinkling around its tiny, dark red, seedlinglike leaves; it is so small that it can easily be misinterpreted as part of the gravel bottom, or as a seedling of a larger marsh plant. Although in the Arctic it grows to

Arctic saxifrage *(Saxifraga hirculus)*

be six inches tall, here the plants are infinitesimal, bearing white flowers less than one-sixteenth of an inch across. A cluster of two dozen
easily fits within a penny.

Koenigia was named for Koenig, a pupil of the great eighteenth-
century botanist and classifier Linnaeus, and has been known from
Scandinavian tundra for several centuries. It was first found in the
United States by Scandinavian botanists who collected it on Pikes
Peak in 1913, and it was not found again until 1956. But as its habitat
is recognized, more reports are made of finding it each year.

Koenigia is one of the few true arctic and alpine annuals. It must

Little red elephant or Elephantella
(*Pedicularis groenlandica*)

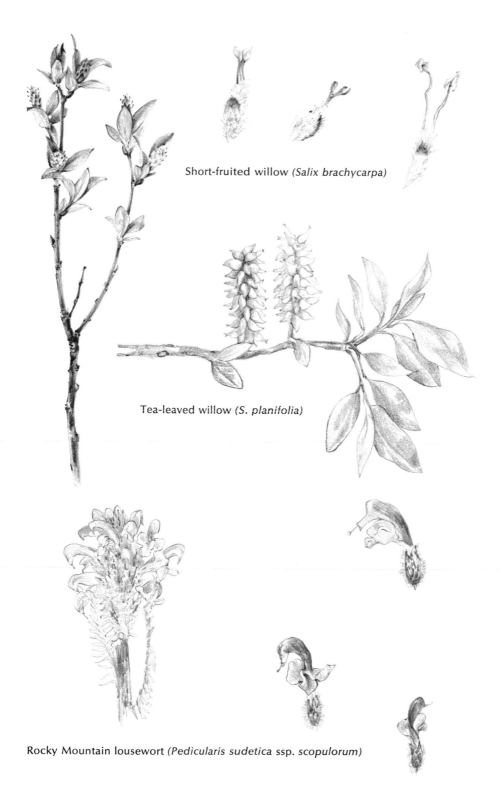

Short-fruited willow *(Salix brachycarpa)*

Tea-leaved willow *(S. planifolia)*

Rocky Mountain lousewort *(Pedicularis sudetica* ssp. *scopulorum)*

germinate from seed, carry on plant production at high rates in cold temperatures, flower, set seed, and all in the few short weeks of alpine summer. Koenigia is generally confined to sites where the immediate maximum surface temperature on windless days, in full sun, does not exceed 46 degrees F. If it does not grow at the edge of running water provided by snowmelt, melting ice masses imbedded in adjacent tussocks of sedge may provide water. These areas remain damp until fall freeze and evaporating water maintains the necessary coolness. Over a third of the plants that grow with koenigia grow only in this specialized community and nowhere else. This exclusiveness is the most absolute shown by any plants in the alpine tundra and indicates the narrowness of the environment.

Icegrass grows in some of the same sites and is most apt to be growing, nearly submerged, in midstream. It was named for C. J. Phipps, a British arctic navigator of the eighteenth century. Icegrass is almost as hard to find as koenigia since it ranges from one-third to one and one-half inches tall, and cannot be firmly identified without a hand lens. One can learn to sight it by its tousled appearance, the leaves and stems seeming to go every which way, and by the barely perceptible bluish tinge which separates it from the tiny deeper green rushes.

These rushes grow widely in open gravelly areas of wet alpine marshes and out into the running water, building their own tiny bottlecaps full of soil, adding perceptible green to the gravel bars and seeps. Soil development in the koenigia microecosystem is negligible. Small clumps of rush may accumulate tufts of organic debris, but these are minute. Koenigia roots either in bare gravel, in moss, or in small pieces of humus dropped from the luxuriant Rocky Mountain sedge tussocks. Like the sedge-marsh community, a koenigia community is in stable equilibrium with the soil water and frost activity that control it, a mature vegetation depending upon the interaction of topography and soil moisture, not climate, for its persistence. There are no developmental phases either into or from either the marsh or the koenigia communities; they stand apart from successional trends, self-contained and unique.

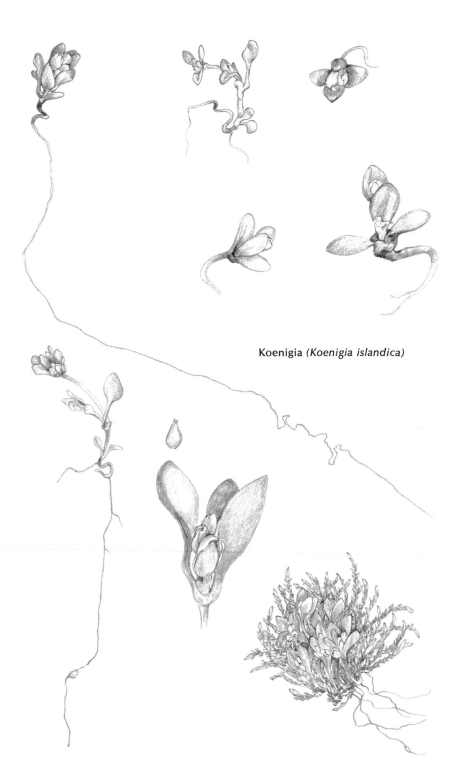

Koenigia *(Koenigia islandica)*

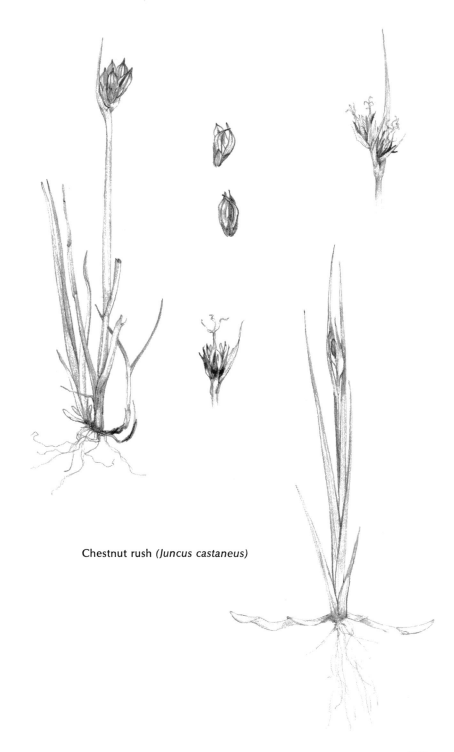

Chestnut rush *(Juncus castaneus)*

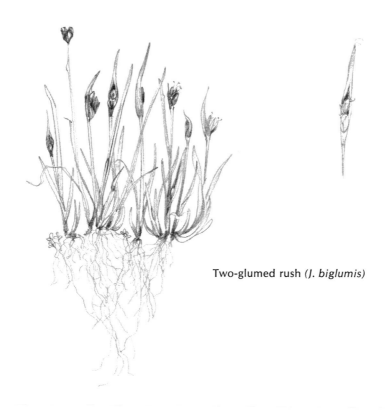

Two-glumed rush *(J. biglumis)*

Three-glumed rush *(J. triglumis)*

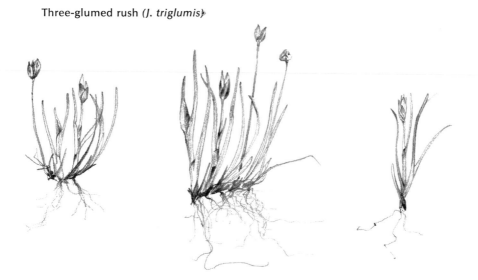

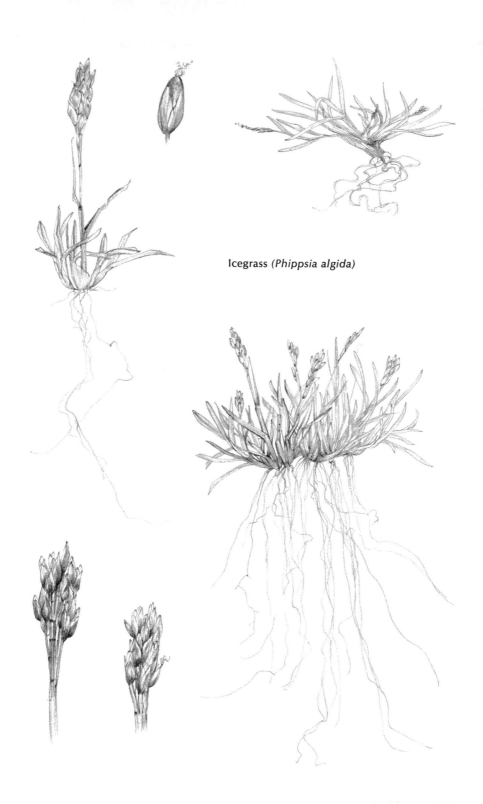

Icegrass *(Phippsia algida)*

An alpine lake lies below a cirque that holds snow all summer long. The water drains out from beneath the snow at a volume hard to equate with the seemingly stationary snowbank. Between the bottom of the cirque and the lake, the flowing water cavorts through a sloping area of marsh. The water is a ventriloquist; just as one identifies a little waterfall squeezing through a six-inch gully bounded by rock and bank, hidden by overhanging turf, another sound appears, slightly different in tone, more sonorous or more hollow or more determined. The stream disappears, sounding faintly below. Then a window in the turf opens and the sound deepens. The water surfaces again, filtering through terraces of ice-frosted moss, a rich black-green that would be dull but for the animation of the water.

This is the area for other rare plants of an alpine marsh, tucked beneath an overhanging bank or rock, secreted beneath a sheltering tussock or behind a thick screen of grasses and sedges. Most are circumpolar, occurring around the world in polar regions and extending down into southern latitudes only in isolated arctic environments at high altitude.

Moss (*Calliergon sarmentosum*)

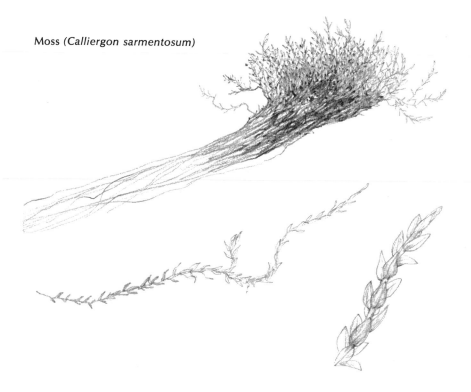

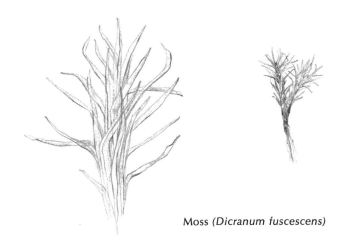

Moss *(Dicranum fuscescens)*

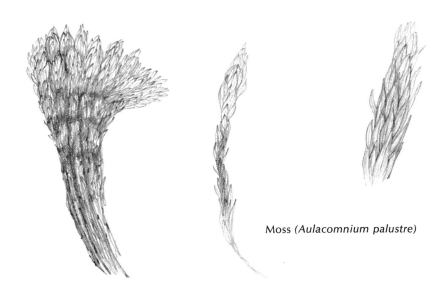

Moss *(Aulacomnium palustre)*

Pygmy buttercup *(Ranunculus pygmaeus)*

Pygmy buttercup is largely restricted to the Arctic and is rare in the Rockies. It is a diminutive perennial, usually one-flowered, less than a quarter of an inch tall, the whole plant spread about the width of a quarter. It is scarcely larger than the moss in which it grows; the pale yellow petals fall away early, leaving only a tiny seed head not much larger than a grain of rice.

Leafy saxifrage also grows within mossy tufts. It has only rudimentary petals or none at all, four greenish sepals and bright apple red bulblets which are almost too tiny to see without a hand lens. Often the whole plant can fit onto a penny. Alpine brook saxifrage is frail and white-flowered. Golden saxifrage is delicate and rare, found only near tiny waterfalls or where it overhangs narrow deep channels of water and receives wetting spray. It has four bright greenish-yellow sepals and no petals, with tiny lobed succulent leaves forming a collar just below the flowers. The seeds form in an ellipsoid ovary less than a quarter of an inch long; when ripe the ovary splits open to form a nest for seeds that look like tiny golden bronze beads.

Leafy saxifrage (*Saxifraga foliolosa*)

These little treasures of the alpine world are worth the wet feet and knees, cricked back and strained eyesight. All of them are bigger, more abundant and less specific in their Arctic habitats. Here they are miniature holdouts, persisting in a teacup environment, needing a hand lens to be appreciated. I suspect they are rather an esoteric and acquired taste. The human mind has always been fascinated by the odd, the rare and the uncommon; the exquisite, the precise and the miniature—of which these tiny alpine plants are the quintessence.

I walk around the lake, angling up to higher ground in order to keep the lake and the marsh in view as long as possible. Heavy clouds are rolling over the western ridges and I hurry to avoid being caught in an afternoon storm. By chance I glance across the slope above. A white

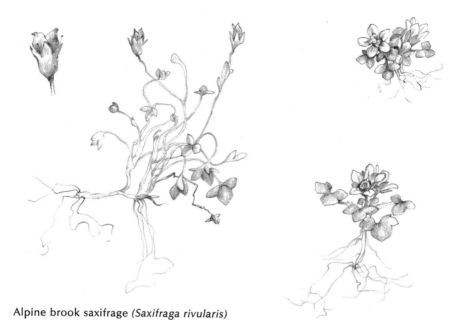

Alpine brook saxifrage *(Saxifraga rivularis)*

Golden saxifrage *(Chrysosplenium tetrandrum)*

patch moves and I stop, suddenly realizing that there are nine bighorn ewes grazing there. As they feed they follow the same angle as the slope, their color matching the drying grasses on it, almost invisible until a white rump patch moves again. Although the ewes are more commonly seen than the rams, this is the first time I have ever seen them so close. One raises her head and turns in my direction and I can see the slightly curved short horns. The ewes are smaller than expected, about forty inches high at the shoulder. They move unhurriedly upslope, out of view behind a rock wall.

Well over half of the bighorn sheep of Colorado live on the eastern slope of the Front Range where there are protected rocky prominences and snow-free winter food. The sheep roam above treelimit in the Rockies, from the Canadian border to Mexico. They formerly occurred regularly on the Great Plains and throughout desert regions of western America. Here in the Rockies they feed primarily on herbaceous plants and shrubs: dwarf clover, viviparous bistort, bluegrass and sedge, and paw through the winter snow for forage. They migrate somewhat between summer and winter feeding grounds, but are most at home in the alpine region. If they descend to the lowlands they are preyed upon by mountain lions and coyotes. The herds are more seriously thinned by lungworm, a parasite whose alternate host is a minute snail often ingested by the sheep.

Males are polygamous; each ram has eight to ten ewes in his harem. If there are too many rams the competition may become so fierce for females that only a few lambs are produced. The males have massive curling horns forming a near circle, and the head-on battles during mating season may be so frequent that they reduce the vigor of the males. Lambs are born between May and July on inaccessible ledges where they are almost completely safe from all predators except those from the sky. They are as agile as their mothers three days after birth.

I continue around the lake and stop to rest on an outcrop that faces a rugged ridge towards the east, illuminated by the last light of the afternoon. Far away, almost totally camouflaged against the gray-tan granite, visible only in silhouette, stands a single bighorn ram. His majestic stance and proud head symbolize all that one has ever heard about bighorn sheep: independent, alert, wild, at home in a world of precipitous crags and rocky ledges, in cold and storm, in which he exists, elusive and free, a symbol of the freedom of the alpine tundra.

15 : The Sierra Nevada

Gray clouds hang over the eastern flank of the Sierra Nevada, and there are only occasional glimpses of white snow patterns caught in rough gray rock. The clouds filter and fume through the peaks, alternately veiling and baring the sharp horns and arêtes chopping the skyline. At the base of the facade, moraines extend out into alluvial fans, marking the extent of the glaciers' paths. The repetitious white patterns remaining in the scooped-out cirques are all that remain of the glaciers. For a few brilliant moments, the clouds sift away completely, and the ragged gray-white peaks catch a shaft of sunlight, spotlighting the stark ramparts.

The weathered Rockies seem very middle-aged by comparison. From the air this morning, the rolling tundra slopes had been softly green, interspersed with a few gently rounded summits which bore light traces of snow. But the Sierra Nevada bears stark patterns, etched in harder, younger rock by bigger burring ice masses. Peaks are so rough that no green shows from this angle at all. From this bird's-eye view, the rock is a colder gray than the feldspar pink of Rocky Mountain granite, and the steely color adds to their forbiddingness. Portions of the farther phalanx of peaks are in striking contrast to the gray-white granites: reds, yellows and browns, remnants of old seabed sediments, streak through like marble cake. In all there is a severity, a stern warning, in the repetition of vertical shadows and sharp-tilted peaks. So they must have looked to the early Spanish explorers who named them: *sierra* meaning "saw" or "mountain," *nevada* meaning "of snow," for their glistening crests.

More than 400 million years ago the area of the Sierra Nevada was covered by a shallow arm of the Pacific Ocean. Sediments accumulated, were uplifted and folded into low mountains. Streams formed in the north-south valleys among the folds. These mountains were eroded and the land again inundated by the sea. New strata formed and crumpled, to be invaded at least 140 million years ago by molten granite from below forming a giant granite block 400 miles long, 80 to 100 miles wide. This rock mass later uplifted like a trap door, hinged on the west, opening on the east. The new mountain range began to erode, exposing rugged gray-white granites over large areas. The ancient stream patterns changed in part from north-south rivers to north-south headwaters, turning abruptly west as the tilting progressed, new streams forming on the sheer east face.

The second uplift series occurred during the Pliocene epoch, pushing the Sierra Nevada to their present 14,000-foot-and-above level, steepening the grade to the west. At the same time, the Owens Valley–Mono Lake region downfaulted, adding to the austere drama of the eastern face which seems to rise straight up out of the valley floor.

The drama of the Sierra Nevada backdrop is reiterated in the contrast between cascading white-water streams flanked with green and the immutable rocky slopes bearing only the scantest vegetation.

In many places, the prevalent rockiness, the deep snow in the high cirques and the lack of soil on precipitous slopes forbid tree growth. Treelimit is patchy and irregular, as low as 10,000 feet or as high as 12,000 feet, and Sierran alpine tundra is best developed between 10,500 and 13,000 feet. The thin soil of steep slopes is often insufficient to permit even shallow-rooted trees to survive. At treelimit white-barked

Sierra or Muir's primrose
(Primula suffrutescens)

pine and mountain hemlock stand stark against the crags; higher, white-barked pine forms krummholz tree islands. These treelimit Sierran trees are infected with the same black fungus caused by late-lying snow that is found in the Rockies.

There are rocky crags and boulder fields in picturesque profusion, since the Sierran granites are young and do not disintegrate easily. One of the rare and endemic plants of this impoverished habitat is Muir's primrose (commemorating John Muir, whose name is almost synonymous with the Sierra Nevada); its rosy stain is visible long before one climbs to its site. Deep pink flowers spring out of shiny rosettes of evergreen leaves. Hundreds bloom on open rock ledges. Most alpine flowers are scattered, but these primroses are so massed that their already vivid color is intensified, complemented by a yellow eye. Below them, red-pink heather spreads in the gravels, feeding a whirring hummingbird. A few rosy paintbrushes echo the intensity of pink;

even the delicate woodrushes seem flushed with a tinge of rose-red varnish. Muir's primroses grow only in such isolated and almost pure stands in the Sierra. Here, on the edge of a boulder field, they receive minerals for nourishment, protection from the weather and freedom from competition.

Above the primrose-imprinted cliffs lies a small tarn. At 38 degrees F it anesthetizes the hands. It was formed by a moraine deposited during the recent stage of Sierran glaciation. The moraine is a hodgepodge of different-sized rocks, from gravels to boulders. The crags surrounding the lake are metamorphic rock, almost a Wedgwood gray-blue turning unmistakably navy blue in shadow, a color and rock born of heat and pressure applied to a volcanic matrix. On these crags ice has sculpted intricate Victorian designs. The high-hanging snowbank above, wreathed with more primroses and tinged with pink snow, reflects in wind-blown fragments in the lake.

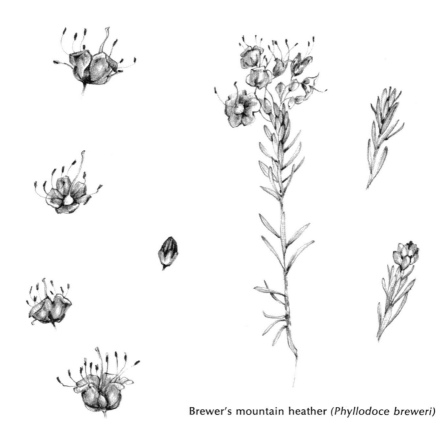

Brewer's mountain heather (*Phyllodoce breweri*)

Forked woodrush *(Luzula divaricata)*

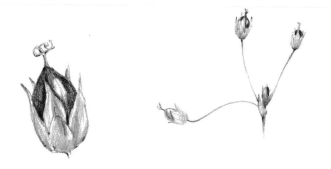

Bud saxifrage *(Saxifraga bryophora)*

An icy trickle slides from beneath the snowbank and flows over a stone pavement to feed the lake. Each stone is juxtaposed as if a stonemason had carefully fitted each one, pressing it neatly into the wet, soft soil. Snow pressure and sliding, well-moistened soils, and some frost heaving, form patterns of this sort beneath long-lasting snow cover and are very common in far northern countries. In spite of the cold, planarian worms, wet ribbons of life, have been found lurking beneath the stones.

The ground around the edge of the lake is characteristic of the Sierran alpine: luxuriant growth within a few feet of the water, marked aridity beyond. Where it is damp, the ground is crowded with rosy-brown Drummond's rush. Tiny threadlike bud saxifrages rise a mere three inches. Miniature alpine willowherbs with hair-thin stems dangle spaghetti-shaped buds and flowers with barely discernible rose petals. Arctic willows web an area where snow lies late.

But as the bank rises and the soil is porous and dry, desert-type plants appear, grayed with hairs for survival on a dry baked soil: a small waterleaf, many buckwheats, several phlox, pussypaws, Tolmie saxifrage, pink rock fringe. Buckwheats belong to a genus which evolution has elaborated out of all reason in the California mountains. Ostensibly, they are all more or less the same in the alpine tundra: usually tiny yellow, white or pinkish flowers, clustered in a rounded head atop a leafless stem, springing from a dense cushion of gray flannel leaves. But there are innumerable variations on the theme, and most of them infinitesimal.

The Sierran alpine flora lacks many of the most commonly distributed alpine plants. Instead, it has had an evolution of high-altitude species, in genera common to the California and adjacent Great Basin flora of somewhat lower elevations, along with many plants that are endemic, like Muir's primrose. A region with such diverse geologic history and rock types, with such a variety of climates as well as topography, contains many more or less isolated niches where plant species may develop in different directions. This large number of local species and subspecies results in a flora with some members from a few very large genera which have been much elaborated, such as milkvetch, lupine, cinquefoil, penstemon and buckwheat. The resultant Sierran alpine flora is nearly as large as that of the Southern Rocky Mountains.

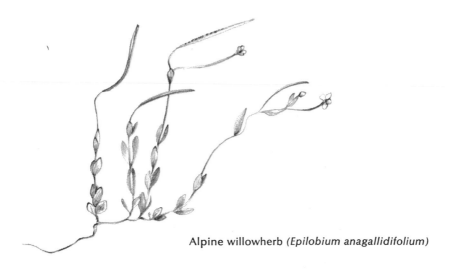

Alpine willowherb *(Epilobium anagallidifolium)*

Alpine phlox *(Phlox condensata)*

The Sierran buckwheats provide good practice in using botanical keys: at each point in identification there is a choice of two alternatives, and by careful observation and denying oneself the luxury of reading the end of the mystery story first, the reader proceeds step by step until the choice ends in the plant at one's feet. What one learns in addition is the value of precise and careful observation, which may be as helpful as the name itself. Once named, it becomes part of one's experience. Then there is the semantic satisfaction of new names, many of which have delectable convoluted syllables, like *Cerastium beeringianum* and *Eritrichium aretioides,* with each syllable enunciated.

Often specific names are descriptive. The pale pink buckwheat I key out is *ovalifolium* or "oval-leafed." Often the names tell of local history and bear the names of ship captains and surgeons and botanists who explored the area a century earlier: Menzies, Tolmie, Eschscholtz. One also learns in subliminal ways by using plant keys, recalling with the next strange plant those characteristics one has read before, and thumbing back to find them.

The richest development of alpine communities in the Sierra Nevada lies on the few unglaciated high plateaus—"nunataks"—that served as refuges for alpine plants otherwise eliminated by glacial inundation.

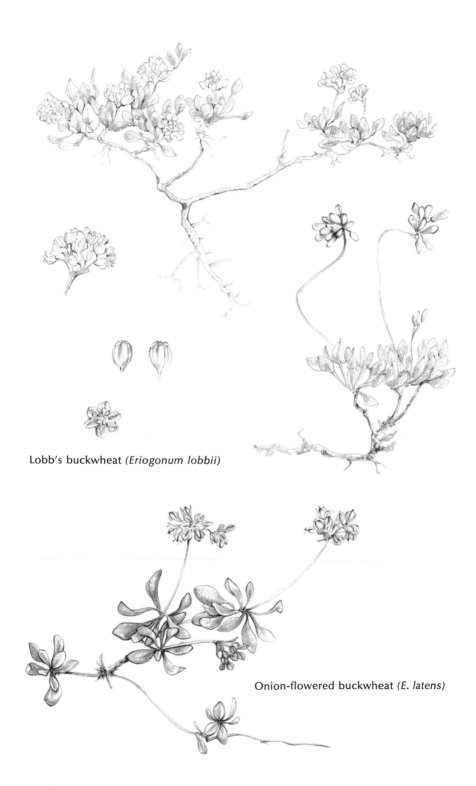

Lobb's buckwheat *(Eriogonum lobbii)*

Onion-flowered buckwheat *(E. latens)*

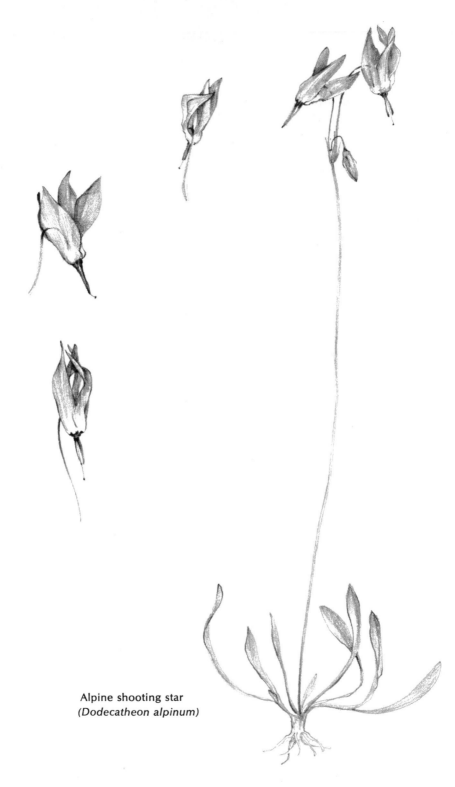

Alpine shooting star
(*Dodecatheon alpinum*)

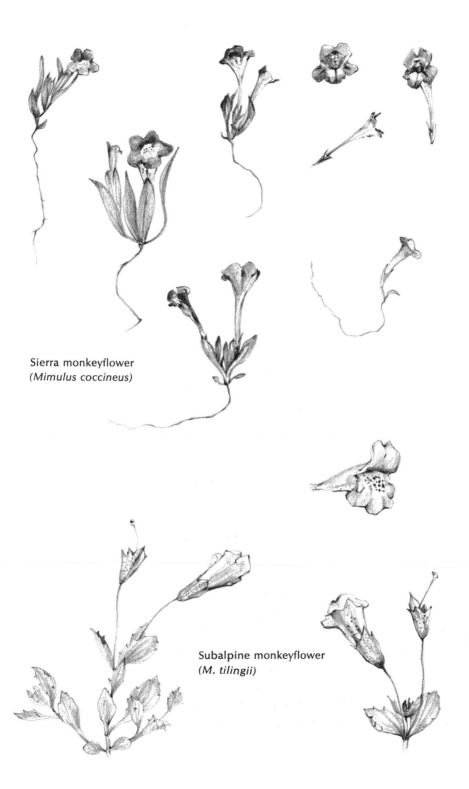

Sierra monkeyflower
(*Mimulus coccineus*)

Subalpine monkeyflower
(*M. tilingii*)

Western bell heather *(Cassiope mertensiana)*

The long walk up to one of these plateaus that lies between 11,200 and 12,000 feet is lightened by cascading streams deeply green with subalpine flowers, phasing into those that prefer higher altitudes. Little yellow-faced monkeyflowers with orange dotted throats and alpine shooting stars grow in tangled profusion. Infinitesimal carpet clovers string mats of matted stems; the flowers are less than a quarter of an inch, translucently white. As long as one follows the streams, the lush greenness persists, but leave them and the ground is dry. At treelimit gnarled whitebark pines cast a light shade over a slope densely carpeted with bell heather illuminated by its tiny white bells. They look like single lily-of-the-valley flowers wired by a red stem to a branch covered with scalelike leaves.

The walk, continuing into a higher valley, culminates in a scramble on all fours up a precipitous slope that marks the edge of the plateau. The slope is a former cirque wall, now stuffed with huge tussocks of sedge and hairgrass that wobble with every step. In the shelter of the leaves are dozens of starworts, bright little flowers all facing upwards that might easily be missed were not one scratching a handhold among them. A large rock stream flows down the flank, angular rocks held so loosely that they clatter down the glacier-sheared flanks at the slightest touch.

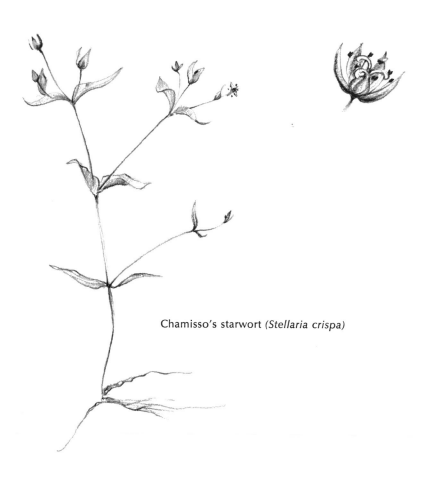

Chamisso's starwort *(Stellaria crispa)*

Carpet clover *(Trifolium monanthum)*

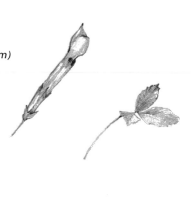

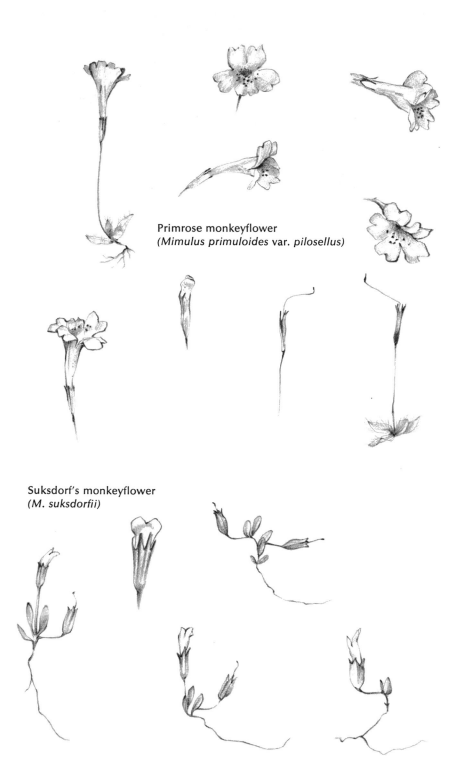

Primrose monkeyflower
(Mimulus primuloides var. *pilosellus)*

Suksdorf's monkeyflower
(M. suksdorfii)

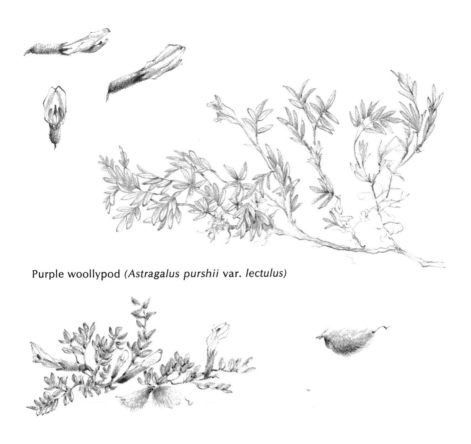

Purple woollypod *(Astragalus purshii* var. *lectulus)*

Dana milkvetch *(A. kentrophyta* var. *danaus)*

Dana lupine *(Lupinus lyallii var. danaeus)*

Almost a square mile of alpine tundra flows out across the top of the plateau, a gently rolling and reminiscent terrain looking very much like the high Rockies. There are a number of these unglaciated plateaus in the Sierra, all of which formed important refuges for plants during the Ice Age, acting as vast storehouses where soils developed uninterrupted over many centuries. Glaciation was much more extensive in the Sierra than in most of the Rockies because of the greater proximity of the Sierra to moisture-laden Pacific air masses.

The more widespread circumpolar alpine plants (so prevalent in the Rockies and East Coast tundras) were cut off in their southern migration from the north to the Sierra by the discontinuity of favorable paths for migration. The Sierra Nevada is separated from northern plant sources by the widely spaced younger Cascade peaks. Only about ten percent of the species here belong to the circumpolar high-latitude vegetation that crept south along the mountain chains of western North America and survived glacial periods.

Some of the Sierran alpine plants are related to Pacific coastal plants that have been able to ascend high into the mountains by developing alpine climatic races. A third group is native to the arid continental Great Basin, either creeping up the mountains from the east or rising with them when they were uplifted. And there remains a group of local high-altitude species that may have existed in refuges during the heaviest glaciation. Such are the minute Dana lupines that unfurl soft lavender and white quarter-inch flowers, the gray-pink dwarf paintbrush and the small alpine hulsea and orange-yellow goldenweeds— all under four inches high.

Vegetation on the plateau is sparse. There is much open rocky ground. The sandy Sierran granite slopes and ridges, lacking the Rocky Mountain sprinkler system of almost daily precipitation, are so well-drained that drought conditions prevail most of the summer. The Rockies receive summer precipitation from frequent local thunderstorms and from the occasional Gulf of Mexico air masses that move northwest over the plains; the Sierran mountains are adjacent to two desert basins. Even though annual precipitation is high in the Sierra, it is concentrated in the form of snow in the nongrowing season, which partially explains the absence of so many common alpine plants. There is just not enough moisture to support them. A shift towards a colder, drier climate has occurred within the last million years or so, accom-

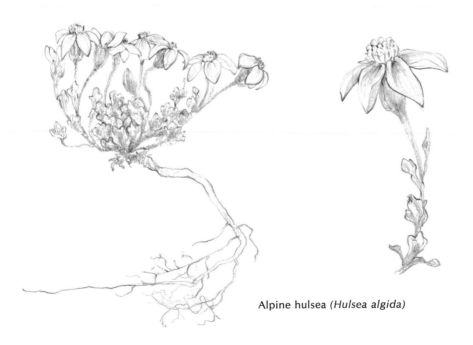

Alpine hulsea (*Hulsea algida*)

Dana goldenweed *(Haplopappus apargioides)*

panied by a shift towards winter precipitation rather than evenly distributed yearly moisture. This lack of summer precipitation, coupled with intense alpine illumination, hinders soil formation and brings about near-desert conditions in many Sierran alpine areas. Usually only the turfs below long-lasting snowbanks receive enough moisture to remain green through the summer.

Sierra saxifrage (*Saxifraga aprica*)

All the major tundra communities that occur in the Southern Rockies are present on this high plateau except animal-disturbed areas. There are no pocket gophers on this plateau although there are probably mice and shrews. But the plant communities are not as rich in species, development, or total acreage, a reflection of the poorly developed soil and general aridity. The snowbed indicator plants, flake lichen and the snow liverwort *Anthelia*, coat the soil where the snow lies late. An old river bed creases the plateau, but there is so little water that only a small marsh community forms, and there are no habitats for koenigia

or other arctic plants. The precise environment which a plant like koenigia must have probably does not exist in the Sierra. There are more
annuals in the Sierra than in the Rockies, but these grow mostly on the
warmer, drier and sandier sites, such as south-facing slopes.

Much of the plateau is covered by a fellfield, the plants of which are
uniformly small: tiny lupines and milkvetches, diminutive saxifrages,
close patches of lavender daisies, minute monkeyflowers with faces
smaller than a little fingernail, and the omnipresent buckwheats. One of
the milkvetches is so prickly and matted that it is uncomfortable to
handle; the other has fuzzy white pods like miniature ermine muffs.
Saxifrages form salmon rosettes, and the white flowers have salmon
anthers, an attenuated version of the snowball saxifrage of the Rockies.
Broad cushions of phlox next to handsome ivory-apricot prickly gilia.
This plant has a name to roll on the tongue: *Leptodactylon pungens*.
It is indeed *pungens* with a peculiar smell like an old caramel candy. A
tiny yellow draba is here, the same as that which grows in the Rockies,
and two more named after early western naturalists: John Lemmon, a
pioneer botanist, and William Brewer (after whom red heather and a
cinquefoil are also named), a Sierran geologist.

Spreading phlox (*Phlox diffusa*)

Alpine bitterroot (*Lewisia pygmaea* ssp. *glandulosa*)

Prickly gilia (*Leptodactylon pungens*)

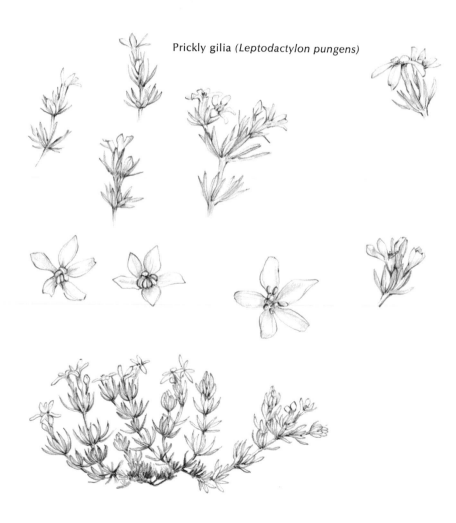

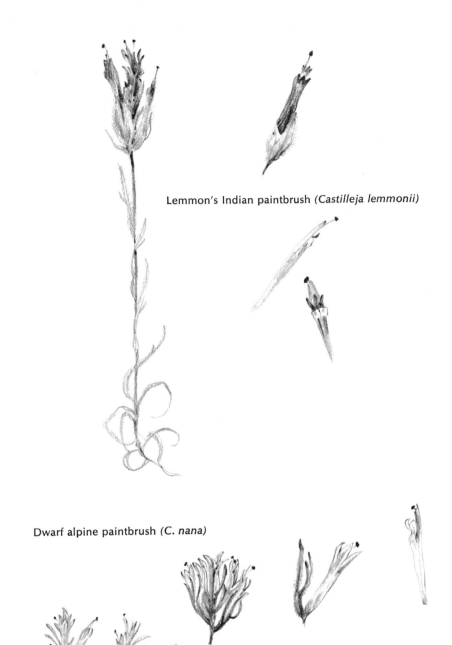

Lemmon's Indian paintbrush (*Castilleja lemmonii*)

Dwarf alpine paintbrush (*C. nana*)

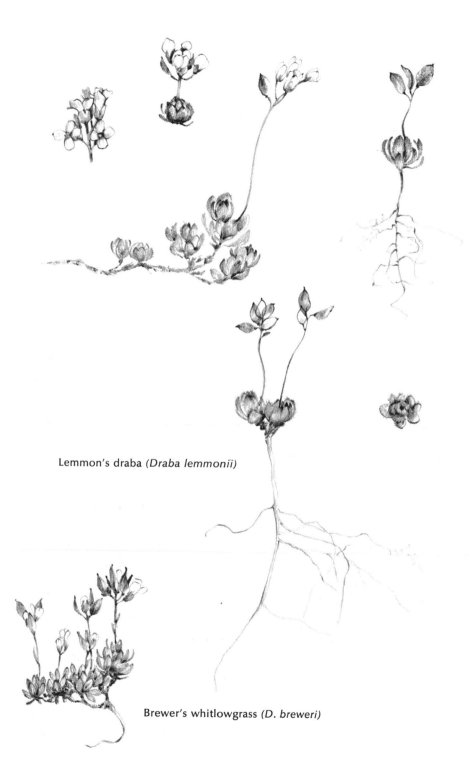

Lemmon's draba *(Draba lemmonii)*

Brewer's whitlowgrass *(D. breweri)*

Creeping penstemon (*Penstemon davidsonii*)

The plateau is a dusty salmon-pink and old ivory grisaille, a combination of soft flower colors and grayed leaves on open granite soil. The one brighter color belongs to low-growing creeping penstemon that has lavender-blue flowers big enough to put a finger inside, although the whole plant is only a couple of inches high. Creeping penstemon is one of the first flowering plants to become established on raw slopes, clinging in a crevice on a rock face with the tenacity and persistence usually associated with lichens. It is sometimes classed as a shrub because of its woody stem and evergreen, somewhat succulent leaves. Its brighter color does not perceptibly change the overall aspect of the landscape but seems instead to imitate lavender-shadowed pockets in the terrain, melding from a distance into an overall evenness of color. The feeling of the plateau seems encapsulated in a minuscule dwarf paintbrush: dotted with tiny protruding black-balled stamens, surrounded by the dusty white lobes of the bracts, it is almost the same subdued pink as the stony soil upon which it grows.

In the center of the up-tilted eastern edge of the plateau is a sheer protruding rock prominence, left by quarrying east-slope glaciers. It projects out into nothingness, like the prow of a ship. It is a solitary place, a place above and beyond. The wind blows continuously and harshly here. The bare-bone rocks are scoured, lichens patched only on their protected leeward undersides. The desolation and isolation force one to measure oneself against the magnificence of a mountain and its stringent hostile environment.

Sierra parsley *(Podistera nevadensis)*

Gordon's ivesia (*Ivesia gordonii*)

The dry soils here are very young and very raw; only infinitesimal quantities of mineral nutrients are present, with little organic enrichment. They sift through the hand like sand, leaving no trace of moisture or stain of humus. Soil formation is so slow that the crystal forms of the rock minerals are still clear in the fine gravels.

A few phlox cushions and isolated penstemons and Sierran alpine parsley, and an occasional buckwheat, shelter in warm pockets in the lee of the rocks. Ivesia, a small member of the Rose family, has tiny yellow flowers that are much less intricate than the elaborately imbricated leaves. The most color in this subdued landscape of beiges and grays comes from the crustose lichens that form patterns of pale crisp green and intense chartreuse, coating the slanting boulder underfaces on the shaded east and north faces. Concentrations of black lichens veneer the east faces, sheltered from prevailing winter winds.

Map lichen's clear yellow-green cartographs the pale pages of the rock surfaces. Only two soil lichens have been found on the whole plateau: flake lichen and bright yellow-orange *Candelariella aurella.*

The configurations of the huge white plated and pitted granite boulders, resting on acres of fine white sandy-gravel soil, recall some desolate seashore. There is almost the sound of waves breaking in the wind that pours down the plateau, and the smell of salt spray in the misting rain that scarves across the sky.

This Wagnerian weather is uncharacteristic for the Sierra. The dull light tarnishes the ground of the plateau to an odd salmon-tan with stone patterns clearly inscribed across it: stone stripes lie across the fall line of the flat tilt of the slope, pulled down into graceful della Robbia garlands wherever the slope steepens. The stone patterns, lacking soil, are nearly empty of plants, but between them the soil is netted with arctic and snow willows and an occasional rockprimrose or a small bitterroot, sepals tipped with amethyst like drops of molten glass. Beyond, the rest of the plateau seems to slide away, dissolved by the rolling mists.

16 : The White Mountains
of California

The White Mountains lie on the border between Nevada and California, separated from the Sierra Nevada by the narrow Owens Valley. They sleep, hazy and muted, in the morning backlight. They are much less dramatic than the gnawed Sierras even though they contain peaks nearly as high. The Sierra Nevada are youthful by comparison, only 140–400 million years old; in the White Mountains the oldest rocks are 200 to 600 million years old. Because this older rock is largely unglaciated, these gentle-looking mountains lack the serrated profile of the Sierra.

The White Mountains are the westernmost of many Great Basin ranges. The Great Basin, lying between 3000 and 6000 feet, forms an inverted triangle with the base reaching from eastern Oregon through southern Idaho and Nevada to Utah; the apex lies in southern California. The ranges within it run generally north and south; the best-defined are the Inyo Mountains, Funerals, Amaragosas, Ruby Mountains, Panamints, Wallowas, Charleston and Wheeler Peaks. The Wasatch Mountains and the Colorado Plateau bound the Basin on the east, and the Sierra Nevada on the west.

The White Mountains lie in the rain shadow of the Sierra. As wet winds come off the Pacific and rise over the Sierra, they cool. Since cooler air holds less moisture, it falls as rain or snow on the western flanks and crest of the Sierra. As the wrung-out winds sweep on across the Sierra they blow cold and dry across the Owens Valley and the mountains to the east; the average annual precipitation on the summits is only fifteen inches. The White Mountains received their name because of their white rock crests, not because of a heavy snow cover.

Patches of tundra on sandstone or granite soils intermix with bristlecone pine groves on dolomite soils, forming a striking mosaic on the higher flanks of the mountains between 11,000 and 12,000 feet. Dolomite is a pale magnesium-rich sedimentary rock much like limestone, and forms a basic and much colder soil than either granites or sandstones do. The bristlecone pine groves may extend as high as 12,000 feet, containing trees thousands of years old, perhaps the oldest known living things on earth. Plant cover defines the substrata clearly and distinctly, especially where the different soils lie side by side.

After climbing and hiking in the rugged Sierran alpine terrain, the White Mountains are easier going, more gentle, with rolling slopes that are very reminiscent of Rocky Mountain alpine tundra. They differ in the extreme clarity of the patterned ground processes, and the aridity and clarity of an atmosphere almost completely free from moisture. When the Sierra Nevada was heavily glaciated, there was never enough moisture in the form of snow for the White Mountains to bear large glaciers, although a few small ones formed on the eastern side. The slopes have the same aspect as the frost-leveled slopes of the unglaciated uplands of the Rockies. The sparse snow cover that does form here is mostly blown into drifts, leaving slopes and ridges bare, and is usually gone by June. No snowbanks or ice fields whitewash the high ridges. Were it not for the breathlessness that goes along with being above 12,000 feet one would feel in a desert.

The patterning and sorting of ground in the White Mountains took place between 2000 and 8000 years ago, or perhaps longer, correlated with the colder, wetter climate of the Great Basin then. Although the patterned ground on the Sierran plateaus is evident, here in the White Mountains it is dramatic, dark rocks silhouetted against light soil, light rock patterns studding dust-green turf. In only a few areas do plants absorb and obscure the patterns; the extreme slowness of revegetation allows most of the rock stripes and garlands to remain sharply delineated.

The surrounding area is a modified moonscape. The soil is very dry and gritty, paved by small pebbles. Although tundra on the White Mountains fills a large vertical range between 11,500 and the top of White Mountain Peak at 14,246 feet, the number of plant species is limited, probably by lack of water—there are only about a third as many as in the Rockies.

Plant life is sparse but when down on hands and knees there is surprisingly more than expected. The plants tend to be exceedingly hirsute and palely flowered, almost embedded in the pebble mosaic, blending into the soil and rocks to create an amorphous landscape. On the rocks, close to ground level, are many lichens, in shades of charcoal brown, green and tarnished yellow-gold. The only bright pure colors here are airborne: a butterfly with orange wings and several small mountain blues. Small grasshoppers weave among the plants, along with purposeful black ants and very small wolf spiders. The charm is very different from other alpine fellfields where there is more variety and color. This is a scrimshaw field with muted colors and minute plants. And the sun at 12,000 feet is intensely hot, washing out both colors and shadows to an almost desertlike monotony.

A plethora of white feathers is scattered across the ground, three of which I wore in my hat band the rest of the summer as the traditional mark of a less-than-intrepid approach to mountain climbing. The puzzle of what kind of large, white-feathered bird lived here was solved by discovering that animal experiments were conducted in the 1950's. Chickens were brought up to 12,000 feet, where most of them were unable to acclimate. The few that did survive adjusted to the high altitude and began to thrive, and the population returned to its original number. Autopsies on these showed that considerable enlargement of internal organs had taken place, a physiological change occurring in most animals, including humans, who live consistently at very high altitudes.

Dwarf daisy (*Erigeron pygmaeus*)

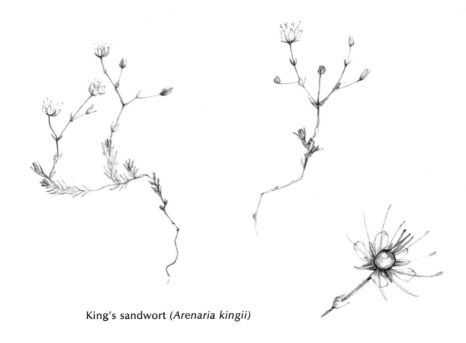

King's sandwort *(Arenaria kingii)*

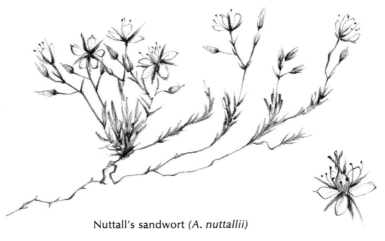

Nuttall's sandwort *(A. nuttallii)*

Along the way every rock seems to hold a marmot marinating in the sunshine, in addition to trotting marmots, snoozing marmots, listening marmots, cavorting marmots, everywhere marmots. At a sound, a marmot moves off like a child's pull toy, legs on an eccentric gear, flowing lumpily across the landscape. Their golden-brown ruffs gleam in the sunlight.

Some of the alpine meadows are thick with hairgrass and bluegrass, and the marmots have ample food to support a healthy population. Near the remains of a sheepherder's cabin the grasses are knee-high. The remains of the cabin stand lonely and forlorn and somehow out of place in the tall grass. One can only wonder what kind of existence it might have been, here above nowhere, with only the wind, the grass, the marmots and the sheep for company.

A snow accumulation area in the White Mountains, after the mucky late-covered areas of the Rockies, looks more like a fellfield. Snow holds here, in the lee of a rock ridge, sometimes until mid-August. But after a dry winter with little snow, by late July the desertlike aspect is marked. It is hard to believe that there really are buttercups growing in damp ground in wet years, for in dry ones the heat vibrates off the rocks. The ground is pebbly and rocky, with many small loose flat stones the size of a hand scattered on the surface. Often the rock seems more vivid than the plants tucked between. Dusty lavender dwarf daisies, pale lavender lupines, soft yellow actineas, an ashen Mono clover with five leaflets (instead of the usual three) bare very little green. There are many thumb-high dwarf paintbrushes, small cushions of phlox, sprigs of both fescue and bluegrass, and a few Nuttall's sandworts among the rocks.

The ubiquitous buckwheats are plentiful, splayed rosettes forming circles against the angular patterns of the rocks. Oval-leaved buckwheat carries flowers seemingly made of rose tissue paper striped with red, the leaves of roughly cut velour. The compact spherical heads are checkered with pale red and cream, depending upon how long the

Alpine meadowrue
(*Thalictrum alpinum*)

Oval-leaved buckwheat
(*Eriogonum ovalifolium* ssp. *vineum*)

Onion-flowered buckwheat *(E. latens)*

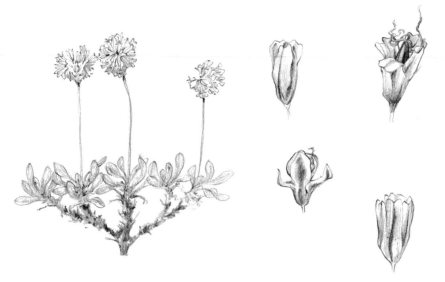

individual flowers have been in bloom; the older ones turn cinnamon red with age. Onion-flowered buckwheat has greener leaves with flowers arranged in a looser head, maroon in bud, white with maroon stripes when open.

The last thing one would expect to see in this oven of a rocky snowbed is an alpine meadowrue. In the Rockies alpine meadowrue grows mainly within kobresia stands, a snow-free area that is comparatively moist, where the small plants are semishaded by taller ones. Here it grows where there is winter snowcover, actually in a snowbed community where in wetter years water trickles all summer, but that now seems a more hostile habitat than a Rocky Mountain fellfield.

The alpine meadowrues of the White Mountains were part of a plant comparison study with the same species growing in Alaska. When grown in a uniform environment, the two populations differed in several ways, most significantly in their light requirements and photosynthetic ability. The internal differences were visible in the leaf color: some of the Alaskan plants had dark green, more lustrous leaves, with about a quarter more chlorophyll. The California plants had an extra layer of plant cells that made the leaves appear paler green. The Alaskan plants were more efficient under longer hours of daylight; the California ones were better adapted to shorter daylight hours and the more intense light and higher temperatures of alpine regions. The differences persisted when the plants were grown in a common environment.

The California plants, like most others, all had two sets of chromosomes; the Alaskan had both two and three. Every plant contains a group of genes gathered together in sets of chromosomes that lie in the cell nucleus and determine the plant's heredity—the color of its flower, the time of flowering, the shape of leaves, etc. When a plant grows in isolation over a period of time, it may, by recombination and beneficial mutations, very gradually develop a different gene system so that eventually it cannot interbreed with its original parent group. It has then become a new and separate species. This kind of evolutionary change takes centuries and centuries to accomplish.

But there is an immediate manner in which a new species may arise: polyploidy. There is no gene change involved because polyploidy is simply doubling or tripling the original chromosome number as a whole, or sometimes even doubling the first doubling. If the original diploid plant had ten chromosomes, the new polyploid will have twenty or thirty and sometimes even forty chromosomes, a process familiar to hybridizers who develop many fancy garden plants in this manner. The reason that polyploids spring into existence in nature is not completely known. Polyploidy may be related to ultraviolet radiation or sharp changes in weather during fruiting that disturb the normal process of sexual cell division, or it may be controlled genetically.

Doubling or tripling of chromosome sets often produces physiological changes much like those produced by slow mutation: cell size in polyploids is usually larger, as are the leaves, flowers and fruits. The whole physiology of the plant may be altered so that it becomes better adapted to a different environment. Often a polyploid can enter a slightly different habitat from that occupied by its parents, and may have a greater latitude than either parent alone. This adaptability can be of great use to a plant invading new areas, such as the barren pockets left after glacial retreat.

Polyploidy occurs in nearly all major plant groups. It is most frequent in the Grass, Sedge, Pink, Mustard and Rose families, all of which are well represented in arctic and alpine regions. On some Arctic islands seventy to eighty percent of the plants are polyploids, while about thirty to thirty-five percent of the plants in temperate climates are. The most widespread genus of the alpine tundra, the Sedge, also has the most varied and irregular chromosome counts.

Chromosome counts and polyploid studies are still incomplete. Future exploration could tell a great deal about this "instant" method of creating new species, the relationships between arctic and alpine plants, and how plants recolonized areas left open by retreating glaciers. They can tell which species are more primitive (those with lower counts) and which are more developed. They may differentiate plants which superficially look alike into distinct species and suggest which has proved more able to populate more strenuous environments.

The beginning sensations of heat exhaustion—flushed face, slight dizziness, dehydration—are becoming unpleasantly apparent in this White Mountain snowbed-fellfield. My pulse feels fast. Heat seems to be billowing from the soil. No afternoon clouds materialize. By this time

Coville's phlox *(Phlox covillei)*

of the afternoon in the Rockies, it is usually raining, sleeting, or snowing, or all three, and at the very least, clouds bleaken the sky. One would have been sitting on the ground to keep out of the wind and stay warm, thankful for the small warmth rising from the morning-heated soil. Here in the White Mountains, only a few degrees farther south in latitude, it is uncomfortably hot. The thin long-sleeved cotton shirt I wear for protection against severe sunburn is too hot.

The White Mountains and surrounding regions of the southwestern United States are exposed to very intense solar radiation. Such radiation, which also exists above 10,000 feet in the Rockies although to a lesser extent, is the result of a somewhat singular combination of very thin high-altitude atmosphere and clear air, and a low humidity and cloud cover. The heat load advancing on the alpine tundra as the sun bursts on the morning slopes has been described as an "avalanche." Part of the radiation received on earth is ultraviolet. At sea level most ultraviolet light is absorbed by the intervening atmosphere. On a clear day, the intensity of direct ultraviolet radiation from the sun increases with an increase in altitude; here twice as much is received as at sea level. The effect of such strong radiation on plants has only been tentatively explored. Some chlorophyll damage at high altitude may be caused by ultraviolet radiation, and changes in pigment and structure may occur. Natural filtration by epidermal pigments, such as the red anthocyanins, is a likely adaptation, along with small hairy leaves, and leaves with a thick outer coating and buried stomates.

All the plants here must be able to survive intense radiation or they simply could not survive at all. It would be easier to understand how plants endure this alpine desert if one could also see some of those that have not. The elements of success can be too easily misinterpreted. Many plants here have extremely hairy leaves, adapted for a near-desert environment. Nestled among the rocks and boulders are some clear yellow ragworts and a large yellow draba, the flowers set against very dark green leaves densely covered with hairs that catch sand grains. A phlox cushion has needlelike leaves coated with stiff hairs. The flowers are not only undiminished in size; many have an extra petal. They are delicately fragrant, a small cushion of tenacious beauty in a wicked climate.

Every plant leaf, it seems, has a different kind of covering: soft and silky, crinkled, stellate, glandular, thickly matted and furry, protecting tender green tissue beneath. Many leaves are thick and some are finely divided, protecting against high evaporation and cold. Most are relatively light-colored, reflecting rather than absorbing radiation. The slope is a rock garden containing minute plants that sizzle beneath a blazing sun, moisture locked inside, able to send down long roots to cooler soils and traces of underground water. They smolder under an afternoon sun that washes out shadows and glares on rocks, able to survive the freezing temperatures in a dry night atmosphere that loses its daytime warmth the instant the sun goes down.

The whole landscape shimmers in a blinding liquid heat. It is impossible to tell if the flight of a small white butterfly is truly hesitant, or if it is merely the distortion caused by heat radiating above the soil.

17 : The Southern Cascades

The widely separated peaks of the Southern Cascades are aligned inverted cornucopias, divided by miles of dark green wooded hills and
valleys. The Cascade Plateau, from which the individual cones rise, is
in itself an impressive structure: a broad ridge rising to between 6000
and 8000 feet, fifty to a hundred miles wide and seven hundred miles
long, oriented generally northwest-southeast.

On the western side, when the Plateau formed, pelting water gnawed
it into a complex series of corrugated valleys and hills, and threaded it
with streams and rivers. By the late Pliocene period, this "first floor" of
the Cascade Range was mainly finished. Then cracks and fissures
opened at intervals along its length, erupting molten rock and pumice,
hot ash and cinder, in a callioped crescendo of mountain building:
Mount Baker, Glacier Peak, Mount Rainier, Mounts Adams and Saint
Helen's in Washington; Mounts Hood, Jefferson, Mazama and Three
Sisters in Oregon; Mounts Shasta and Lassen in California, along with
lesser intervening peaks. Molten rock ran down the flanks of the cones,
the lava sometimes spreading ten miles out before it cooled and solidi-

fied. Volcanic bombs and debris shot out and landed on snowcovered slopes, melting and mixing into oozing mudflows. When the cones became too high for lava to rise to their tops, it forced its way out of side cracks and formed lateral cones and new ridges in the already wrought terrain. Pumice sprayed out the tops, froth from gas-rich lava that hardened before the gas could escape, so light that it floated over hundreds of square miles of the countryside.

As the Plateau rose, it forced up the wet winds sweeping in from the Pacific and cooled them to rain or snow, spawning the great glaciers that still endure. The western slopes of the Cascades have rainfalls of

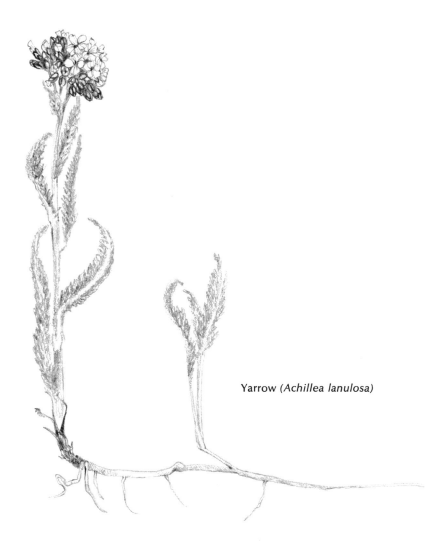

Yarrow (*Achillea lanulosa*)

Sulphurflower (*Eriogonum umbellatum* ssp. *covillei*)

between eighty to a hundred inches yearly; the eastern side gets only about a fifth as much. In the rainshadow of the Plateau it is hot and dry in summer, cold and dry in winter. But the volcanic cones bear snow and ice all year, floating in the morning haze like a Hokusai print of Fujiyama.

Mount Hood is an individual and grand mountain, with its own particular crisp grace. It soars sharply upward in splendid isolation as do all the peaks of the Southern Cascades. Its pumiced flanks seem to curve inward like the Eiffel Tower, culminating in a sparse pinnacled summit.

On Mount Hood treelimit is inscribed around 7000 feet; beyond it the rock is covered deeply with pumice into which each footstep sinks, sending up plumes of fine dust. The sun reflects off the light-colored ground with dehydrating intensity. The mountain's aspect is light in color, the pale lavas broken by weathering and glacial action into a pale powdery soil; it is characteristic for each lava flow to have its own individuality of plant cover and color, and here both are colored dust.

There are almost no plants to brighten the ridge or provide excuses for botanical reconnaissance or a rest. Small plants of yarrow, occasionally low-spreading sulphurflowers with rusty buds, once in a while a gray-pink pussypaws or a dusty Lyall lupine, are all so dust-coated that they are almost undifferentiated from the soil itself. Newberry knotweed straggles along the ground; a few phlox cling to the sharp slope. A single sedge and a few grasses nod languidly in the furtive breeze that hesitantly insinuates itself up the slope, a slope that has been free of glacial ice for only about twenty-five years and has achieved only a sparse plant cover. Above, the ridge tapers out into nothingness in a steep rocky talus slope that sweeps upwards to the snowcapped summit of Mount Hood.

Beneath the spur lies the spent end of a glacier, webbed and cracked, crisscrossed with dirt and debris. The sparkling whiteness of distant glaciers, sculpted in monumental curves and cornices and overhangs, is lost in this myopic view. Debris encrusts the surface, making it look like a white marble floor that needs a good sweeping. Rocks have tumbled down on it from adjacent ridges, adding to the general dishevelment. The hummocked surfaces tell of wasting and evaporation that mark a glacier's retreat.

If a glacier is advancing, the front end is steep and bulging. If it is retreating, it is more gently sloping with hummocks and a puckered surface. The lower the ice wedge creeps, the more a glacier is subject to melting. When melt and advance rates are equal, the glacier stabilizes, appearing to sleep on its slope, waiting for the heavy snows of winter to nourish it into life again. Melting water from its base and evaporation from its surface nibble away at its bulk. The glacier languishes in the sunshine that is slowly depleting it, seems to draw within itself.

In the Cascades (as in the Sierra Nevada and the Rockies) deeper cirques formed on the eastern than on the western flanks. On the coastal side, the maritime climate is more even and moderate; the continental climate on the east side is sharper, with wider temperature fluctuations accompanied by more freezing and thawing. Snow also blows over and deposits on the lee side, the mountain ridges acting like gigantic snow fences. As the glacier moves grindingly downslope, crevasses are slashed open, and in them the layers of recent years appear in dark stripes of summer dirt separated by white stripes of winter snow. Crevasses open and close according to glacial stresses created by the configuration of the ground beneath. As a glacier flows over a ridge in the terrain beneath, it breaks across the top at more or less right angles to its flow. Crevasses, when hidden beneath a fresh snowfall, are one of the greatest hazards to mountain climbers crossing a glacier.

The base of the glacier lies like a dirty white paw upon the gouge it has made in the mountain. It looks menacing, still able to rise and claw. Over the last one hundred fifty years, glaciers have been generally shrinking in the Cascades, as they have been over the Northern Hemisphere because of less snowfall and temperatures more often above freezing; only a few have made slight local advances in the 1950's and early 1960's. But the amount of snow and ice here is white witness that the prevailing cold at this altitude and the amount of winter moisture nearly balance summer warmth and drought, and the glacier's recession is very slow.

In the dry summer air, a milky trickle catches the light as it licks out from under the glacier, filtering through cobbles and detritus: the glacier's life blood seeping its way to the Columbia River.

Atop an older moraine is a plateau only about half-covered with a sparse fellfield vegetation—mauve lupines, deeper lavender asters, white phlox, a few pussypaws, a scattering of yellow parsleys, the ever-present buckwheats (some yellow, others grayish-white), all muted by a light pall of dust. The soil lacks both nourishment and moisture to produce a thicker plant cover, and the wind keeps it unstable. Most of the plants ring boulders or follow cracks in the soil, or flower in hollows somewhat protected from the worrying wind. The plateau has an other-worldly quality, an ivory sameness of color, as if individual plant colors were reduced to the common denominator of ground color.

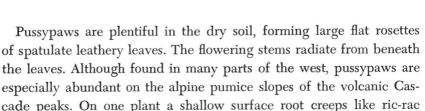

Pussypaws (*Calyptridium umbellatum* var. *caudiciferum*)

Pussypaws are plentiful in the dry soil, forming large flat rosettes of spatulate leathery leaves. The flowering stems radiate from beneath the leaves. Although found in many parts of the west, pussypaws are especially abundant on the alpine pumice slopes of the volcanic Cascade peaks. On one plant a shallow surface root creeps like ric-rac braid, just under the dry windblown soil, before quirking downward. The flowers fade and fall early, but the papery bracts holding them remain, compacted into spheres that cluster together to resemble the tender pads of a cat's paw.

Short-beaked agoseris flowers gild the ground, the only bright spots of color. Lomatium smells strongly of parsley, to which family it belongs; the cluster of tiny flowers looks like the alpine parsley of the Rockies and the finely divided leaves look like kitchen parsley. A few sandworts almost exhaust the list of plants in this very sparse and almost monotone fellfield.

The plants are small and isolated, typical fellfield cushions with a low growth profile and long root systems. These porous volcanic soils allow water to percolate so quickly beyond shallow root depth that in order to survive all of these plants have developed extended taproots. By comparison, Rocky Mountain fellfields even at their sparsest have more color and variety. The difference lies in the type of soil and the

Short-beaked agoseris *(Agoseris glauca* var. *dasycephala)*

amount of summer moisture, and probably most critically in the age of the surface. Although Rocky Mountain fellfields contain only rudimentary soil, it is much more stable and less volatile than the volcanic soil of the Cascades, able to hold, even if only briefly, the moisture from the summer showers that roll across the tundra.

A snowbank lies near 7600 feet. Water threads hesitantly out from beneath the snow, as if the dryness in the air and pumice soil make the snow reluctant to give up any of its moisture. The soil is darkened where the water seeps, but so porous that there is scarcely any dampness available for plants.

Cascade lomatium (*Lomatium angustatum*)

Tolmie's saxifrage *(Saxifraga tolmiei)*

Tolmie saxifrages cluster under overhanging and sheltering boulders. At first glance the leaves look like those of a sedum, almost as round as they are long, tightly packed into fat shiny evergreen rosettes that cluster into a crescent at the base of the rocks. Some of the plants are just uncovered, and some have been free for a week or so, and the saxifrage ranges from bud to full bloom within a few feet: plants in this arid situation must mature very quickly since the ground may be desert-dry almost immediately after the snowbank retreats. Saxifrages develop with watchlike precision: there are ten filaments, each holding a dark purple pollen-covered anther; the five corresponding to the petals ripen first, and then the second set, offering pollen for cross-pollination over an extended period of time. In full fruit, the large prominent follicles turn rosy red. This little saxifrage is named for Dr. William Tolmie, a Hudson's Bay Company officer and avid plant collector. In 1833, he was the first botanist to visit Mount Rainier, where he found several new plant species, among them this saxifrage.

Although it is a sparse site as far as plant cover is concerned, and a few feet away from the snowbank the fellfield takes over, there are many insects in evidence. A brown grasshopper leaps across the soil with great verve, and there are several kinds of flies, including a small cranefly which wafts around in indecisive cranefly fashion. There are white cabbage butterflies, and a large orange-brown one that wheels by too quickly for identification. But the overall impression is of a less energetic world than most tundra areas, a world more self-contained, less joyous in growth, yet with the precise appeal of plants growing in the absolute minimum needed for survival.

There are only a few communities on this side of Mount Hood: a fellfield shading into a scree community, a sparse open turf, and a rudimentary snowbed. There are no lush meadows and no real marshes. It is an austere environment. The isolated mountain stands triumphant over the lowlands way of life. Mount Hood is a hostile and unforgiving mountain with a bare beauty of form.

The southeastern approach to Mount Rainier takes one through opulent undergrowth that skirts the huge straight firs and red cedars, white pines and western hemlock of the Washington forests. The forest light, sifting through layer upon layer of leaves, illuminates the pale "underherbs" of the forest floor with a limpid green glow usually seen underwater, and one feels almost submerged in the liquid greenness.

Suddenly there is an opening in the trees and Mount Rainier magically fills the horizon with glowing white, textured with blue shadows, fresh-washed in the afternoon light. A few clouds still pay court at its base; above them the summit gleams in massive splendor. Every mountain range has its own personality, as do the higher peaks within it. Pikes Peak, rising alone over the lower ridges of the Colorado Front Range, has a certain visual impressiveness because it is the highest mountain in the Range's immediate profile. The Sierra Nevada with its craggy and forbidding eastern face presents a phalanx of peaks, few visually more important than another in spite of the fact that Mount Whitney, the highest mountain in the continental United States, is among them. But Mount Rainier's volcanic cone has not only majesty of proportion and size but a dramatic isolation, rising 8000 feet above its 6000-foot plateau, covering a hundred square miles. Its full size and solitude, like that of the other Southern Cascade peaks, can only be grasped from the air or from a distant hillside. There is a visual impact of majesty and venerability, of sheer monumentality, ceremonially clothed in white even in August, completely dominating the view. It would be no surprise to hear crashing chords by Liszt, with kettle drums and French horns, crescendos and cymbals, all fortissimo.

The building of Mount Rainier began about a million years ago. Lava spouted from a vent in the earth's crust, and layer after layer of molten rock streamed out. As the core built, it caught the winter snows. Breccias, formed of lava and rocks and debris, sizzled on the ice and snow-covered flanks, and mixed with them to form hot mudflows that thundered downslope. Clouds of gas cauliflowered out of the vents and lightning crackled in the gray clouds. Occasionally explosive bursts plumed the sky with smoke and steam, spewing hot cinder, ash and pumice in a Roman orgy of insolent belching. Most of the pumice thrown out by Rainier in the last thousand centuries lies to the east of the mountain, caught by the westerly winds and carried like millions of gray butterflies. Rainier's last major eruptions ended about 6000 years ago.

At its greatest height, about 75,000 years ago, Rainier was 1000 feet higher, with nearly half again as much volume as it has today. Between 50,000 and 8000 years ago massive erosion from glaciers, debris and mudflows, and avalanches reduced Rainier's size to roughly that of the present. Between 2500 and 2000 years ago, Rainier briefly erupted several times, leaving new drifts of pumice on its eastern side and producing a new volcanic cone on its own summit. The new cone is about 1000 feet high and a mile across at its base. That it seems scarcely noticeable is indicative of the scale of the present massif, although from some angles the more even sides of the younger cone, virtually unmarred by erosion, contrast vividly with the grandfatherly configuration of Rainier itself, its flanks wrinkled by ice and water.

Rainier is snow- and ice-covered all year, since eighty percent of its precipitation falls as snow. Record snow depths for the United States have been recorded at Rainier. Glacial ice covers about forty-five square miles on the peak. The snow extends below 4000 feet in the winter and spring; in the summer, heat pulls cascades of water out from under the glacier's icy toes, and bare rock masses cleave and define the twenty-six resident glaciers. Most of Rainier's glaciers are retreating or relatively stable. Only half a dozen of Rainier's glaciers begin from ice at the summit; the rest originate some 2000–3000 feet below, where precipitation is greater.

These glaciers may have insects and scraps of windblown lichen and debris on their surfaces. A few mosses grow in the steam-heated crater of the summit, and lichens rim it at 14,300 feet, but no vascular plants are known to exist above the 10,000-foot line.

Several long ridges radiate out from Rainier's main core, looking flat and wide and dark from below, like monstrous beached whales. Like other large ridges of the same character in the Cascades, they were formed several thousand years ago when thick lava flowed down the deep canyons surrounding the mountain. Because these flows of resistant lava do not erode as quickly as the softer rock surrounding them, they remain as ridges above the carved-out valleys. Porous ash and pumice later drifted tens of feet deep on top of the laval spines. These pumice layers drain so rapidly that little erosion occurs to destroy the flat broad summits, and those that lie in the rainshadow of the mountain receive considerably less rain than the 106 inches that fall on Rainier's high western flanks.

A krummholz of whitebark pine, subalpine fir, Engelmann spruce and yellow cedar along a ridge flank is brightened in the summer by drifts of white anemones, some in flower, some with huge white dish-mop seed heads. Treelimit can be as low as 5500 feet at Rainier; the mosaic of trees and tree islands often spreads over a thousand-foot band, lower on north-facing slopes, higher on south-facing. Local soil conditions may bring treelimit even lower; the raw coarse pumice soils from recent eruptions on a more southerly Cascade cone, Mount Saint Helen's, where the mountain core is less than 2000 years old, depress treelimit to around 4500 feet. The thirty or so square miles of alpine tundra above 5500 feet on Mount Rainier are sandwiched narrowly between these last outliers of timber and the zone of permanent ice

Drummond's anemone
(*Anemone drummondii*)

and snow. The firn line on Rainier, the line at which melting reaches its highest point for the year, is well above 6500 feet, but in sheltered areas may extend below 5000 feet. Therefore only a very narrow band of open ground remains for alpine plant growth.

A hoary marmot hitches himself up onto a nearby rock, tilting his head in typical marmot fashion. Life is extremely difficult for Rainier's animals: rocky slopes above treelimit are covered with very deep snow except where they are blown free by strong winds. Pacific fronts often bring storms that cover all exposed surfaces with ice, making food completely unavailable for weeks at a time. Only one other large mammal lives here, a mountain goat, although pika, ground squirrels and chipmunks are plentiful.

The remaining animal populations are summer birds, the same species that inhabit the alpine Rockies: horned larks, gray-crowned rosy finches, water pipits and white-tailed ptarmigan.

The marmot's look is so lugubrious and wistful that I have the uneasy feeling that he wishes me gone, leaving him the days and years of his mountain. Given a marmot's particular questioning expression and tilt of head, it is difficult not to believe that it is sentient.

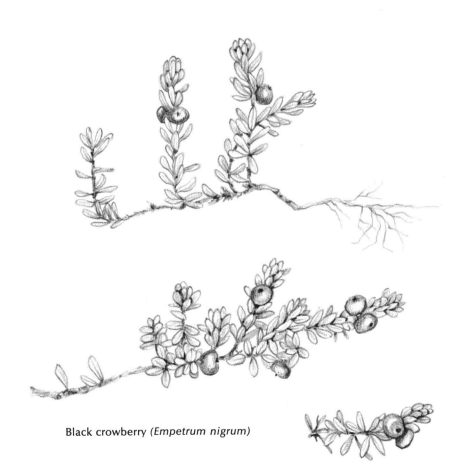

Black crowberry (*Empetrum nigrum*)

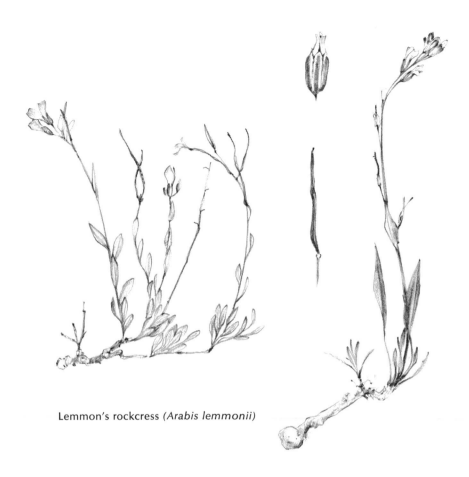

Lemmon's rockcress (*Arabis lemmonii*)

The rising slopes between treelimit and the crest of the ridge range from gentle to steep, and all are mantled with dark gray volcanic soil. The ground covers are all adapted to grabbing into this shifting substrate. Crowberry creeps along the ground, forming a web of tangled branches and stems which catch the blowing soil. The word *empetrum*, part of its scientific name, derives from the Greek and means "upon rock." Near the base of the ridge they are in shiny black berry but near the top a few are still in bloom. With evergreen needlelike leaves, crowberry looks much like a heather although it belongs to a completely different family, a case of parallel adaptation to similar environmental requirements. Crowberry fulfills the same role as the evergreen mountain dryad that stabilizes steep Rocky Mountain slopes.

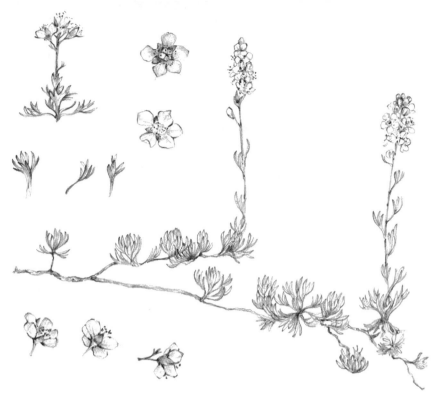

Luetkea or Partridge foot *(Luetkea pectinata)*

A clump of resoundingly scarlet flowers, the cliff Indian paint-brush, contrasts with the dark gray volcanic soil. Although many at lower elevations are red, most alpine paintbrushes are dusty rose or orange or yellow. (In fact, there are almost no pure red flowers in the United States alpine tundra at all.) Lemmon's rockcress grows within a cluster of rocks; the green of leaves and stems is neutralized by the red pigments in them so that the little plant is nearly the color of the shadows. Tight rows of Tolmie saxifrage dovetail with the rocks, and big mats of luetkea string upslope above them.

Luetkea, a dainty ground-hugging shrub that belongs to the Rose family, is named for Count Luetke, a Russian captain on a ship chart-ing the Alaskan coast in the nineteenth century. It often grows with Tolmie saxifrage, a frequent combination on the steep scree slopes of the Cascades and Olympics. Immediately after snowmelt the leaves of luetkea are flat on the ground; they lift with warmth and dryness.

Spikes of ivory-white flowers rise on four-inch stems, the masses of yellow stamens making them look creamy yellow from a distance.

Both luetkea and Tolmie saxifrage are extremely important soil holders in the northwest, since volcanic soil is one of the most difficult for plant life. It contains little nourishment. It drains so quickly that humus has almost no chance to form in the cool alpine climate. It is extremely abrasive, and this is one of the main reasons that alpine plant communities of the Pacific Northwest are not nearly as developed as those of the Rockies. In addition, these soils are so recently formed that they have not had time to develop any horizons indicating approaching maturity, and have large amounts of bare rock and rubble. Along with a short growing season of about two months, strong drying winds and a limited water supply, especially in the rainshadow of the mountain, the soil prevents any extensive development of alpine plant communities.

The soil is as hard as ground glass to the touch, and as gritty. Although the soil is damp in the shadows, it maintains its separateness as individual grains. As it dries, it floats away with a breath of wind, neither able to hold or be held.

On the steep north face of the ridge, the snow still holds in shaded lozenges and ovals. The open slopes between are nearly vertical. The pumice soil slithers downward in unbroken slides, the smooth contours indicating the freshness of descent. The snowbanks covering the path are very slippery; I negotiate two of them but lose courage on the third and decide to leave the path and cross above the snow. The soil is so unstable, the slope so precipitous and the footing so insecure that each footstep loosens black feathers of pumice downslope. I finally sit down and edge across, undignified and dusty, but somehow more reassured.

Over the last short rise the horizon suddenly opens. The crest of the ridge is bright and sunny after the closeted shade of the north slope, with a clear light wind that vibrates the carpeting of flowers. There seem to be double the number of clear lemon yellow agoseris, triple the number of pussypaws, and quadruple the number of lavender and white lupines, lilac asters and golden daisies in the constant movement.

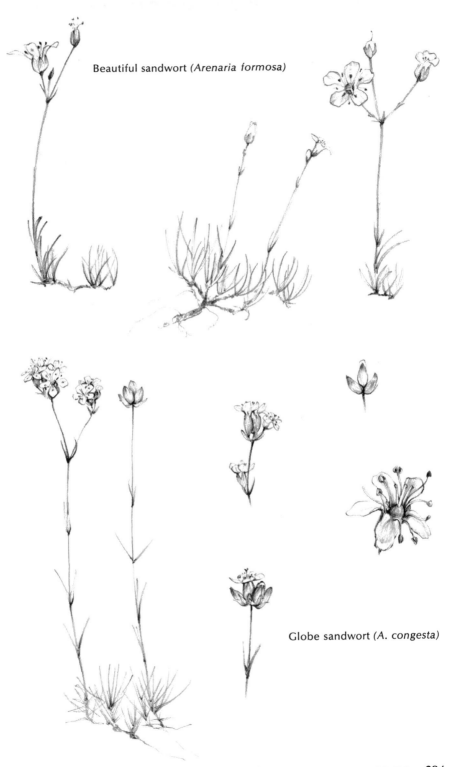

Beautiful sandwort (*Arenaria formosa*)

Globe sandwort (*A. congesta*)

Coiled-beak lousewort *(Pedicularis contorta)*

Since all the plants fit closely and compactly to the ground, they suffuse the dark soil like the border of a Byzantine mosaic. Looming in the near distance is the summit of Rainier itself, so close that it cannot be taken in one glance but has to be read, beginning on the left with Little Tahoma Peak, crossing glacier and outcrop and glacier, and finally coming up and over the summit to the right margin, the end of a white page against a pale blue Washington sky. And instead of feeling dwarfed, one feels larger than life for it is the kind of a time and place that makes one feel totally attuned to the natural world: one could soar like a hawk or draw forth a thunderbolt or scribe the sky with a rainbow. I know at this moment precisely how the gods on Mount Olympus must have felt.

The wind spoons up eddies of soil with every footstep, and boots leave lug-soled patterns that are shot out by the next arrow of wind. No plant rises over eight inches, and the general cushion of vegetation lies between two and four inches, topped only by spike trisetum and woodrush. The entire ridgetop is a giant fellfield, with patches of turf, open to unrelenting winds, in full searing sunlight, surviving by the grace of frequent showers and protective cloud cover. The plants all bear the impress of the climate: hirsute or thick-leaved cushions with a prostrate growth pattern, and deep anchoring root systems that can tap any wisps of moisture and hold against the insistent wind. The growth forms and adaptations here are similar to those of White Mountain alpine plants, although the plants here are larger and more luxuriant in the cooler, moister climate.

Only about a third of the ground is covered with vegetation. Big patches of empty pumice surround undulating ribboned islands of plants. Although there are many plants in number on this vast ridgetop, there are relatively few species, only about a fourth or fifth the number of plant species in a Rocky Mountain fellfield. Many are hardy grasses, sedges and rushes. There are no annuals at all.

Sometimes a buckwheat root snakes over the ground a foot or two before connecting a flower at one end with its ground hold at the other. The long smooth roots are unbranched and dry, abraded clean, bearing no root hairs. Full-blooming cushions of phlox lie far away from where their crooked roots take ground. The continual wind alternately covers and uncovers the roots, and the plants migrate in the most propitious

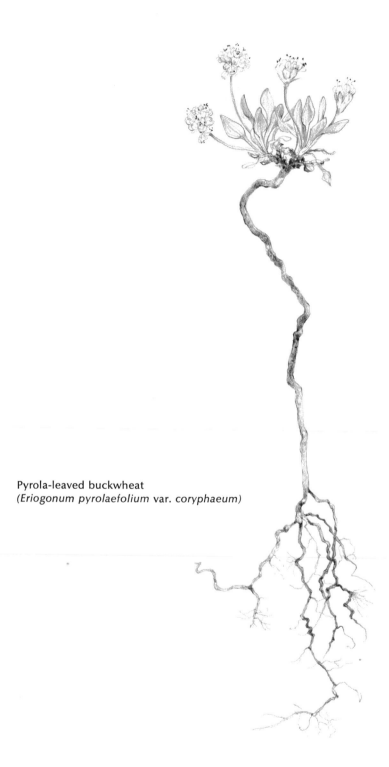

Pyrola-leaved buckwheat
(*Eriogonum pyrolaefolium* var. *coryphaeum*)

direction, a growth pattern typical of scree slope plants existing here on the flat.

There are hundreds of dwarf Lyall lupines, the quarter- to half-inch flowers arranged in stacked whorls around the stem so that from above the flower head looks like lavender-blue wheels the size of a fifty-cent piece. The word "lupine" comes from the Latin word for wolf because of an old superstition that lupines robbed the soil, a curious conclusion since in fact legumes add much-needed nitrogen to the soil. These dwarf alpines belong to a large, diverse and widespread Western genus with members growing from the seashore to the mountaintops, from the plains of Texas to the Arctic. Lyall lupine ranges through the Cascades south into the Sierra Nevada, a characteristic plant of pumice fields. The stems, leaves and calyces holding the pealike blossoms are covered with dense silvery hairs, a device that protects the plant from the severe radiation of the mountain heights and probably reduces moisture loss.

Spreading phlox *(Phlox diffusa)*

Alpine yellow daisy *(Erigeron aureus)*

Alpine aster *(Aster alpigenus)*

Yellow alpine daisies stipple the lupines and enhance their lilac hue as in a Seurat landscape. These are appropriately specified as *aureus* for their deep bright golden yellow. While neither Lyall lupine nor the yellow daisy is limited to this area, this particular intermixing of the two seems to be characteristic of the alpine gardens of the Washington Cascades.

Entwined in the roots of a lupine are those of Newberry knotweed, a plant typical of open pumice areas in the Cascades. It grows here in the open areas between plant islands, where it has no competition. Newberry knotweed has small, inconspicuous cream and red flowers, and large simple green leaves on rhubarb red stems. While not as colorfully endowed as the lupines and daisies, it is an important ground cover where loose soils limit soil lichen growth. In early spring the leaves are pale vermillion, and in late fall they turn soft apricot.

On the other side of the ridge, the ground takes a slight southeasterly tilt downwards, unnoticeable except for an increasing lushness of vegetation marking the more protected microenvironment. Interwoven with the lupines are bright blue penstemons. The ground is plaited in amethyst and mauve and alabaster, with gilt threads of yellow alpine daisies and cinquefoils. A few bistort twinkle above the low plants, along with satiny grasses and sedges. Each flower in the head of ivory lousewort is twisted to the right. Late afternoon shadows deepen in small hollows, blurring the sharp clarity of the noontime. The sweet-pea odor of the lupines swirls around my head. The richly figured medieval foreground and the great white cone of Rainier intensify each other, and there is a resolution of plane and solid, of light and shadow, of all the elements of a mountain world in the slanting shafts of afternoon sunlight.

Alpine penstemon *(Penstemon tolmiei)*

Ivory or Yellow mountain heather
(*Phyllodoce glanduliflora*)

The eastern slope of the ridge has been severely trampled. Although the path on the north slope is paved partway and well marked, it is also obstructed with large snowbanks late into the summer, so the tendency is for hikers to take a different pathway down, especially early in the year when the snowbanks are formidable. Where there is no marked path, as here, hikers take their own individual routes depending upon their stride, the difficulty of the descent, and their judgment of what is the shortest distance between two points.

The pressure of a boot scraping downward on loose soil sends a pall of dust over adjacent plants, to clog plant pores with every step. A human's weight is easily able to crush and break fragile stems. Rocks roll and tear. Gravel slides and smothers. Only the most hardy plants endure, either between rocks or in patches that are too small to put a boot into: a few saxifrages, a few buckwheats, a scattering of sedges and grasses, and some scraggling carpets of crowberry losing the battle of soil-holding.

The plants that ought to grow here unhindered, carpeting the ground with a profusion of tiny pink and white flowers, are tucked away in shelters or far off the traveled areas. Ivory heather and pink heather, penstemons and luxuriant mats of crowberry lurk in untrodden corners. Ivory heather, sticky with glands, lights a hidden slope with hundreds of minute lanterns. Crowberry next to it forms a crisp interlocking of soil-holding roots and stems.

There are few alpine plant community possibilities on Mount Rainier: fellfield, late snowbed, open turf, boulder field and shrubby heath. The latter is nearly missing at this end of the ridge although it should be flourishing here. It is fragmented and almost eliminated by human traffic. After the euphoria felt in the lupine and daisy meadow, the destitution caused by thoughtlessness and ignorance is doubly depressing. This community, even if cloistered from this moment on, will not recover in our lifetimes.

18 : The Olympic Mountains

From the air, solid clouds at the base of the Olympic Mountains look like snowcovered foothills. Although it is late afternoon, it is far enough north so that the sun is still high. The air is soft, and the mountains and ocean are visible in subtle nuances of blues and grays and greens. Ultramarine shadows lengthen behind outcrops and spurs, accentuating snow-starched summits. The even-toothed peaks stretch continuously southward and westward to an amorphous horizon in which sky light merges with mountain light.

The next morning the fog clings so thickly at the base of the mountains that trees and boulders suddenly loom out of the mist, ominous in the milky morning. At 5000 feet the mists shred, and within a few seconds the clouds are below, gently lapping the mountain walls like waves from a foamy ocean.

Ahead, the glacier-covered peaks of the Olympics catch the morning light, dark rock crags radiant with bright snow and sunshine, but with a softness of contour that reflects the moisture in the summer air, much different from the crystalline clarity of dry-air light in the Rockies

Glacier lily *(Erythronium grandiflorum)*

Snowbed buttercup *(Ranunculus eschscholtzii)*

and Sierra Nevada. Tall lupines and orange paintbrush along the road-side give the illusion of having been painted in water color on damp paper, the soft light so furs the edges. Then the white bobbins of bistort appear among them. The subalpine fir, Engelmann spruce and yellow cedar thin and become more stunted.

At treelimit glacier lilies bloom, late because of a deep late-lying snowbed and a record winter snowfall. The hillsides below are stalked with thousands of long stems swaying with heavy seed pods. The upper field has a Midas touch: the golden lilies are molded of buttered sunshine, and between them blow gilded snowbed buttercups. Beyond there are more fields—hip-high lupines and tousle-headed grasses, orange paintbrushes and butterworts, yellow and purple louseworts silhouetted against a dark green island of subalpine fir, luxuriant meadows fed by heavy snowfall and snow blown across from higher alpine ridges.

Beyond the thick high subalpine–low alpine meadows, the ground cover thins and diminishes. The terrain steepens and becomes so gravel-covered that no taller plants persist. Puddles of luetkea spread across the ground, hundreds of them stabilizing the shale-scree slope. Below lies a solifluction terrace formed in a now-empty cirque, still active in the wet scrabbly soil. In spite of the instability, there are huge pads of moss on the wet surface, studded with minute yellow monkeyflowers and stalked with sedges locking the soil with their strong root systems.

The top of the cirque is a ridge, stretching towards the northeast. A path strings across the unblemished fall of the wall, twining across the steep scree flank, looking gray and dusty and empty. Where the ridge traces southward no snowcover holds. Opposite, to the west, the remote, massive Mount Olympus carries a glacial necklace fed by the wettest winds in the United States. This contrast of terrains is engendered because the ridge lies on the northeast side of the Olympics, in the rainshadow of the mountain mass. The heavy precipitation that forms the windward rainforests comes mostly from the southwest; on the western side of the Olympics, rainfall reaches two hundred fifty inches a year, supporting luxuriant growth. On the eastern side eighty inches fall, and here on this ridge, forty inches, all within a twenty-five-mile horizontal distance. Although this is much heavier than the rainfall in the Rockies and Sierra, the steepness of the ridge flanks and the porosity and mobility of its soil maintain nearly barren inclines.

In spite of this preliminary view of impoverished scree slopes, with exploration the most diverse and developed tundra outside the Rocky Mountains unfolds: rock crevice, scree, fellfield, turf, snowbed marsh, and heath, each determined by the turn and tilt of the terrain. Around a sharp projecting rock spine of charcoal-gray shale there is a total surprise: an alpine rock garden as richly stocked as if planted by a skilled landscape architect and maintained by a master gardener. The change from the rather sparsely flowered scree slope is sudden, and coming around the corner is like opening a florist's box. The whole slope, which now faces southeast and holds extra snowcover in the winter, is embroidered: lavender against yellow, pale opaque blue

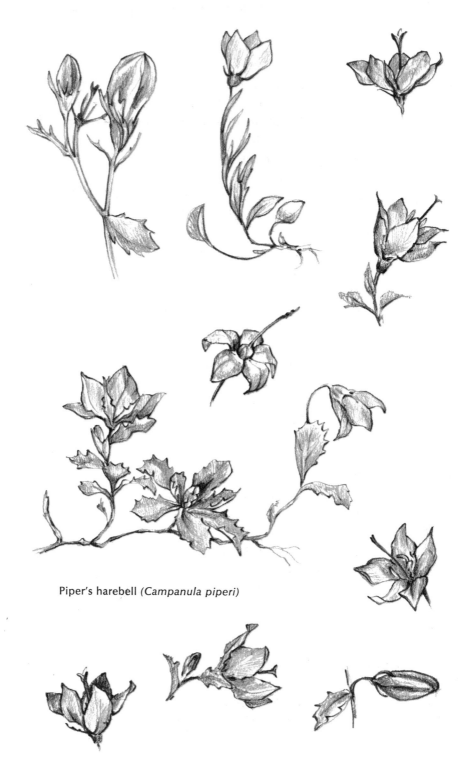

Piper's harebell (*Campanula piperi*)

against dark gray-blue rock, ivory against dark slate, with just enough magenta to add warmth, and enough white to add light. The garden is protected by the sliding talus slope beneath it as effectively as if by a ten-foot fence. The flowers spread upslope, from just above my head to almost fifty feet, crevices and hollows and ledges packed with flowers in an opulent display.

Olympic violets spring from a dirt-filled crevice, smaller than the cultivated variety but with an intensity of color set off by emerald green leaves. Most of the spurs have holes nipped in them, probably by enterprising bees after nectar. Piper's harebells (named for Dr. Charles Piper, the first resident botanist at Mount Rainier) grow in a blue line following rock cracks, the rows of tiny pale cerulean bells open wide to the sun, on just enough stem to raise them off the rock. Both are small plants, fitted into sharp ledges and interstices in the slate, snugged against the rocks so that their contour seems merely brighter lodes of color. By slithering up the slope and holding on by my fingernails, I can just look into the harebells. The profusion of flowers almost covers their tiny toothed leaves, the particular blue repeated up the rock wall in rococo scrolls, flourishing where they receive warmth, protection and good drainage.

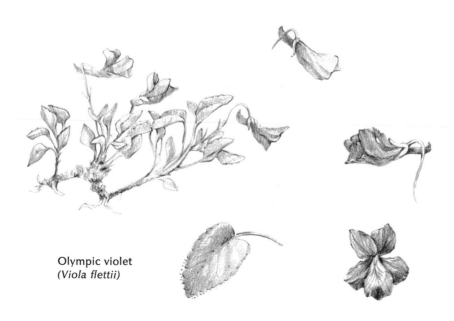

Olympic violet
(Viola flettii)

White-flowered willowherb
(*Epilobium lactiflorum*)

Hornemann's willowherb
(*E. hornemannii*)

Western sweetbroom
(Hedysarum occidentale)

Alpine alumroot *(Heuchera glabra)*

Besides the wealth of tiny plants tucked into rock cracks, other plants richly embroider the steep sliding slope between outcrops. Several tiny magenta-pink fireweeds resemble silk French knots on couched stems. Tall creamy alumroot and bright lavender-pink sweetbroom grow ten inches tall. Sweetbroom, with its sweet-pea-like blossoms stitched on tall stalks, also dangles scalloped seedpods. Tiny white larvae occupy a few of these instead of seeds. Luetkea makes nets sewed in feather stitch. The flowers of cliff douglasia, a small primrose named for the Scottish botanist David Douglas, seem satin stitched in resonant pink. Dotted and tufted saxifrages and anemones look bullion knotted in white. Larkspur puts shafts of royal purple fourteen inches high above rosy red leaves. All the hairs on the larkspur's stem point downward, a deterrent to crawling insects in a bee-pollinated plant. Heads of arnica rotate to the sunshine. White asters make opulent clumps. Black-and-white sedges, fishbone stitched in black on thin silken green stems, add linear grace to top-heavy thistles and butterweeds with beet red leaves and stems.

After the profusion of plants in the rock garden, the scree slope beyond seems distinguished only by the paucity, hardiness and tenacity of the

Cliff douglasia *(Douglasia laevigata)*

Flathead larkspur
(*Delphinium glareosum*)

Olympic aster *(Aster paucicapitatus)*

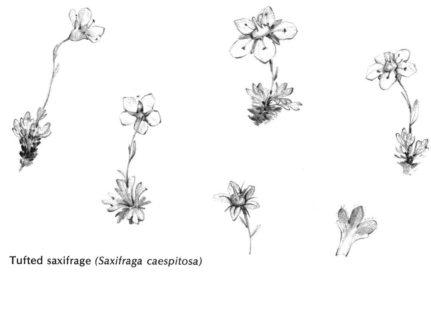

Tufted saxifrage *(Saxifraga caespitosa)*

Shrubby cinquefoil *(Potentilla fruticosa)*

plants that survive there. These southwest-facing screes appear as well-drained and dry as the volcanic soils of the Cascades, but streams and ribbons and saucers of plant growth polka-dotting the gravels suggest deeper-down moisture. Clumps of buckwheat proliferate wherever a lessening of slant gives them a chance to become established, along with nuggets of short-beaked agoseris that flourish in the empty slope. A summer wind twitches the plants, a drier wind than those that carry the winter and spring storms. The westerlies that bring heavy precipitation are pulled northward in the summer, and the

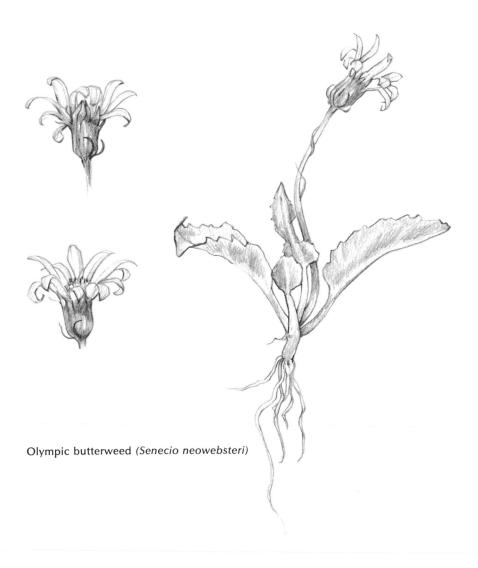

Olympic butterweed *(Senecio neowebsteri)*

Olympic summers can be remarkably dry except for fog at lower altitudes. Only the briefness of the summer, the oceanic situation and the coolness of the northerly latitude prevent severe drought conditions from occurring. Both subalpine and alpine areas may receive frost any day of the year, and the coastal areas may get only half the amount of possible sunshine. There are always more deterrents to plant growth in the alpine tundra than there are encouragements.

Shrubby cinquefoil sprawls down the forty-degree slope, six-foot patches alternating with scree on a wide length of path. Here the west-

Parry's catchfly *(Silene parryi)*

southwest exposure is covered with dry loose gravel, lying at such a steep angle that the surface slides and moves most of the time. At lower altitudes in the Rockies shrubby cinquefoil grows to be a three-foot shrub, only rarely extending into the alpine reaches. Here it is less than hand high and scraggles along in a disheveled mat, but otherwise leaves and flowers look the same. It grows well in the full sunlight and there is inordinate pleasure at finding it so far from where I know it so well.

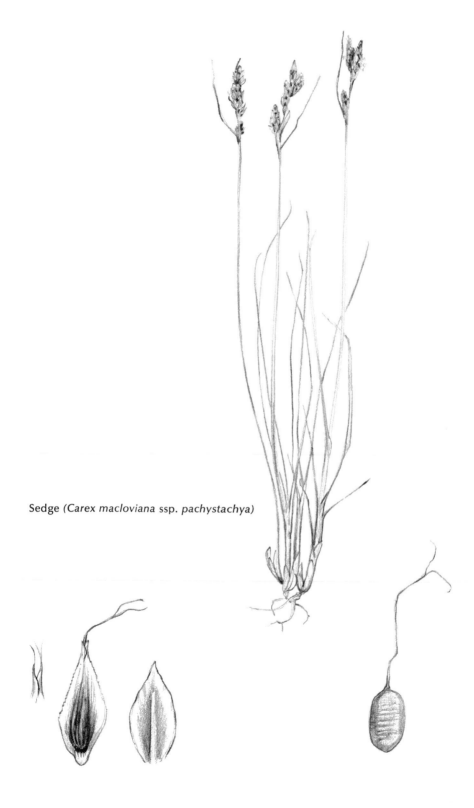

Sedge *(Carex macloviana* ssp. *pachystachya)*

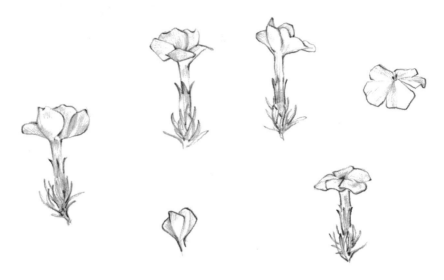

Spreading phlox *(Phlox diffusa)*

Talus collomia *(Collomia larsenii)*

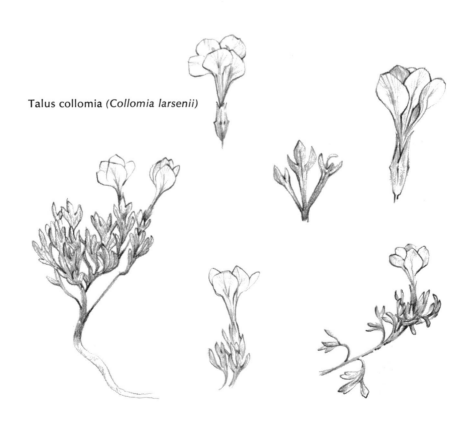

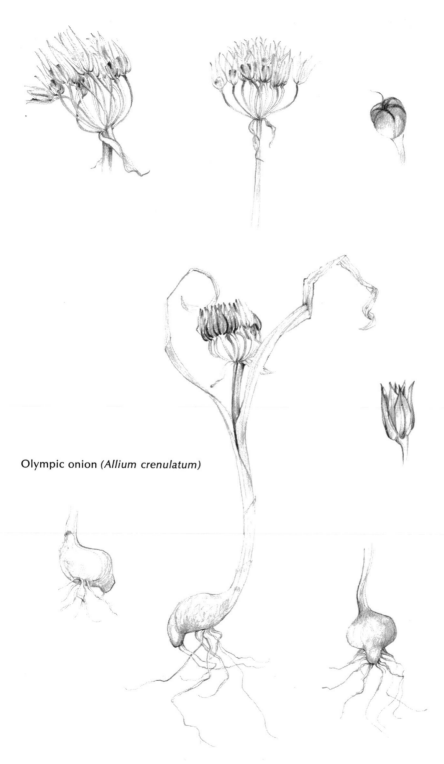

Olympic onion (*Allium crenulatum*)

Rich blue-gray patches define areas of slate that contrast with the paler areas of tan scree. The slate lies in slabs so loose that practically no plants root here; a card-sized piece bounces down the incline with a hollow musical clanking, tiddlywinking smaller pieces along with it, disappearing while the metallic notes still ring. Where the slate is temporarily stabilized by the path, a few nearly spherical cushions of collomia cling. Its name comes from the Greek word for glue because the seeds are mucilaginous when wet. The small flowers are mauve tinged and the stems are rose, nestled in balls of extremely glandular foliage; the stamens are pale baby blue. It grows from a very long taproot which extends deep into the soil to hold it fast against the slipping terrain. The color and hirsuteness of collomia indicate that it is adapted to survive on just such a sun-parched slope as this, with seeds that adhere where they fall rather than blowing or rolling down the slide. Just a few feet beyond, where the slope briefly has less of a tilt, a purple onion nods and a few plants of stonecrop put out

Three-forked sage
(Artemisia trifurcata)

Olympic fernleaf candytuft *(Smelowskia ovalis)*

star-shaped soft yellow flowers. A locoweed takes tentative foothold. But the minute the slope steepens again and becomes dry and dusty, it is bereft of plants.

Another turn in the path, and the slope levels out to a small, sunny meadow. The slight change in terrain allows more moisture to remain in the soil, and a turf very reminiscent of those in the Rocky Mountains is growing. There is a profusion of plants and insects and movement. A large clump of catchfly has peppermint-striped flowers, and

Explorer's gentian
(*Gentiana calycosa*)

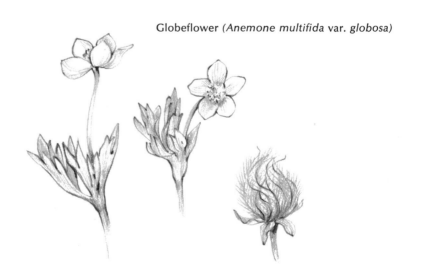

Globeflower (*Anemone multifida* var. *globosa*)

is as sticky as fly paper to touch. A portentous bumblebee, back legs full of orange pollen, works the foot-high lupines. Sedges and grasses and rushes quiver in the sunlit breeze; three-forked sage silvers the background. Wall flowers and Olympic fernleaf candytuft beat like yellow and white pendulums , timing the summer day. Daisies nod and toss. The feathery seedheads of alpine avens blur in the noontime breeze. Many of these same species grow in the Rockies above 11,500 feet; here they bloom at 6800 feet, depressed by the more northerly latitude. The topography and precipitation support a rich alpine meadow that seems to be woven of grass, flower color and high summer.

A deep bottle-blue explorer's gentian in a secretive moist pocket marks the beginning of autumn blooming. It grows six inches high, surrounded by many plants already in seed, witness to the greater water-holding capacity of the turf since gentians require moisture. They bloom late because they require a longer growing period. The brocade of other plants is woven of harmonious greens, mellow whites and rose, against which the gentians glow like a handful of scattered sapphires.

The view from the meadow encompasses the main body of the Olympic Mountains, directly across the horizon. Of the 5000 square miles of the Olympic Peninsula, 4000 square miles are mountainous. The highest is Mount Olympus at nearly 9000 feet, with others in the 7500-foot range. Although there are no volcanic cones in the Olympics, the old lavas which were laid under sea water and later raised were eroded into pinnacles called The Needles which contrast with the more smoothly notched profile of the Range. The names of the rivers and creeks that fan out from the peaks are euphonious: Soleduck, Calawah, Bogachiel, Hoh, Queets, Satsop, Skokomish, Duckabush, Dosewallips, Quilcene and Dungeness.

The uplifts which raised the Olympics began fifty-six to sixty million years ago and alternated with periods of erosion and depression until the birth of the present mountain system fifteen to twenty million years ago. The mountains as they stand today reached their present height about eleven million years ago during the cataclysmic events that brought both the Cascade and Olympic Mountains into being.

Over the eons, these uplifts so bent, contorted and fractured the rocks that the geology of the Olympic Peninsula is some of the most elaborate and complex in the world.

The snowline—that elevation above which snow remains all year round—scribes the peaks around 6000 feet, the lowest snowline in the contiguous United States, rising somewhat higher on the eastern side, which gets less direct snow. The Olympics and the Cascades contain most of the major glaciers in the United States, for in these areas conditions are most favorable for glacier formation: cool summers combined with heavy winter and spring snowfalls. There are approximately sixty glaciers in the Olympics, remnants of those spawned during the Little Ice Age, but still large and complex by comparison with other glaciated areas.

Today the glaciers retreat up their U-shaped valleys toward the cirque wombs that bore them. They are probably half as large now as they were during their greatest development, and are now melting back at the rate of about forty feet per year, shown by extensive studies made from the air, since none of the Olympic glaciers are easily accessible. In the summer sun, the peaks look as if they have been carelessly frosted, the knife scraping some of the ridges bare and leaving crumbs of outcrops on the surface.

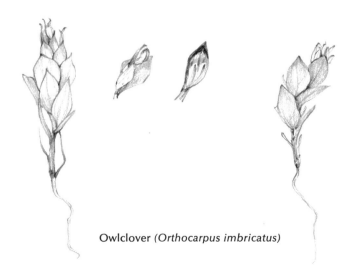

Owlclover (*Orthocarpus imbricatus*)

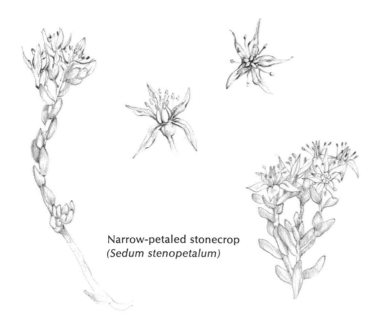

Narrow-petaled stonecrop
(*Sedum stenopetalum*)

The Range disappears from view over the crest of the knife-edge ridgetop. Such sharp ridges reflect the interaction of softer and more easily quarried sedimentary rocks with the deep, persistent, nearly all-encompassing glaciers of the Olympics. Little if any surface was left for plant growth during the major glacial periods here. The surfaces are young, but the rock is not as young as in the Cascades; the amount of soil and plant cover reflects this, as does the instability of this northeast-facing steep slope. From the slope just climbed, the aspect of the sheer scree-covered walls of the empty cirque below nearly give one vertigo.

On the shaded side of the ridge, snow still clings in large, porous patches. Where it has recently melted, minuscule gray cauliflowers of lichen foam over the wet ground. A few buttercups bloom at the edges of the snowbank, and a few globeflowers and sibbaldia. What is not already in bloom by late August probably will not come to bloom before autumn storms seal the summer in snow.

A well-developed fellfield lies above a patch of misty rose heather. In some places the plants grow close enough together so that they almost

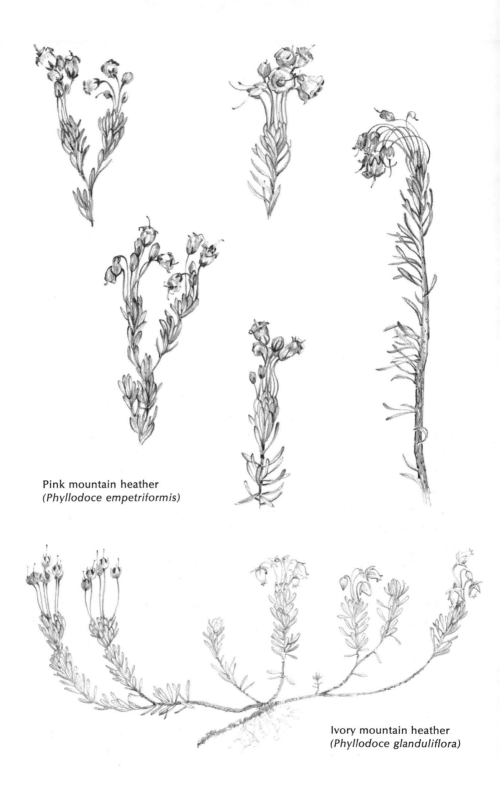

Pink mountain heather
(*Phyllodoce empetriformis*)

Ivory mountain heather
(*Phyllodoce glanduliflora*)

form a turf, but the open areas indicate that neither soil nor cover is advanced enough to be called anything but a fellfield. A few small owlclovers, sandworts, alpine avens, buckwheats, Lyall lupines, sedum and hawksbeard and spike woodrush compose a variegated field of small chips of color.

The pink mountain heather beyond carpets the ground, protected from the wind, receiving moisture from above but still high enough on the slope to be well-drained. It is intermixed with ivory mountain heather, patterning a low continuous cover like all heath communities. Lavender-pink or yellow-white bells hover over profuse tiny leaves and leathery tough creeping branches. The dusky shadows of late afternoon curl into the heathers, and all the plants on the slope come to share in the same amethyst softness.

19 : Mount Washington

I huddle in the felsenmeer at the summit, a sea of rocks embossed with mosses and lichens and sedges. The boulders tilt at odd angles, huge and frost-cracked, ringing small patches of dark green turf, wedged with mosses, surfeited with lichens. Haircap mosses, almost as big as a small grass, are in full capsule. Mists steam across the summit, curling down among the boulders, catching in the lichens, seething as if the whole summit were a giant cauldron. The whole landscape is dark olive green and gray and damp, unrelieved by blue sky or warm colors, and the wind is the same. With no horizon and the crazy lie of the boulders there is an uncomfortable disorientation.

Bigelow's sedge crowds between the rocks, dark heads snapping in the wind. Iceland lichen crinkles in patches fist deep; in the wet and damp they are as resilient underfoot as a wet sponge. Rocktripe lichen, which scabs the rocks in the Rockies where there is relatively little surface moisture, here forms opulent three-dimensional gray roses. At the edge of rocks, Greenland sandwort pioneers in tiny thimbles of soil, forming erect patches from an inch to the width of a hand. A tuft of dwarf bilberry snugs to a rock. The low plants, tucked into all the rock crannies, enjoy a more equitable climate, warmer by degrees, less snarled by the wind, than the weather at head height. Spike rush and bluegrass crop up between the rocks, above the stolid mats, caught in a multiplicity of movement.

There is almost no color here but green and gray and a salting of white, yet the ground between the rocks is almost totally covered. Dark bare spots indicate rock movement by soil ice, but they are slowly being invaded. Sedges are everywhere. Composing most of the plant cover, they are adapted to this incessant fog and wind and cold, able to proceed with photosynthesis in this half light, where skies are cloudy three-quarters or more of the summer growing season, and the highest recorded wind velocities in the world howl and bellow.

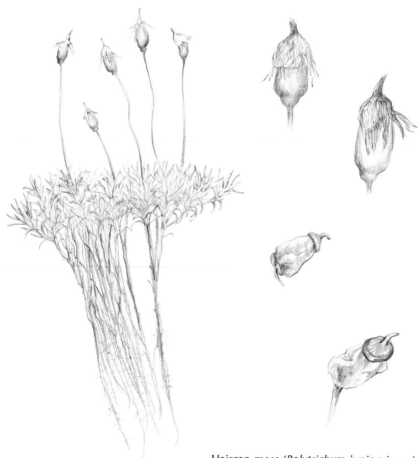

Haircap moss (Polytrichum juniperinum)

The soil lies cold and damp in the hand; it is quite sandy, peppered with dark humus, dark brown and unassimilated. It sifts through the fingers with no cohesion. The sedge rhizomes thread it and the lichens veneer it, but it is not a rich soil. The wind, the prevalent cold and the frost action hinder soil formation. Although it is moist, it is not wet; water percolates through it like ocean through a sandy beach.

Starting downslope, the mists fume and swirl in hollow enveloping scarves. The wind keeps one constantly off balance. It is stinging bitter. Each vapor consumes me in a helix of cold smoke, engendering a sense of vertigo. Some of the cold gray-green rocks are so encrusted with map lichens that they look like mottled green marble. The plants are so cloud-caught that they appear gray. Green rocks, gray plants: a Norse landscape.

Diapensia (*Diapensia lapponica*)

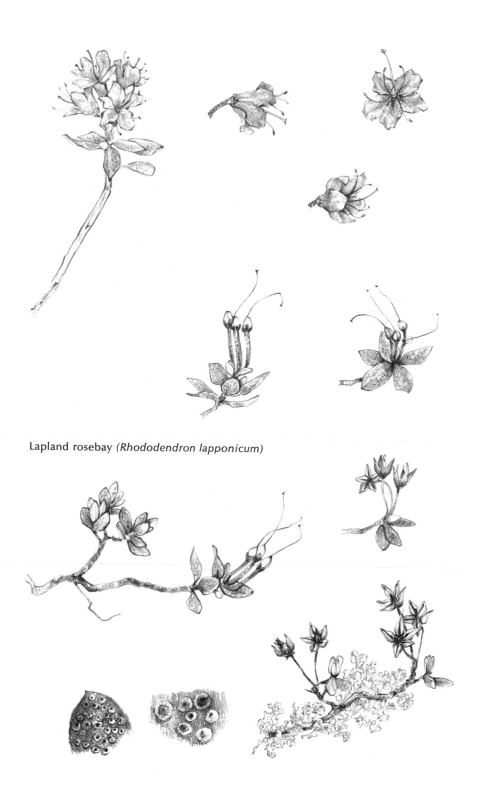

Lapland rosebay *(Rhododendron lapponicum)*

The dull somber green of the plants is due not only to the lack of sunlight but also to the dark green leaves of the evergreens. Mats of diapensia are in bloom in a careless heap of boulders. The flowers have fallen off whole and unwilted, with stamens still attached to the flower tube. Although they are nearly finished flowering, the plants appear awash with blossoms. Diapensia is slow-growing, adding only a few evergreen leaves a year. It is an arctic-alpine plant that reaches its southern limit here. And here it withstands the greatest exposure to wind of any flowering plant.

Lapland rosebay flowers lie shattered from the recent storm and a few last flowers snag in the mat of shiny evergreen leaves, petals blasted almost translucent. Both leaf surfaces are scabbed with minute rings, varying from clear to rust, depending on age, odd freckles that can be lifted off with a fingernail. There was an ice and snow storm two days ago, of which this weather is the bitter holdout. Although the flowers look beaten, these tough-leaved plants are undamaged. Even with a period of five days below freezing in the summer, they can continue to bloom and set seed. Diapensia and Lapland rosebay, like most fellfield flowers, are very early blooming, depending on reserves built up during the last growing season.

Alpine azalea is also able to withstand water loss from frozen soils, enduring on the highest and most wind-exposed slopes. The mats rise only a quarter of an inch high, a dwarf among dwarves. They are so low and so compact that in spite of the wind they do not even quiver. This area is half bare ground and maintains little snow cover, a true fellfield community.

Little stone rings, made of pebbles and as wide across as a hand or boot, parquet the ground, produced by freezing and thawing of these damp soils. With open soil and little snow protection, there is active frost action in the spring and fall when temperatures alternate rapidly and frequently between freezing and thawing. Such frost action does not disturb a dry Rocky Mountain fellfield nor a shifting pumice ridge in the Cascades.

The tremendous boulders that form a towering ring around me were formed by frost action in the past. The crustose lichens that

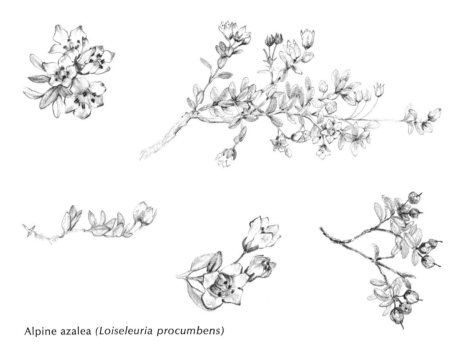

Alpine azalea *(Loiseleuria procumbens)*

clothe them now bear witness to centuries of stability. These rocks are hard and unyielding, little altered by weathering, in contrast to the granites of the Rockies. Feeling the viciousness of the weather that can create only the modest pebble patterns of today, one is struck suddenly by the fearsomeness of a climate that could have levered boulders.

The clouds blow upslope so fast that continuous walking is impossible; as each blast gallops by one must wait until it clears to see ahead. The rain doesn't fall; it appears, condensing on jacket and face, blurring in the eyelashes, making a plastic-covered notebook too slippery to grasp. The wet mosses and lichens hold no imprinted footsteps, only momentary puddles of water before they spring up again. Sometimes the moss mounds billow up around and consume small stones. It seems so cold that it ought to be sleeting. The wind is more than I can walk against, at once strong and steady, and then gusting when I am not prepared for it, nearly toppling me over. The mists and fog and vapors and rain devour shapes and forms, bleaching all colors gray. They consume the landscape like an amorphous, ravenous, ice-breathing dragon. It is summer on Mount Washington.

Juneberry
(*Amelanchier bartramiana*)

Dwarf raspberry
(*Rubus pubescens*)

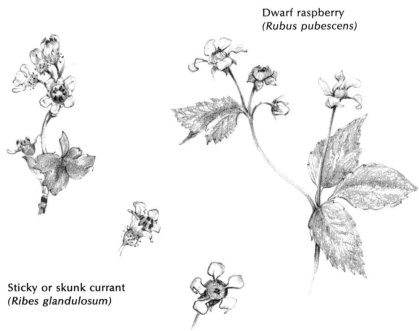

Sticky or skunk currant
(*Ribes glandulosum*)

The next day on the mountain is sunny and clear. The slopes bask in a four- or five-day period of higher-pressure air between storms. There are no clouds on the summit today, unusual for Mount Washington. The wind is less on this eastern slope, too, making a pleasant bright day reminiscent of western mountain days except for the moisture in the air that softens distant vistas.

Cairns follow the curve of the cirque lip, placed there for guidance in bad weather. Their closeness suggests how very limited visibility is when the clouds come in. A large cairn blocks the path at the top of a rise, posted with a neatly lettered sign:

> THE AREA AHEAD HAS THE WORST WEATHER
> IN AMERICA. MANY HAVE DIED THERE FROM
> EXPOSURE. EVEN IN THE SUMMER. TURN
> BACK NOW IF THE WEATHER IS BAD.
> WHITE MOUNTAIN NATIONAL FOREST

Had I not skirmished with clouds and contended with wind on the summit I would be tempted to disbelief. Nineteen people have perished here, a sobering thought on a clear day.

The trail is clearly marked, in being both well-trodden and posted with cairns, but it is difficult walking. Large rocks are everywhere, to be skirted, hopped over, or tripped on, glacial till deposited by retreating continental glaciers. In spite of the polish of the path, Greenland sandworts have rooted at every protective rock edge, and tussocks of sedge and balls of diapensia invade at the path's periphery. In spite of having to pick one's way around the rocks, the walking is physiologically easy, for I am at a lower altitude than that at which I live in Colorado.

The path parallels the edge of a high empty cirque that drops nearly vertically below. Called "gulfs" locally, they indent the whole Presidential Range on eastern and northern slopes, bitten out by local glaciers. Continental glaciation striated the mountains' open stone faces and left alien rock in high fields. The U-shaped valley below is now mantled with trees.

Frail sedge *(Carex debilis)*

Alpine holygrass *(Hierochloe alpina)*

The texture of the forest across the ravine is not like that of a western forest; the latter contains only spired evergreens at high altitude. Here the round shapes of deciduous trees are interspersed, changing both the color and pattern. Down the mountain side, krummholz begins around 4200 feet, also containing the lighter open greens of wild raspberry and Juneberry bushes. Here the tundra itself is such a dark green from the profusion of heaths and low shrubs, and contains so much gray rock and so many rough crags outcropping everywhere that they dilute the definitive color contrast common in the West.

Treelimit may be retreating in some of the northeastern mountains and there is considerable fluctuation on Mount Washington. As in the Rockies, treelimit is generally climatic, although all the interacting factors cannot be easily separated. A combination of winter snow-cover, slope exposure, frozen soil, low temperatures and wind all interact. Wind seems to be predominant, in both increasing plant desiccation and mechanical pruning. The winds of Mount Washington are legendary. Summit winds reach two hundred miles per hour in December, January, February and March, and can achieve a hundred miles per hour every month of the year. They may blow continually at high velocities for weeks at a time. Combined with the sleet and ice storms that rake the summit, it is no wonder that more ambitious stretches of krummholz are frequently killed back. Their trunks usually core out to a hundred years or less, although the root systems may be much older, supporting different generations that have become established through layering. In the Rocky Mountains, krummholz is much older, probably because of less severe growing conditions.

Many trees form krummholz here. White birch and mountain ash grow in it at the lower reaches, with black spruce and balsam fir becoming more prominent on the upper fringe. The upward extent of krummholz is sporadic, varying between 4800 and 5300 feet, depending largely on exposure and snowcover. Fir and spruce may extend up to 5700 feet in shelter behind rocks, fitting into the rocks' contours on the lee, growing up to a foot or so in height, while they rise only a few inches on lower more exposed slopes.

In wind-exposed areas, 4400 feet is the upper limit of krummholz.

Krummholz here is often tucked neatly between the rocks so that the landscape seems to be a level patchwork of gray rock and dark green, giving no hint of ground twenty to thirty inches beneath. The plenitude of large rocks provides many niches in which dwarf trees can survive in spite of the climate. Because of the prevailing low altitudes of the Presidential and other ranges in the northeast, alpine areas are limited in extent, about seven and one-half square miles in the Presidential Range, plus small areas on Mount Katahdin in Maine and Mount Marcy in New York, and the Green Mountains of Vermont. Treelimit on Mount Washington makes a crucial comment about the severity of the climate: it lies at least 6000 feet below that of the Rockies, and sometimes more.

The path quirks slowly across the slope. Drifts of white alpine bluets spring in hollows at its edge. Bright yellow Mount Washington avens are the only visible yellow flowers across this whole view. Like Rocky Mountain avens, many are centered with black flies. Rushes make dark-fringed clumps, taut bronze wires against the paler green-leaved herbs. Grasses shine in the wind, reflections glimmering up and down their stems. White three-toothed cinquefoils brighten a rock terrace where snow has lain and protected them through the winter. An idle spider relishes the warmth near the ground where the wind is still, luxuriating in its private gazebo of sedges and cinquefoils. The mosaic of tundra communities here is morticed in a tight interwoven pattern, determined by the amount and duration of winter snow, soil moisture, and in some instances the amount of active frost action: swatches of fellfield lie immediately adjacent to pockets of bluets blooming where snow lasts late.

One community here is composed of dwarf shrubs, heaths and highland rushes, often growing within the center of large stone rings. The rushes' stems separate into two or three leaves above, all linear, so that it is hard to tell which is leaf and which is stem. This combination of rushes and shrubs and heaths forms the most common alpine community in the Presidential Range.

Mount Washington avens
(*Geum peckii*)

Highland rush *(Juncus trifidus)*

Bog bilberry leafs out in May, flowering with small pale pink bells in June and July. It is the most prevalent dwarf shrub in the northeastern alpine region, growing in nearly every community, its mat a paler duller blue-green than that of the evergreen heaths so that one soon learns to recognize it from a distance. The delicious dark berries ripen in August. Many berries remain from last season; they look remarkably fresh, and one wonders why the bushes are not stripped by Mount Washington animals. There are few residents, but one cannot help but envision a little redbacked mouse, fruit rotated in tiny paws, having a bilberry feast, comfortably hidden from marauding hawks under the thick protective thatch.

Mountain cranberry creeps along the ground, with shiny thickish evergreen leaves and tight-clustered branches. The buds are rose, opening to four-lobed flowers: in a group of nearly homogeneous plants, a variation of even one petal is a great help in identification. Alpine bearberry, the only deciduous member of the genus, looking like a tiny willow, opens its flowers at the same time as its leaves, their top surface heavily veined with a puckered leathery texture. The dark purple-black berries, unlike the red ones of the Rockies, are sweet tasting. Three-toothed cinquefoil bears white flowers above evergreen leaves. The red anthers have gilt edgings of pollen which blend to look like brown horseshoes to the naked eye.

Bog bilberry (*Vaccinium uliginosum*)

Mountain cranberry
(*Vaccinium vitis-idaea* var. *minus*)

Although there are lichens between the rocks, there are almost no mosses; the soil is drier and warmer here, not as well suited. But larger herbs grow better in the warmer, sunnier environment of the east-facing slope, and there is considerable variety in these plant communities. A few cushion plants of the more exposed fellfield situations invade the bare spots, but they are both less developed and less prevalent than on the high north slopes. Greenland sandwort is the most plentiful, lurking in every cranny. But diapensia is impoverished, round clusters of leaves like marbles at the end of string roots that lead back to where the main root descends. Some of the cushions are salmon red, and some look bronze with the empty calyces turned rose.

Three-toothed cinquefoil or Sibbaldiopsis
(Potentilla tridentata)

A White Mountain butterfly momentarily flowers one. The rocks through which the plant insinuates itself are more plant-green than the diapensia itself.

A rock has fallen away from beside the path, opening a cross-section of soil. The rock has been pulled away long enough for some soil erosion to occur, but dirt still clings to its face, not yet washed clean by summer rains. The roots of alpine bilberry spread out through the top inch of soil; sedge roots go straighter and deeper, but there are no long taproots that are so prevalent in dry western soils because here the soil is damp all the way down. The horizons are fairly clear in spite of the short amount of time warmth is available to encourage decomposition. Humus composes half or more of the dark top horizon, decreasing as the soil deepens. The large amount of sand in the soil rolls between the fingers, gritty and fine. Like the soil on the summit, it is very damp but not wet. Worked in the hand it is different from the pale dry granite soils of the west—in texture, in coldness, in the amount of moisture.

Soil moisture remains high here throughout the growing season. Except for brief periods in frost-disturbed and windswept areas, alpine soils are damp all summer. Drought conditions do not occur here, and wilting seldom takes place. Therefore there are no heavily hirsute or succulent plants adapted to endure water stress. All the herbs are a bright fresh green and relatively broad-leaved, offering wide leaf surfaces at right angles to the sun.

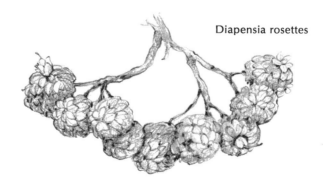

Diapensia rosettes

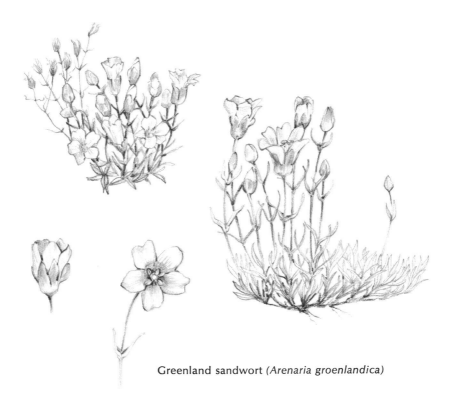

Greenland sandwort *(Arenaria groenlandica)*

The path breaks abruptly at a small stream that works its way downward, more visible in the proliferation of various bright green mosses than in its own course. It is deceptive; what looks like a solid piece of turf sinks two inches into black water with the weight of a footstep. Nutrients and minerals are dissolved from rocks above and flushed down, a phenomenon typical of locales with high rainfall; these added enrichments are a major factor in making this a luxuriant plant community.

The stream spreads almost a yard across, many small quiet channels braiding together as one, then unravelling again. The feeder spring originates high above, from under the summit cone. The vegetation is so thick that there is little sound, no larking or chortling, just a silent flowing interpolated with a light sibilant whisper.

Big willows and mountain alder are waist high, making a Gothic tracery over honeysuckle and birch. Mountain fly honeysuckle is pale green with joined double ovaries from which pairs of pale yellow

Mountain alder *(Alnus viridus* ssp. *crispa)*

flowers extend. Small-flowered woodrushes hang graceful clusters of flowers, their stems making tiercerons.

Away from the stream but where it is still moist, bearberry willows, named after their resemblance to the bearberry of the Heath family, form tight mats. The catkins seem disproportionately large and bright above gray-green leaves. As it twists and twines over the rocks its espaliered driftwood branches are exposed.

Alpine marsh communities everywhere have a basic resemblance: they are lusher and greener than turfs and fellfields, and are animated by light and running water, a pleasant sound to add to that of the wind. They also tend to be graced with taller and more tender herbs, many of which may move up into the alpine region from lower elevations. The color here is nearly all shades of bright green, with furtive

Mountain fly honeysuckle *(Lonicera villosa)*

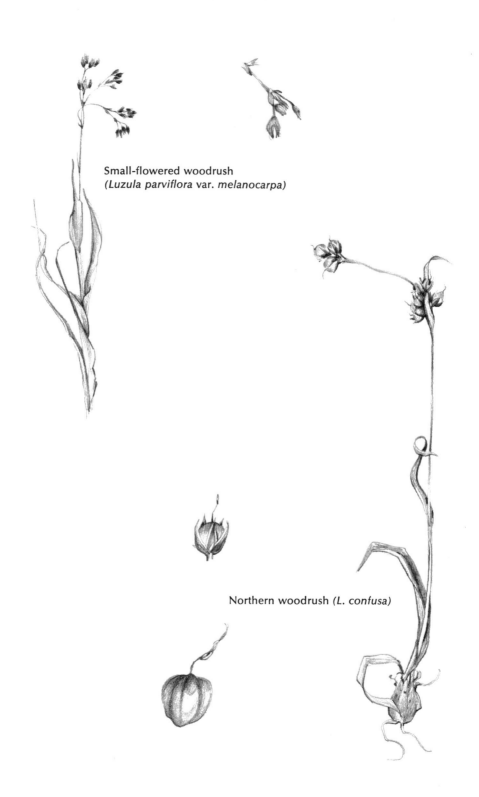

Small-flowered woodrush
(*Luzula parviflora* var. *melanocarpa*)

Northern woodrush (*L. confusa*)

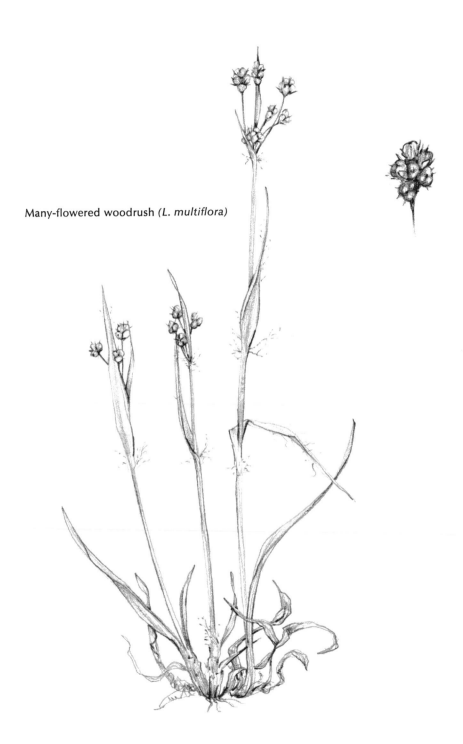

Many-flowered woodrush *(L. multiflora)*

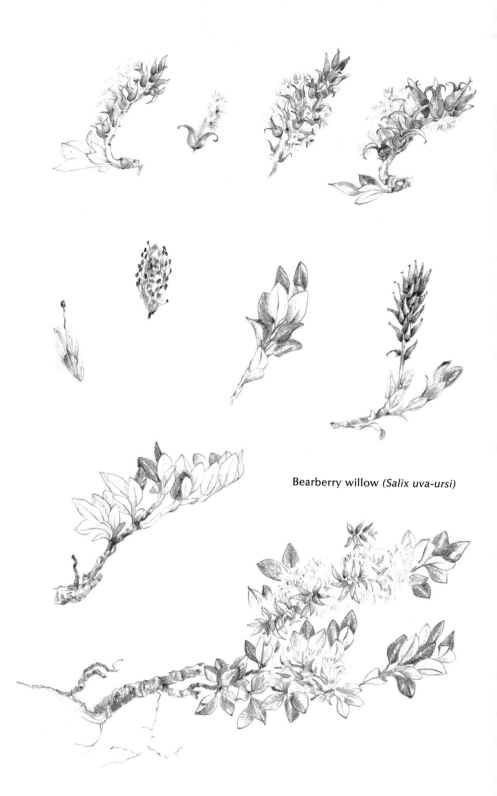

Bearberry willow *(Salix uva-ursi)*

whites and tenuous yellows. There are none of the vivid colors of a Rockies or Sierran marsh. The continuous green is elegant and striking, the variety of shape, not the colors, making it individual: lozenge and elliptical leaves, hatched and quilted, polished and crinkled, and an infinite combination of vein and shape and size in a rich multistoried community.

Up the mountainside, above the marsh, is a narrow horizontal snowbank. Almost gone, it is seemingly stuck on the side of the summit cone to be peeled off in this week's warmth; it is the only snow left across this whole slope. Large solifluction terraces scalloped with smaller lobes hang beneath the snowbank, possibly still active. Gravity pulls the freezing and thawing soil downward, while big rocks and outcrops of solid bedrock and tough plants hold it back. When the rate of movement is faster than the growth of the stabilizing plants, the whole soil mass pulls apart and slips slowly downhill.

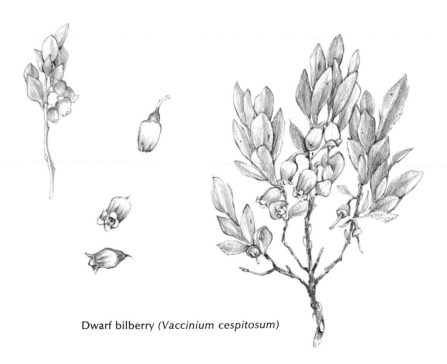

Dwarf bilberry *(Vaccinium cespitosum)*

Mountain heather *(Phyllodoce caerulea)*

Many lowland plant species creep upward and grow well here, although they may not be able to set seed. This community contains the largest number of plant species of any on Mount Washington, and some are restricted to it alone. Dwarf bilberry makes thick small clumps up to four inches high. The coral flowers are longer than most of the bilberries, dripping down along the length of the branch. Mountain heath grows in a sunny crevice, lavender-pink bells on glandular sandy red stems, the brightest color for yards around. Cornlily stands above the other growth, stalky and quite unalpine-looking. Beadlilies dangle luteous flowers from the top of eight or nine inch stalks. Goldenrod blooms at the end of summer with small clustered yellow heads. Woodrushes quiver in the breeze.

Beadlily *(Clintonia borealis)*

Small-flowered woodrush
(*Luzula parviflora* var. *melanocarpa*)

False lily-of-the-valley
(*Maianthemum canadense*)

Bunchberry (*Cornus canadensis*)

Alpine bluets
(*Houstonia caerulea* var. *faxonorum*)

Bluets are blue at lower elevations, but here they are pure white, pert flowers all facing upwards, growing in gentle drifts several feet long. Flies and small bees land on the petals to probe the yellow-ringed centers, their weight sufficient to bend the plant. Not as high as a finger, they grow below the heavy winds. Bunchberry flowers are small with black ovaries and rose stigmas, surrounded by four large ivory bracts. Four-petaled flowers like the bluets and bunchberry have a simple square appearance. Five-petaled flowers connote round-ness. Four-petaled flowers have a clarity of shape that makes a bank of bunchberry or a drift of bluets a simple fundamental statement of precise flower fact.

False lily-of-the-valley bears clustered, creamy white flowers. Gold-

Goldthread *(Coptis groenlandica)*

thread has evergreen leaves above which a delicate half-inch white flower shows. The roots are bright yellow, hence its name. The petals are shaped like white porcelain mittens. Yellow-orange stamens center starflowers which often have seven white sepals, a difficult number to draw after one's hand is trained to threes, fours and fives. Plant cover is almost total, formed of green plants growing in clumps and drifts and banks; all the flowers are white or nearly so. A western snowbed community is often impoverished and more clearly signaled by specific indicator plants, with ground lichens if not obvious at least very prevalent, and a great deal of bare ground if the bank melts out late.

Mount Washington snowbed communities do not have the sharp gradients of Rocky Mountain snowbeds, but they do have their indicators. Dwarf willow grows where snow melts early, round half-inch leaves crowded on tight stems, bearing tiny rosy catkins. Where snow goes by early June, hairgrass flourishes. Minute moss plant grows where snow disappears by the end of June. Most Mount Washington snow-

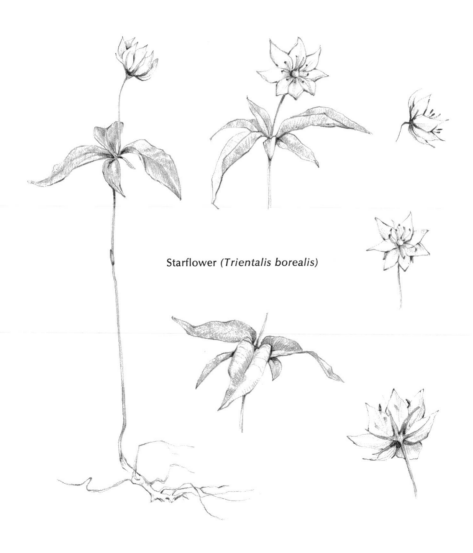

Starflower (*Trientalis borealis*)

banks are gone, at the latest, in early July, and their protective aspect is more important than their restriction on growing season. A Mount Washington snowbed community is stalked, sedged, and staffed with greenness, the other end of a scale beginning with the windswept snowfree diapensia community.

Around the north of the summit cone, the variety of greens narrows in a sedge meadow. Stone stripes ribbon roughly downslope and stone rings tile the turf with cantaloupe- to watermelon-sized rocks, marbled with lichens. Although mosses and alpine bilberry and a few club-mosses intermix, the visual impression is of solid sedge.

Cushions of moss chink the rocks. Rocktripe lichens, dry today, crunch like crackers underfoot. There are no orange jewel lichens that would indicate the presence of a stable animal population. The loose rocks warble like a shingle beach as one picks a path across them. On this north-facing slope there is more cloud cover and wind, and although it is the same elevation as the mixed turfs on the east side, the environment is sufficiently colder and wetter to form an almost pure sedge stand, green and greener still.

Dwarf willow (*Salix herbacea*)

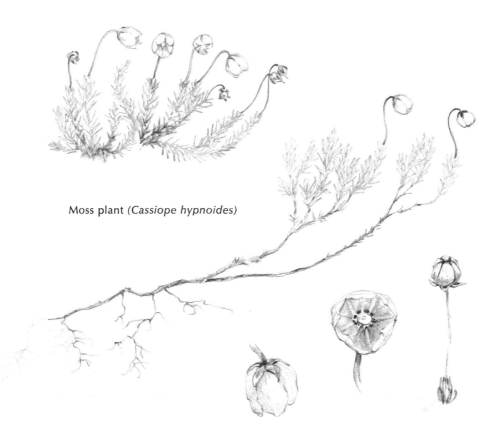

Moss plant *(Cassiope hypnoides)*

My first reaction to a dwarf shrub heath community is that all resident plants look much alike: dense low shrubs not over four or five inches high, with evergreen leaves, all with many small leaves and numerous small bell-like flowers. But like many first judgments in the alpine tundra, the aspect is misleading. The variations on a theme are often more elaborate than first glance admits, and even a cursory examination begins to reveal diversity. These heath communities flourish just above treelimit and are a striking characteristic of eastern tundra, especially to a westerner who sees few of them. This is a sunny community, with an intricacy of outline in the reiterated leaf shapes; tiny leaves and tiny shadows forming a pointillistic landscape.

Spiraea or Meadowsweet
(*Spiraea latifolia*)

The heaths scroll among the rocky benches which lie across the slope. The stiff branches are not easily whipped by the wind and broken; the wind threads through them in much the same way that it works through spruce and pine needles, with a hollow whistling that does not disturb the firm leaves. All the plants are shallow-rooted, spreading more widely above ground. They trundle across the rocks, grope up banks in an almost total cover, interspersed with lichens and clubmosses and an occasional beadlily or spiraea. If a plant looks taller it is usually because it has espaliered over a rock beneath and is simply following the hidden contour. A thick batting of leaves and debris collects in the shrubs, and those that nestle in pockets are probably protected by winter snow.

Velvet-leaf blueberry *(Vaccinium myrtilloides)*

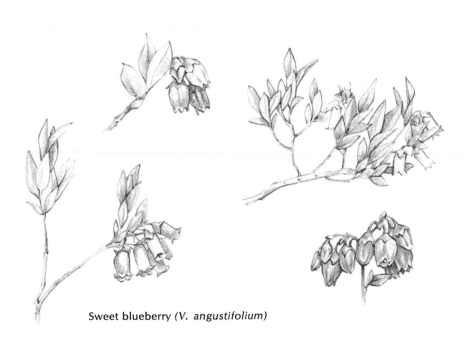

Sweet blueberry *(V. angustifolium)*

Small cranberry (*Vaccinium oxycoccos*)

Alpine bilberry grows luxuriantly here, as it seems to nearly everywhere in the New England alpine region. Sweet blueberry and velvet-leaf blueberry are also here, the latter with softly haired leaves. A small cranberry laces over the rocks, the threadlike stems raising it only a half an inch above the minute leaves; tiny pink shooting-star flowers develop into berries that seem impossibly large for such a small plant.

Labrador tea bears feathery white flowers in clusters that light the banks of dark leaves. Bumblebees, who prefer blue flowers, are hard put to find one on this tundra, and are busily exploring the white heads. The leaves have a peculiar rusty covering beneath, like a rusted steel-wool pad. Bog laurel, also evergreen, bears fine rosy-purple flowers. The anthers are held in little pleated pockets until ripe and released by an insect's weight. Rockberry, like the northwestern species, has black berries and tiny needlelike leaves.

Beneath the wealth of heaths various clubmosses inch over the soil, producing no flowers or fruit, only minuscule spores. They are primitive plants; important both as ground cover and soil holders, they have a neatness of structure that matches the branch of a spruce tree. The commonest clubmoss above treelimit holds its spore cases like yellow beans tucked in the leaves. Below the heaths they are sheltered, warmed by the still sunlight, undisturbed by the wind that twitches the plants above them.

Labrador tea (*Ledum groenlandicum*)

Bog laurel (*Kalmia polifolia*)

Fir clubmoss *(Huperzia selago)*

Bristly clubmoss
(Lycopodium annotinum var. *pungens)*

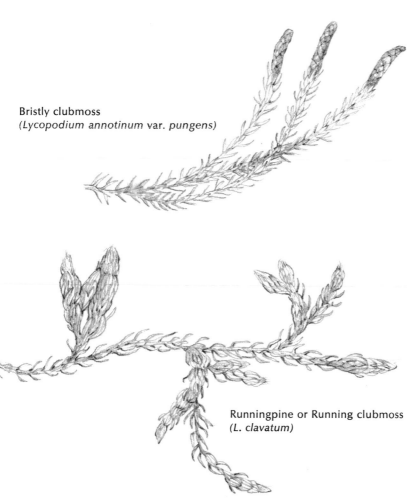

Runningpine or Running clubmoss
(L. clavatum)

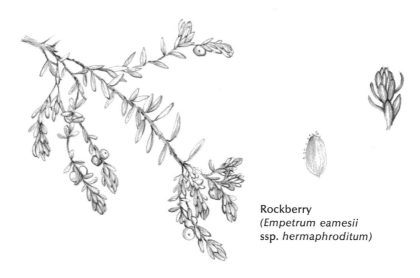

Rockberry
(*Empetrum eamesii*
ssp. *hermaphroditum*)

There are Iceland lichens, crisp masses from the size of a hand to the size of a small table top, intertangling in masses that cover the ground as profusely as the heaths. When they are dry they crackle and crunch like crumpled brown tissue paper. They blend together with the heaths to the warm rich faded colors of an old Oriental rug, the blues gone to bronze, only some of the rose reds and old greens remaining, the warp showing through here and there.

The heath community—low, largely evergreen, shrubby and dense —more closely resembles the arctic than the western alpine. The climate of Mount Washington is also more arctic: high levels of atmospheric moisture in fog and rain, long periods of cloud cover, and warmth beginning earlier in the spring. Western alpine climates are drier and sunnier. Yearly precipitation on Mount Washington averages 73.5 inches, evenly distributed throughout the year, while the Colorado Front Range alpine tundra averages 25 inches.

The large amount of lichen and moss cover, especially on the darker more windswept slopes, is also reminiscent of the Arctic. Lichens carry on photosynthesis more effectively at low light and high moisture, environmental factors characteristic of the Arctic and East Coast tundras. In the Rockies, Iceland lichen is found in mere snippets; on Mount Washington it is bigger, more extensive, infinitely elaborated into frizzled scrolls and curves. In the Rockies and West Coast ranges crustose forms of lichen are more prominent, whether on soil or rock. On Mount Washington, as in the Arctic, fruticose forms are more prevalent, branched and storied above the ground; these are most numerous in sites unprotected by winter snow.

About three-quarters of Mount Washington's plants probably migrated south in advance of the continental ice sheet, and followed north when the ice receded. They retreated to the mountain tops, closely followed by the trees of the boreal forest, with which they cannot grow. Only on the highest mountains are there refuges for arctic plants south of their main body of distribution, and nearly two-thirds of the plants of Mount Washington today are arctic outliers.

The arctic plants of the southern Rockies are often restricted in habitat to wet marshes, usually existing in the southernmost area of their distribution, and are much smaller than their arctic counterparts, such as koenigia and the arctic species of rush, saxifrage and buttercup. The arctic plants of Mount Washington have wide ecological amplitude and are present in many communities. Diapensia, Bigelow's sedge, highland rush, alpine bilberry, mountain cranberry and others are close counterparts in size and growth pattern to plants of these species in southwestern Greenland, northern Norway and Alaska.

The remaining plants of Mount Washington are cold-loving subalpine and boreal plants extending upward in favorable habitats of krummholz, dwarf shrub, streamside and snowbed communities. The western mountains also contain many plants related to lower-elevation species. Some are subalpine forest species that extend their range into protected tundra microenvironments, but many others have close affinities to desert plants, such as the buckwheats of the Sierra Nevada and the *Hymenoxys* of the Rockies, a juxtaposition not existing in the East.

The color scheme of Mount Washington, like much of the arctic tundra, is monochromatic—a Pre-Raphaelite background, muted, close-held and self-contained. Even where heather or bog laurel or Mount Washington avens enliven the greens, they are either so small or so few that the color does not carry. In the marsh, even the flowers seem as close to green as possible.

The late afternoon sunshine fades the surrounding hills to a flowing milky blue. But the tundra-burnished slopes of Mount Washington are imbricated in bronze and olivine, verdigris and stony, stony gray.

Part Three

MAN AND THE TUNDRA

20 : Man and the Tundra

Of what value is the alpine tundra to man except as a pretty wilderness? Does its preservation matter, since no one lives here? And in these days of growing population and economic pressures, is such a wilderness too expensive to afford?

In Colorado, three and one-half percent of the total acreage of the state contributes twenty percent of the stream flow. That acreage is alpine tundra. It is like a great sponge, hoarding snow and melt water and releasing it throughout the summer, crucial for dry Colorado. If all the available water were released in the early spring, it would be too early for plants to be sprouting on the plains, nor could frozen soils absorb water. Snowbanks, maintained by low alpine temperatures, melt throughout the summer to provide metered water to agriculture below.

The melting of frozen alpine reservoirs on Mount Rainier insures a steady feed of water for hydroelectric power for the region, regardless of season. Water stored in the high-caught snowbanks of the Three Sisters, also in the Cascades, aids in stabilizing the summer flow of the McKenzie River, supplies water for Eugene, Oregon, and vicinity, and hydroelectric power and irrigation. Mount Shasta is the source of the Sacramento River. Water for the city of Los Angeles comes largely from alpine sources in the Sierra Nevada.

With population pressures and the need for more water, hydrological engineers are exploring means of making the tundra more effective as a snow storage area. At the top of Independence and Loveland Passes, above 12,000 feet, there are snow fences which catch snow in their lee and prevent it from blowing off to the subalpine forests, and also help prevent avalanching. On a vast scale, this could make decisive changes in vegetation. If the accumulation areas are snow-free fellfields and meadows, snowcover would destroy many cushion plants and climax sedges. The meadows would become snow-bed communities, with a relatively small number of plants and a very short growing season. The stability of alpine soils would be endangered because the holding roots of turf grasses and sedges would be destroyed; solifluction would become active with more water. With the turf, grasses and sedges destroyed, the whole ground surface could be strongly eroded during summer, with possible catastrophic results downslope.

Alpine tundra catches radioactive fallout over its vast surface. Fallout blankets snowbanks, filtered from the air by snowflakes; and as the banks melt out, fallout accumulates on the tundra surface, much of it concentrating in lichens. As it begins to soak into the ground and trickle downward, it is sieved by acres of closely held sedge and grass root fibers. Measured at the top of a tundra streamlet, the water is highly radioactive; measured at the base of the tundra, radioactive particles have been filtered out by the intervening vegetation, making it safe for drinking, and the water supply of many foothill cities comes from sources above treelimit. If the tundra vegetation is eliminated or reduced, radioactivity will increase in such water supply.

For city-oriented people, whose water comes out of a tap, who may never see a mountain or care to, alpine tundra has little meaning. In some way, people who will never see the alpine tundra must come to have a feel for the preservation of its tenuous windy reaches. For some, it is forever too strenuous an environment to enter, to enjoy, or to endure. For others, it is the breath of life against which a lowland world seems prosaic by comparison. But for everyone, it is a safety factor that helps to preserve our lowland world.

Following a path on Trail Ridge in the Colorado Rockies that moccasined feet padded thousands of years ago, one can gain not only a vast view of tundra slopes but of other mountain tops. Prehistoric man used this ridge as an east-west traverse across the Front Range during the summer, hence the name of Trail Ridge. The narrow single-file path has been used for at least 6000 years, and some archeological evidence suggests that it may have been in use as long as 15,000 years ago. It was a trail used mainly by women and children and is an easy passage over the top of the Ridge. But so slow is tundra vegetation to recover from disturbance that the trail is still clear, raveling across the landscape like a brown thread, even though it has been little used in the nearly forty years since the modern paved road was laid.

At the base of the slope the trail crosses a fellfield paved with lichened rocks and small gray-green plants set in hard soil. A little higher up a tumble of boulders contains pika, usually seen and always heard. Alpine coral bells, cinquefoils, alpine sorrel and an occasional dwarf bilberry grow in the rocks' protection. A Parry primrose, usually found along subalpine streams, shelters beneath an overhang. Leaning down to enjoy its resonant magenta color one gets a sniff of its resonant odor instead—a pungent and distinctive smell.

Pussytoes fringe a rug of kobresia. A pocket-gopher-worked area is dotted with bright blues and yellows of sky pilot and Rydbergia and chiming bells. Going up takes an inordinately long time because there is so much to see: an iridescent beetle riding a curled rock sedge leaf like a roller coaster; a cluster of wand lilies just out, a willow area where ptarmigan roosted during the last storm, the last harebells of summer and the first arctic gentians. I cannot help but wonder if the Indian women and children who used this part of the trail enjoyed the plants that they saw, if they had names for them, and if so, what they were. And I wonder, when they walked towards the plains at the end of summer, if they too felt a sense of sadness at a summer's ending.

On top of the Ridge, the wind birrs across, swooping up from the

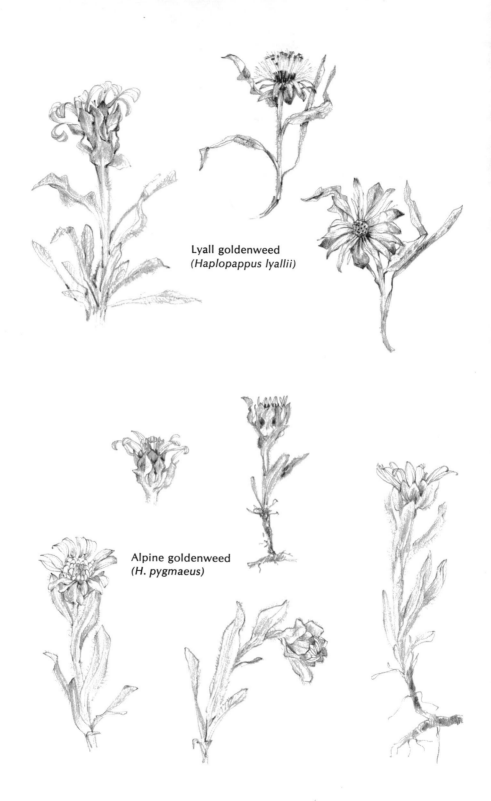

Lyall goldenweed
(*Haplopappus lyallii*)

Alpine goldenweed
(*H. pygmaeus*)

deep dark green valley below. There is something about an alpine wind: it can blear the eyes and chill the fingers and be exceedingly irksome, but it seems to come from the back of beyond, carrying tangles of trees and warps of willows in its passing. Across the valley, other tundra areas seem close enough to step to, cleanly outlined in the alpine light. It seems unreasonable to have to accept that they are separated by miles of arduous hiking. It is an untouched and untroubled landscape, a peaceful one in spite of the restless wind, an uncluttered landscape, a landscape of ultimate isolation.

In a sheltered niche, back to a warm rock, under the wind, I watch the paved highway winding across the Ridge, its firm sinuous curve in contrast to the wavering foot path. The cars look no bigger than the beetle I watched on the way up, and their sound does not carry this high. But their swift purposeful going is a reminder that Trail Ridge is one of Colorado's alpine areas where man's presence is heavily felt.

Over a million people visit Trail Ridge in the summer; nearly 400,000 travel the road to the summit of Pikes Peak. Visitor pressure concentrates where there are parking areas and scenic overlooks. With overcrowding, parking areas are sometimes full, and more and more people pull off to the side of the road and walk out onto the tundra on their own. There are almost no signs telling them not to. But there are other clear signs for the knowledgeable to read.

When the present Trail Ridge Road was built, the Old Fall River Road was blocked off where it crossed the tundra. It was scarified and all attempts were made to delete any evidence of its presence. It is protected from use. In the nearly forty years since, it is still clearly visible. Strips of sod along the new road, laid to stabilize cut banks, are still almost as separate as the day they were laid, the dirt lines between them empty of vegetation.

Enclosures were established by Dr. Beatrice Willard in cooperation with the National Park Service in 1959 in order to measure the recovery of alpine plant communities that have been intensively trampled or destroyed. The study has documented the recovery rate of damaged plants and areas, and is a technique which has value in other heavily used natural areas. In the short time between May 30 and

August 25, 1958, the path people made crossing a fellfield removed two-thirds to nine-tenths of the pad of cushion plants. It requires only eight weeks to abrade cushion plants to the crown with trampling, and only two weeks for the top horizon of thin fellfield soils to begin to erode. If, after one season of trampling, the fellfield is protected, recovery begins within the month, but it is not complete for more than two decades. Longer degradation causes even slower recovery. Notably missing for many years are the important soil-building and soil-holding ground lichens and mosses.

At Mount Rainier some of the heavily used high subalpine and low alpine slopes have been webbed with paths. In spite of established trails, hikers take the shortest distance between two points, or simply strike off on their own. Attempts are being made to reestablish vegetation by scarification, reseeding and replanting, blocking the paths off and covering them with mesh and burlap to prevent washing. It is necessary to restore their original aspect since any trace of a path is an invitation to use it again. The Park Superintendent estimated that $250,000 is needed for two seasons for full restoration, requiring five men plus machines, plants and water.

It seems obvious that it is easier to prevent damage on the alpine tundra than repair it. Where plants and animals grow at the outer limits of their existence, recovery is marginal and extremely slow.

Not all alpine areas open to automobiles are so fortunate as to have a paved road. The road to the summit of Pikes Peak is a dirt road, excellently maintained. It is wide, safe, constantly checked for washing and erosion, continually patrolled. But it is gravel and dirt in a windy area. On the downslope side of the switchbacks, the plants are so coated with dust that they are almost invisible, and in most places the constant sliding of the fine loose gravel soil has simply inundated them, reducing the slopes between to the most impoverished and constantly eroding scree slides.

Since the Pikes Peak Hiway is well patrolled, cars remain on the road. But in the remote interior passes roadsides are often crisscrossed with four-wheel-drive tracks, made by drivers who take off across the tundra with no thought except that of pitting their vehicles against nature, with no realization that their tracks may remain for years and centuries, causing erosion and damage not only to the immediate but to nearby areas.

In recent years, access to high mountain country has been made possible by four-wheel-drive vehicles, trailbikes, and in the winter, snowmobiles. Areas previously closed are now open all winter, and the invasion of noise and people into previously cloistered areas has disturbed both larger animals and ptarmigan, pushing them out of previously peaceful winter pasture and disrupting breeding areas. And during fall and winter, when tundra plants are at their most fragile, vehicle tracking is most damaging.

The litter barrels on Trail Ridge are stuffed with refuse. It is an almost impossible task to keep them emptied. Paper plates, paper towels, disposable bottles and cans are easier to throw away than wash up or return. Some National Forest areas have tried removing all containers and posting the entrance with the notice that everyone is responsible for carrying out his own trash. This is so recent an idea that its effectiveness is not known. The more usual method is constant pick-up; this fall, members of the Sierra Club anticipate picking up between 10,000 and 15,000 pounds of litter along the Adirondack hiking trails. A helicopter goes into the Mount Whitney area to air lift the trash out. The *in loco parentis* philosophy of the Park Service and conservation organizations does not encourage personal responsibility. The mother who always picks up after her children soon finds that that is all she does.

In the lowlands, a crumpled cigarette pack would probably decompose within the season. On the tundra, it will take several summers. Meanwhile it cuts the light to the plants it covers, killing them within a few weeks. When it blows a few inches away, it leaves a dead plant and a bare spot. A bottle cap encompasses a nascent cushion of moss campion. Bottle caps and metal cans do not disintegrate for at least a hundred years on the tundra. Fifty to one hundred years of plant growth can be snuffed out by a beer can.

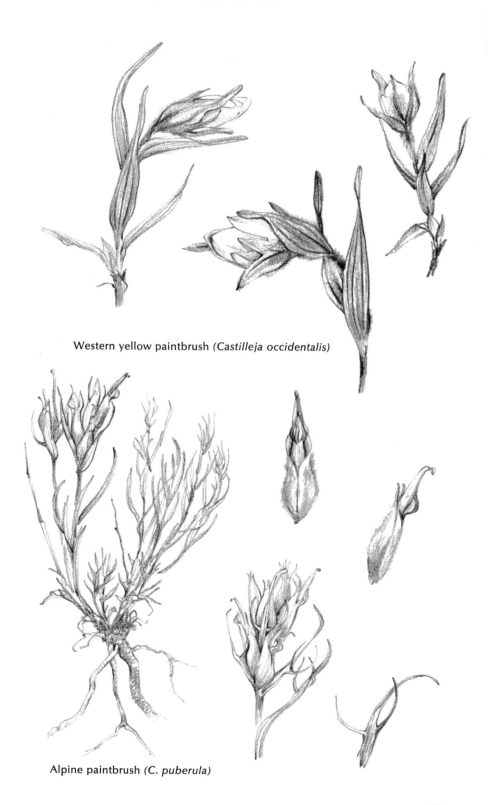

Western yellow paintbrush *(Castilleja occidentalis)*

Alpine paintbrush *(C. puberula)*

If there is anything for which the alpine tundra has been used with any consistency, it is grazing. There are areas in the Rockies that have been grazed by sheep, and damage is still clear many years later. That there is not more grazing is probably due to changed grazing allotments, along with the paucity of good graze—plant productivity is very low although nutrition in proportion to weight is high. Grasses and sedges are the most nourishing, and survive fairly well because they can continue growing when leaves and stems are nipped off. Most herbs cannot, and tend to be deleted. Trampling also damages plants, especially on steep slopes.

Where only a few sheep have grazed, the turfs seem to have recovered, but where too many have fed, bare ground still remains. Damage is especially severe in fellfields. Many of the same tall short-lived plants which appear after pocket gopher disturbance also tend to come in after grazing. Pasture land in the high European Alps, which is fertilized, has been used for centuries, and it is also better watered. But in the dry western mountains of the United States, alpine grazing has not been economically worthwhile and in most areas has been terminated by default if not by direction.

The West has been populated largely by people who originally lived in the East, where revegetation took place in a matter of weeks, recovery in a matter of months. Western mountain slopes still bear the scars of timbering and mining of a century ago because reforestation is so slow in the cool, arid climate. The alpine tundra is fragile far beyond all forests. The tenacity of alpine plants, their adaptation for endurance and survival, is tremendous, but they cannot withstand mass abuse.

The wilderness has never been thought of as a museum in which the treasures of the natural world are preserved, against which man can measure himself and see how human habitation alters his environment. Wilderness has been ours to enjoy and use, and often misuse. There was always more. Until recently, no one ever thought of wilderness as an irreplaceable, exhaustible resource. Now we know that the wilderness can be exhausted, and this is most poignantly true of the alpine tundra.

The alpine tundra has remained, until recent years, almost a total wilderness because no one is able to live here. With the exception of the Sherpas of the Himalayas and the Tibetans, and some Andean Indians, almost no one lives above treelimit year round. Eskimos and Lapps utilize the Arctic tundra. But with that, man's habitation of the tundra ends. Miners sometimes lived above treelimit in the Rockies; their still-standing cabins are mute reminders of the slowness of decay in the tundra, and that only very strong economic reasons give a man cause to stay here.

The growing season is too short and too cold to raise food crops, to say nothing of the poorness of the soil and steep rocky slopes. Unless one lives near a lake, there is no stable water supply, and that is frozen in winter. There is no wood for heating. Mechanical means can make winter above treelimit possible, but then there are physiological problems: disorientation, sapping of energy, rapid weight loss even though on special high protein–high fat diets, and a continual fight against cold and frostbite that consumes so much energy that there is little left for work. These are all effects noted by men working in arctic climates, compounded by the lack of oxygen at high altitudes.

People vary in their tolerance of oxygen starvation, or hypoxia, at high altitude, and individual tolerances vary with other factors: fatigue, time of acclimation, etc. The lower oxygen content of the atmosphere at high altitude provides too little oxygen. The body compensates to a certain extent by deeper breathing, but there are changes in the blood itself, such as the necessity for the blood to contain a higher proportion of oxygen-carrying red corpuscles. Heart patients should not be at high altitude at all, and if there, should be as inactive as possible.

Hypoxia comes on very slowly and insidiously, beginning with a sense of euphoria, followed by headache, a slowing of reactions, and a general dulling of feelings. Disorientation is frequent. Night vision is impaired. A physical warning is often blueness at the base of the fingernails. Hypoxia can occur at any altitude above 10,000 feet, and sometimes lower for particularly sensitive people.

For people walking on the tundra, rest step hiking, in which each step has a hesitation, eases high-altitude strain. Extreme fatigue and breathlessness require additional rest stops. Mountain climbers advocate taking one breath through the mouth per step when suffering from breathlessness. Forced slow deep breathing, or "overbreathing," to hyperventilate the lungs is of help. But too rapid breathing can increase the amount of carbon dioxide expelled, thus lowering its concentration in the blood, actually slowing heart action, the opposite of what one needs to do. Dizziness, tingling of hands and feet, nausea, and sometimes unconsciousness, may result. Breathing into a paper bag or one's hands will increase carbon dioxide concentration in the blood, thus speeding the heart; getting bottled oxygen or getting off the mountain should be accomplished immediately.

Most workers at high altitude must build up a tolerance to altitude. Coming up slowly gives the body time to acclimate itself and may avoid many of the common symptoms of headache, nausea and dizziness which may persist for several hours. Even ordinary working on the tundra brings its own peculiar problems. One learns never to go without extra clothing, pomade, sunburn cream, sunglasses and handkerchiefs. Extra liquids are needed to prevent dehydration at high altitude. Extra high energy food is required to make up for greater expenditures of energy needed to navigate rugged terrain.

I have learned to make a list of what plants I want to draw or what I wish to accomplish. One is apt to become forgetful on the tundra. I take notes, no matter what the weather; one's mind does not retain the necessary precise details. It is wise to make careful note of landmarks for it is easy to become disoriented and walk past areas where one has often been before, completely misled by a usually reliable sense of distance and direction.

In spite of the problems of high-altitude work, the end of the short summer comes all too swiftly. In the Rockies, the halcyon days of late September and early October are often stiller on the tundra than any other time of the year. There will have been September snows, dumping a foot or so on the drying ground, mottling it with white. Still there is a sense of sunny peace that does not exist during the intense summer or the brutal winter.

When there are no trees to charge the landscape with autumnal brilliance, the dried grasses and sedges in the alpine turfs have added splendor, glowing against the washed-out colors of the faded fell-fields. Beneath the brilliantly clear September sky, the meadows seem lighted from within. Kobresia is glowing coppery gold, a thick rich color. Within it there are all shades of red: russet red of avens leaves, salmon red of stonecrop rosettes, alizarin crimson, sandy red, beet red of stems, brilliant scarlet, wine red, brick red, Pompeiian red, rose red.

The arctic gentians have turned intense banana orange in their foliage. The leaves of sky pilots are a peculiar plum color, falling off at a touch. Their round seedheads are almost bleached white. Rydbergia has big fat seedheads that fly at a touch, summer floating out across the turf. Stonecrop rosettes range from dark dull mauve to salmon red, still bearing last year's sturdy charcoal-gray seedpods. Sage stalks are dark cinnamon brown, the tiny empty involucres like tufts of snow caught in the branches. Nutmeg brown meadowrue stalks are empty of sepal and seed. The light shines through empty alpine fescue spikes, making them opalescent—thin, pale, luminous. Two shiny dark red beetles with three black stripes down their backs mate beneath a dried Indian paintbrush.

Across the road, a large snowdrift is sculpted with sastrugi, the peculiar peaked patterns made in snow at high altitude by sun and wind. The snow surface feels as firm as paper. The residual heat of summer still holds in the rocky ground and eats away at the snow's underside; water hurries out from beneath.

Beyond, the gray fellfield is drained of its color with the coming of winter. Moss campion is a peculiar brassy bronze, the color of French mustard. Forget-me-nots are gray, snippets of fur left on the ground. And there is one small impoverished alpine avens in yellow bloom. But the other colors of the fellfield are so neutral that the chartreuse map lichens on the rocks seem to be fluorescent.

I shake the grass stems and the seeds sift out and I can feel the slowing of the season in my hand. A tiny black caterpillar noses under a clubmoss. The smooth empty goldenweed seedheads catch the light, glinting like the quartz in the granite. A last lone grasshopper trudges through the dried sedges, too cold to spring. A shadow crosses the ground—two large ravens slowly beating across the sky.

Across to a far slope, the krummholz is spatter-painted charcoal green. Willows stain a soft dark red; those on stream courses seep up into the tundra like ink soaking up into a blotter, tying the tundra to the lowlands in color but never in spirit. The high tundra looks like crushed velvet pulled smooth, dyed tawny Indian red, mottled with chamois and sand, dove gray and mauve gray.

Thin snow lines are stenciled in white chalk along the high saddles, the beginning of winter's magnificent snow cornices. The solifluction terraces hold wavering white lines, colophons of summer. A thin waning moon shines bleakly in a cold pale afternoon sky. Life ticks to a standstill and the winter snows fall on an already withdrawn world.

Comprehensive List of Alpine Plants

The arctic-alpine tundra flora is more widely distributed throughout the world than any other single flora. The following table of the known distribution of the alpine plants of the United States, exclusive of Alaska and Hawaii, indicates the mountain ranges in the United States where these plants grow above treelimit. The World Distribution shows North American, as well as global extent. For example, some plants growing in the low alpine of Mount Washington may grow in the subalpine forests and meadows of the Sierra Nevada or Rockies; the NA shows their wider total distribution exclusive of the alpine. The PR means that that is the only mountain range within the U.S. in which the plant is known to grow in the tundra. Some plants in the Colorado Rockies do not occur again, except in the American and Eurasian Arctic; they are shown as RM and AA, CP.

Color designations have been shown to provide a maximum of information. Those plants with two color forms are shown with a space between the color symbols. Symbols that are hyphenated indicate nuances of color to reduce total symbols used.

The designation of community for the Colorado Rockies and Mount Washington are more accurate than for the other ranges, where few community ecological studies have yet been made.

KEY

Scientific and Common Names	Color	Bloom	Community	U.S. distribution	World distribution
Achillea lanulosa (Yarrow)	W	L	G	RM SN SNC NRM GB PR	AA CP
Acomastylis rossii (Alpine avens)	Y	E-M	E	RM SC OR GB	WNA AA
Adoxa moschatellina (Muskroot)	G	M	B	RM	EN
Agoseris aurantiaca (False dandelion)	O	L	S	RM SN SNC	NA
A. glauca var. *dasycephala* (Short-beaked agoseris)	Y	L	FF	RM SNC OR NRM GB	WNA
A. glauca var. *monticola*	Y	L	FF	SN WH SNC	WNA
Agropyron pringlei (Pringle's wheatgrass)	G	M	SC	SN	EN
A. scribneri (Scribner's wheatgrass)	G	M	D	RM WH NRM	WNA
A. subsecundum	G	M	B	SN	EN
A. trachycaulum (Rough-stemmed wheat-grass)	G	M	T	RM WH SNC PR	NA CA
Agrostis borealis (Northern winter bentgrass)	G	L	S	RM PR	CP
A. idahoensis (Idaho bentgrass)	G	M	T	RM SN SNC	WNA
A. scabra var. *geminata* (Ticklegrass)	G	M	T	RM SN SNC PR	NA
A. thurberiana (Thurber's bentgrass)	G	M	M	RM SN SNC	WNA
A. variabilis (Variable bentgrass)	G	M	M	RM SN SNC GB	WNA
Alder: see *Alnus*					
Allium cernuum (Nodding onion)	P	M	T	RM	WNA
A. crenulatum (Olympic onion)	P	M-L	SC	SNC OR	EN
A. geyeri (Alpine onion)	R	M	D	RM SN SNC NRM	WNA

Scientific and Common Names	Color	Bloom	Community	U.S. distribution	World distribution
Allium obtusum (Red Sierra onion)	G-W	M	FF	SN	EN
Alnus viridis ssp. *crispa* (Mountain alder)	BR	E	ST K	PR	AA
Alplily: see *Lloydia* Alumroot: see *Heuchera*					
Amelanchier bartramiana (Juneberry)	W	M	K B	PR	EN
Anaphalis margaritacea (Pearly everlasting)	W	L	D	SN SC PR	NA
Androsace chamaejasme ssp. *carinata* (Rockjasmine)	W	E	FF	RM	CP
A. septentrionalis (Rockprimrose)	W	E	D T	RM SN WH GB	CP
Anemone drummondii (Drummond's anemone)	W-B	M	SC TA	SN SNC	WNA
A. multifida var. *globosa* (Globeflower)	W	M	T	RM SNC OR PR	NA
A. narcissiflora ssp. *zephyra* (Narcissus-flowered anemone)	W	M	T	RM	CP
A. parviflora (Northern anemone)	W PR	M	M	RM GB PR	NA AA
Angelica grayi (Gray's angelica)	G	M	B	RM	EN
A. lineariloba (Sierra angelica)	G	M	B	SN	EN
Antennaria alpina (Alpine pussytoes)	W	M	T	RM SN WH	WNA
A. corymbosa (Meadow pussytoes)	W	L	SC G	NRM	WNA
A. lanata (Woolly pussytoes)	W	L	SC	RM SNC	WNA

Scientific and Common Names	Color	Bloom	Community	U.S. distribution	World distribution
Antennaria media (Alpine pussytoes)	W	L	T	RM SN SNC NRM	WNA
A. racemosa (Racemose pussytoes)	W	L	SC	RM SNC NRM	WNA
A. rosea (Pink pussytoes)	P	L	SC	RM SN WH	WNA
A. umbrinella (Brown pussytoes)	BR	L	T SC	SN WH	EN
Aquilegia caerulea (Colorado blue columbine)	B-W	M	B	RM	EN
A. pubescens (Coville's columbine)	Y-W-B-P	M	B	SN	EN
A. saximontana (Dwarf columbine)	B-PR	E	B	RM	EN
Arabis covillei (Coville's rockcress)	PR	M	SC	SN GB	WNA
A. drummondii (Drummond's rockcress)	W-P	M	SC	PR RM	NA
A. holboellii var. *pendulocarpa* (Holboell's rockcress)	W-P	M	SC TA	SN WH SNC	WNA
A. inyoensis (Inyo rockcress)	?	M	FF	SN WH	EN
A. lemmonii (Lemmon's rockcress)	PR	M	T	RM SN WH SNC OR	WNA
A. lyallii (Lyall rockcress)	R	M	B SC	RM SN SNC OR	WNA
A. platysperma (Broad-seeded rockcress)	R	M	SC	SN SNC GB	WNA
A. platysperma ssp. *howellii*	R	M	B	SN SC	WNA
A. repanda var. *greenei*	?	M	SC	SN	EN
A. suffrutescens (Woody rockcress)	PR	M	TA FF	SN SC GB	WNA
Arctostaphylos alpina (Alpine bearberry)	Y-G	E	H F	PR	CP

Scientific and Common Names	Color	Bloom	Community	U.S. distribution	World distribution
Arctostaphylos uva-ursi (Kinnikinnik)	P	M	K	SN SC	WNA CP
Arenaria congesta (Globe sandwort)	W	L	T	SN SNC NRM GB	WNA
A. congesta var. *suffrutescens*	W	L	T	SN	WNA
A. fendleri (Fendler's sandwort)	W	E	T FF	RM GB	WNA
A. fendleri var. *tweedyi*	W	E	FF	RM	EN
A. formosa (Beautiful sandwort)	W	M	S FF	SN SNC OR GB	WNA AA
A. groenlandica (Greenland sandwort)	W	M	G	PR	ENA
A. kingii ssp. *compacta*	W	M	FF	SN WH	EN
A. kingii var. *glabrescens* (King's sandwort)	W	M	FF	SN WH	EN
A. marcescens (Northern sandwort)	W	M	G	PR	EN
A. nuttallii (Nutall's sandwort)	W	M	FF	SN WH SNC OR NRM GB	WNA
A. propinqua (Northern sandwort)	W	M	G	RM SN SNC GB	WNA
A. rossii (Ross' sandwort)	W	M	FF	RM SN WH SNC OR	WNA
Armeria maritima ssp. *labradorica* (Thrift)	P	L	S	RM	NA CP
Arnica amplexicaulis (Streambank arnica)	Y	L	R	SN	EN
A. diversifolia (Lawless arnica)	Y	L	M	SN SNC NRM	WNA
A. mollis (Soft-haired arnica)	Y	L	M	RM SN SNC NRM GB PR	NA
A. nevadensis (Sierra arnica)	Y	L	FF	SN SNC GB	WNA

Scientific and Common Names	Color	Bloom	Community	U.S. distribution	World distribution
Arnica rydbergii (Subalpine arnica)	Y	L	T	RM SC GB	WNA
Artemisia arbuscula (Sagebrush)	Y	L	FF	WH	WNA
A. arbuscula ssp. *nova* (Dwarf sagebrush)	Y	L	FF	NRM GB	WNA
A. arctica ssp. *saxicola* (Arctic sage)	Y	L	S	RM SN WH SNC OR	AA CP
A. borealis ssp. *purshii* (Alpine sage)	BR	L	T	RM	EN
A. dracunculus (Dragon sagewort)	Y	L	SC FF	WH	WNA
A. ludoviciana ssp. *incompta* (Western mugwort)	Y	L	FF	SN WH	WNA
A. michauxiana (Michaux's mugwort)	Y	L	FF	WH SNC	WNA
A. pattersonii (Patterson's sage)	Y	M	FF	RM	EN
A. rothrockii (Timberline sagebrush)	Y	L	FF	SN WH	EN
A. scopulorum (Rocky Mountain sage)	Y	M	E	RM NRM	EN
A. trifurcata (Three-forked sage)	Y	L	TA	SNC OR	WNA AA BA
Asplenium viride (Grassfern)	N	N	R B	RM SNC OR	NA
Aster alpigenus (Alpine aster)	PR	L	SC T	SN SNC OR GB	WNA
A. alpinus (Alpine aster)	PR	M	T	RM	CP
A. coloradensis (Colorado aster)	R	M	T	RM	EN
A. foliaceus (Leafy-bracted aster)	PR	L	S	SNC PR	NA
A. foliaceus var. *apricus* (Sun-loving aster)	R	L	S	RM SN SNC PR	NA

Scientific and Common Names	Color	Bloom	Community	U.S. distribution	World distribution
Aster paucicapitatus (Olympic aster)	W	L	T	OR	EN
A. peirsonii (Peirson's aster)	B-PR	L	T G	SN	EN
A. puniceus var. *oligocephalus* (Reddish-purple aster)	R PR	L	T	PR	ENA
A. shastensis var. *montana* (Shasta aster)	W	L	TA	SN WH	EN
Astragalus alpinus (Alpine milkvetch)	PR	M	T D	RM SN GB PR	AA CP
A. austinae (Austin's milkvetch)	Y-W	M	B	SN GB	WNA
A. calycosus (King's rattleweed)	W	M	FF	SN WH	WNA
A. cottonii (Cotton's rattleweed)	G-W	M	TA	OR	EN
A. kentrophyta var. *danaus* (Dana milkvetch)	W B PR	E-L	TA FF SC	SN WH NRM	WNA
A. lentiginosus (Mottled rattleweed)	PR-W	M	T	WH	WNA
A. lentiginosus var. *ineptus*	PR-W	M	T	SN	EN
A. microcystis (Small-pod milkvetch)	P W	M	FF	NC OR NRM	WNA
A. molybdenus (Colorado milkvetch)	B	M	SC	RM	EN
A. occidentalis (Western milkvetch)	P-PR	M	FF	RM	WNA
A. platytropis (Broad-keeled milkvetch)	W	M	SC	SN GB	WNA
A. plumbeus (Alpine milkvetch)	PR	M	SC	RM	EN
A. purshii var. *lectulus* (Purple woollypod)	PR	M	FF	SN SNC GB	WNA
A. ravenii (Raven's milkvetch)	W	M	FF	SN	EN

Scientific and Common Names	Color	Bloom	Community	U.S. distribution	World distribution
Astragalus whitneyi (Whitney milkvetch)	PR	M	FF	SN WH	EN
Athyrium alpestre var. *americanum* (Alpine ladyfern)	N	N	B TA	RM SN WH SC	NA AA CP
A. filix-femina ssp. *angustum* (Ladyfern)	N	N	B	PR	NA CP
Avalanche lily: see *Erythronium*					
Avenochloa hookeri (Mountain oat)	G	M	T	RM	CP
Avens: see *Acomastylis* Azalea: see *Loiseleuria* Baked-apple berry: see *Rubus*					
Barbarea orthoceras (Northern wintercress)	Y	M	K	PR	NA
Bastard toadflax: see *Comandra* Beadlily: see *Clintonia* Bearberry: see *Arctostaphylos* Beardtongue: see *Penstemon* Bedstraw: see *Galium* Beechfern: see *Phegopteris* Bell heather: see *Cassiope* Bentgrass: see *Agrostis; Podagrostis; Ptilagrostis*					
Besseya alpina (Alpine kittentail)	PR	E	F B	RM	EN
B. ritteriana (Kittentail)	Y	L	T	RM	EN
Betula cordifolia (Heart-leaved birch)	BR	E	K S	PR	EN
B. glandulosa (Bog birch)	BR	E	M S	RM SNC OR NRM PR	NA
B. minor (Small birch)	BR	E	M S	PR	EN
B. papyrifera (Paper birch)	BR	E	K ST	PR	NA

Scientific and Common Names	Color	Bloom	Community	U.S. distribution	World distribution
Bilberry: see *Vaccinium*					
Birch: see *Betula*					
Bistort: see *Bistorta*					
Bistorta bistortoides (American bistort)	W	M	E	RM SN SNC OR GB	NA
B. vivipara (Viviparous bistort)	W	M	TM	RM NC PR	CP
Bittercress: see *Cardamine*					
Bitterroot: see *Lewisia*					
Bladderpod: see *Lesquerella, Physaria*					
Bleedingheart: see *Dicentra*					
Blueberry: see *Vaccinium*					
Blue-eyed Mary: see *Collinsia*					
Bluegrass: see *Poa*					
Bluets: see *Houstonia*					
Bog laurel: see *Kalmia*					
Botrychium lunaria	N	N	T	RM	CP
B. simplex (Simple moonwort)	G	M	T	RM	CP
Boykinia: see *Telesonix*					
Braya humilis (Dwarf braya)	Y	M	S	RM	AA CP
Brewer's pea: see *Lathyrus*					
Brittlefern: see *Cystopteris*					
Bromegrass: see *Bromus*					
Broom: see *Hedysarum*					
Bromus porteri (Porter's bromegrass)	G	M	T	WH GB	WNA
Buckwheat: see *Eriogonum*					
Bulrush: see *Scirpus*					
Bunchberry: see *Cornus*					
Bunch evergreen: see *Lycopodium*					
Bupleurum americanum (American thoroughwort)	Y	M	T	RM GB	WNA
B. purpureum (Lavender thoroughwort)	PR	M	T	RM NRM GB	WNA
Buttercup: see *Ranunculus*					
Butterweed: see *Ligularia; Senecio*					

Scientific and Common Names	Color	Bloom	Community	U.S. distribution	World distribution
Butterwort: see *Pinguicula*					
Calamagrostis breweri (Brewer's reedgrass)	G	M	T	SN	EN
Calamagrostis canadensis (Canadian reedgrass)	G	M	M	SN SNC	WNA
C. canadensis var. *scabra*	G	M	M	PR	ENA
C. inexpansa (Narrow-spiked reedgrass)	G	M	M	SN SC	WNA
C. neglecta (Neglected reedgrass)	G	M	M	PR	ENA
C. nubila (Lake-of-the-clouds reedgrass)	G	M	M	PR	EN
C. pickeringii (Pickering's reedgrass)	G	M	M	PR	ENA
C. purpurascens (Alpine reedgrass)	G-PR	M	D	RM SN WH SNC OR	WNA
Callitriche anceps (Water-starwort)	G	M	P	PR	ENA
C. verna (Spring water-starwort)	W	M	P	SN WH SNC OR	WNA CP
Caltha leptosepala (Marsh-marigold)	W	E	M ST	RM SNC OR NRM GB	WNA
Calyptridium roseum (Rosy pussypaws)	P	M	FF	WH GB	WNA
C. umbellatum var. *caudiciferum* (Pussypaws)	P	M	FF	SN WH SNC OR NRM GB	WNA
Campanula gieseckiana (Mt. Washington harebell)	B	L	M	PR	EN
C. parryi (Parry's harebell)	B	M	T	RM	WNA
C. piperi (Piper's harebell)	B	L	R	OR	EN
C. rotundifolia (Mountain harebell)	B	L	D	RM SNC OR GB PR	NA CP
C. scabrella (Rough harebell)	B	M	B	SNC GB	WNA

Scientific and Common Names	Color	Bloom	Community	U.S. distribution	World distribution
Campanula uniflora (One-flowered harebell)	PR	M	T	RM	CP
Campion: see *Melandrium, Silene*					
Candytuft: see *Smelowskia, Thlaspi*					
Cardamine bellidifolia (Alpine bittercress)	W	M	ST	SNC PR	AA CP
C. umbellata (Umbel-flowered bittercress)	W	M	M	RM SNC	WNA AA
Carex ablata (American cold-loving sedge)	BR	M	M	SNC NRM	WNA
C. abrupta (Abruptly-beaked sedge)	BR	M	M	SN SC GB	WNA
C. albonigra (Black-and-white sedge)	BL	M	M	RM SN WH SNC OR	WNA
C. aquatilis ssp. *stans* (Water sedge)	BL	M	M	RM NRM	NA CP
C. arapahoensis (Arapahoe sedge)	BR	M	T	RM	EN
C. atrata	BL	M	T	RM NRM SN	CP
C. atratiformis	BR	M	ST	PR	ENA
C. atrosquama	BR	M	T	RM	EN
C. aurea (Golden sedge)	Y-O	M	T	RM	NA
C. bella (Handsome sedge)	BR	M	T	RM	EN
C. bigelowii (Mt. Washington sedge)	BL	M	F	PR	ENA AA CP
C. brevipes (Short sedge)	G	M	T	RM SN WH SNC OR GB	WNA
C. breweri (Brewer's sedge)	BR	L	S	SN WH SNC	WNA
C. brunnescens (Brownish sedge)	BR	M	D	RM SC PR	NA

Scientific and Common Names	Color	Bloom	Community	U.S. distribution	World distribution
Carex canescens (Silvery sedge)	BR	M	T	PR	NA
C. capillaris (Capillary sedge)	BR	M	M	RM PR	AA CP
C. capitata (Capitate sedge)	BR	M	M	RM SN SNC PR	ENA CP BP
C. chalciolepis (Fish-scale sedge)	BR	M	T	RM	EN
C. congdonii (Congdon's sedge)	BR	M	TA	SN	EN
C. debilis var. *strictior* (Frail sedge)	BR	M	M	PR	NA
C. douglasii (Douglas' sedge)	BR	M	SC	SN WH SNC	WNA
C. ebenea (Ebony sedge)	BL	M	T D	RM	CP
C. egglestonii (Eggleston's sedge)	BR	M	FF	RM	WNA
C. elynoides (Elk sedge)	BR	M	T	RM NRM GB	WNA
C. engelmannii (Engelmann's sedge)	BR	M	T	RM SC	WNA
C. epapillosa (Smooth-fruited sedge)	BL	M	M	RM SN WH SNC	WNA
C. exserta (Short-grass sedge)	BR	M	T	SN SC GB	WNA
C. festivella (Mountain meadow sedge)	BR	M	T	RM	WNA
C. filifolia (Thread-like sedge)	BR	M	T	RM SN WH	WNA
C. foenea	BR	M	D	RM NRM	NA
C. haydeniana (Hayden's sedge)	BL	M	T	RM SN WH	WNA
C. helleri (Heller's sedge)	BR	M	SC	SN WH SC GB	WNA

Scientific and Common Names	Color	Bloom	Community	U.S. distribution	World distribution
Carex heteroneura (Various-nerved sedge)	BL	M	D	RM SN WH GB	WNA
C. hoodii (Hood's sedge)	BR	M	T	SN SNC	WNA
C. illota (Unwashed sedge)	BL	M	M	RM SC	WNA
C. lachenalii (Lachenal's sedge)	BR	M	M	RM	CP
C. lenticularis var. *albi-montana* (Lenticular sedge)	BR	M	B	NRM PR	NA
C. leporinella (Sierra hare sedge)	BR	L	B	SN SNC NRM GB	WNA
C. limosa (Quagmire sedge)	BR	M	M	PR	EN
C. macloviana	BR	M	M	RM	CP
C. magellanica ssp. *irrigua* (Magellan's sedge)	BR	M	M	RM NC GB PR	NA AA CP
C. maritima (Incurved sedge)	BR	L	S	RM	WNA
C. maritima var. *danaensis* (Dana's sedge)	BR	L	S	SN	EN
C. microglochin	BR	M	M	RM	AA CP
C. microptera (Small-winged sedge)	BR	M	T	SN WH SNC NRM	WNA
C. misandra (Man-hater sedge)	BL	M	M	RM	CP
C. nardina var. *hepburnii* (Hepburn's sedge)	BR	M	FF	RM SNC	CP
C. nelsonii (Nelson's sedge)	BL	M	M	RM	EN
C. nigricans (Blackish sedge)	BL	M	M	RM SN SNC NRM	WNA AA BA
C. nova (New sedge)	BL	M	M	RM NRM	EN

Scientific and Common Names	Color	Bloom	Community	U.S. distribution	World distribution
Carex obtusata (Blunt sedge)	BR	M	T	RM	EN
C. oreocharis (Mountain-loving sedge)	BR	M	FF	RM	EN
C. paysonis	BR	M	M	NRM SNC	WNA
C. pelocarpa	BR	M	T	RM	EN
C. perglobosa (Round sedge)	BR	M	FF	RM	EN
C. phaeocephala (Mountain hare sedge)	BR	M	T	RM SN WH SNC OR	WNA
C. praeceptorum	BL	M	T	SN SNC NRM	WNA
C. proposita	BR	M	SC	SN NRM	WNA
C. pseudoscirpoidea	BL	M	T	RM SN SC GB	WNA
C. pyrenaica (Pyrenees sedge)	BR	L	S	RM SNC OR	CP BP
C. rariflora (Few-flowered sedge)	BR	M	M	PR	CP
C. raynoldsii (Raynold's sedge)	BR	M	M	RM SN SNC	WNA
C. rupestris (Rock sedge)	BR	E	T	RM GB	WNA CP
C. saxatilis ssp. *laxa* (Rock-growing sedge)	BR	M	M	RM SNC OR	WNA
C. scirpoidea (Canadian single-spiked sedge)	BL	M	T	SNC NRM PR	NA AA
C. scopulorum (Rocky Mountain sedge)	BL	M	M	RM SN SNC OR NRM	WNA
C. spectabilis (Showy sedge)	BL	M	S	SN SNC NRM	WNA AA
C. stenophylla ssp. *eleocharis* (Narrow-leaved sedge)	BR	M	FF	RM SN GB	WNA

Scientific and Common Names	Color	Bloom	Community	U.S. distribution	World distribution
Carex straminiformis (Mount Shasta sedge)	BR	M	TA	SN SNC NRM	WNA
C. subnigricans	BL	M	TA	SN WH SC NRM GB	WNA
C. tahoensis (Tahoe sedge)	BR	M	TA	SN	EN
C. vernacula (Native sedge)	BR	M	M	RM SN WH GB	WNA
Carrot: see *Oreonana*					
Carpogymnia dryopteris (Oakfern)	N	N	K	PR	NA
Cassiope hypnoides (Moss plant)	W	M	S	PR	AA CP
C. mertensiana (Western bell heather)	W	M	FF ST	SN SNC OR	WNA
C. stellariana (Alaska moss heath)	W	M	FF	SNC	AA BA
C. tetragona (Lapland cassiope)	W	M	FF	NC	AA CP
Castilleja arachnoidea (Cobwebby Indian paintbrush)	Y-R	M	FF	SC	EN
C. breweri (Brewer's Indian paintbrush)	R	M	FF	SN WH	EN
C. chrysantha (Wallowa Indian paintbrush)	W-Y	M	ST	GB	EN
C. cryptantha (Obscure Indian paintbrush)	G-Y	M	T	SC	EN
C. culbertsonii (Culbertson's Indian paintbrush)	PR	M	M	SN	EN
C. fraterna (Fraternal Indian paintbrush)	R	M	W	GB	EN

Scientific and Common Names	Color	Bloom	Community	U.S. distribution	World distribution
Castilleja lemmonii (Lemmon's Indian paintbrush)	PR	M	T	SN SC	WNA
C. nana (Dwarf alpine paintbrush)	P	M	FF	SN WH	EN
C. occidentalis (Western yellow paintbrush)	Y	M	T	RM	EN
C. oreopola (Rosy Indian paintbrush)	R	M	T	SNC OR	EN
C. ownbeyana (Ownbey's Indian paintbrush)	Y PR	M	T	GB	EN
C. payneae (Pumice Indian paintbrush)	O-R	M	FF	SC GB	EN
C. peirsonii (Peirson's paintbrush)	PR	M	B	SN	EN
C. puberula (Alpine paintbrush)	P	M	FF	RM	EN
C. rhexifolia (Rosy paintbrush)	PR	M	M	RM SNC	WNA
C. rubida (Little reddish paintbrush)	PR	M	FF	GB	EN
C. rupicola (Cliff Indian paintbrush)	R	L	FF S	SNC	EN
C. sulphurea (Northern paintbrush)	W-Y	M	M	RM NC PR	NA AA
C. villicaulis (Mt. Adams paintbrush)	Y	M	SC	SC	EN
C. wallowensis (Wallowa purple Indian paintbrush)	PR	M	FF	GB	EN

Scientific and Common Names	Color	Bloom	Community	U.S. distribution	World distribution
Catchfly: see *Silene*					
Cerastium arvense (Field mouse-ear)	W	M	D	RM SC OR GB PR	NA CP
C. beeringianum ssp. *earlei* (Alpine mouse-ear)	W	M	T	RM SN WH GB	NA AA BA
Chaenactis alpigena (Southern Sierra dusty maiden)	W-P	L	SC	SN	EN
C. alpina (Alpine dusty maiden)	W-P	M	SC	RM SN SC GB	WNA
Chamerion angustifolium (Fireweed)	P-PR	L	D	SNC OR PR	NA CP
C. latifolium (Alpine fireweed)	P-PR	M	G	RM SN SNC OR	AA CP
Chickweed: see *Stellaria*					
Chiming bells: see *Mertensia*					
Chionophila jamesii (Snowlover)	W	M	S F	RM	EN
Chrysosplenium tetrandrum (Golden saxifrage)	W-G	M	ST	RM NC	AA CP
Chrysothamnus nauseosus (Rabbitbrush)	Y	L	FF	WH	WNA
Cinquefoil: see *Potentilla*					
Cirsium coloradense (Colorado thistle)	PR	M	TA	RM	EN
C. edule (Edible thistle)	PR	M	SC	SNC OR	WNA
C. scopulorum (Alpine thistle)	W	M	D	RM	EN
C. tioganum (Tioga thistle)	W-PR	M	T	SN	EN
Claytonia bellidifolia (Rydberg's springbeauty)	W	E	FF	SN SC NRM	WNA
C. caroliniana (Springbeauty)	W-P	E	FF	PR	ENA
C. megarhiza (Big-rooted springbeauty)	W-P	E	FF D B F	RM SC NRM GB	WNA

Scientific and Common Names	Color	Bloom	Community	U.S. distribution	World distribution
Claytonia nevadensis (Sierra springbeauty)	W-P	E	FF	SN	EN
C. nivalis (Wenatchee springbeauty)	P	E	TA	NC	EN
Clementsia rhodantha (Queen's or Rose crown)	P	M-L	M	RM	EN
Cliffbrake: see *Pellaea*					
Cliffbush: see *Jamesia*					
Clintonia borealis (Beadlily)	Y-G	M	K	PR	NA
Clover: see *Trifolium*					
Clubmoss: see *Huperzia, Lycopodium; Selaginella*					
Clubrush: see *Scirpus*					
Collinsia parviflora (Small-flowered blue-eyed Mary)	B-PR	M	R	SN SNC NRM	WNA
Collomia debilis (Alpine collomia)	W-PR	L	SC	SNC NRM GB	WNA
C. larsenii (Talus collomia)	W-PR	L	SC	SNC OR	EN
C. tinctoria (Yellow-staining collomia)	P-PR	L	SC	SC GB	WNA
Coltsfoot: see *Petasites*					
Columbine: see *Aquilegia*					
Comandra umbellata (Bastard toadflax)	W	M	T	RM	WNA
Coptis groenlandica (Goldthread)	W	M	T	PR	NA AA
Coralbells: see *Heuchera*					
Cornlily: see *Veratrum*					
Cornus canadensis (Bunchberry)	W	M	K	PR	NA
Cottongrass, Cottonsedge: see *Eriophorum*					
Cow-wheat: see *Melampyrum*					
Cranberry: See *Vaccinium, Viburnum*					
Crepis nana (Dwarf hawksbeard)	Y	M	SC	RM SN SNC OR	NA BA

Scientific and Common Names	Color	Bloom	Community	U.S. distribution	World distribution
Crowberry: see *Empetrum*					
Cryptantha circumscissa var. *hispida* (Cryptantha)	W	M	FF	SN GB	WNA
C. circumscissa var. *rosulata*	W	M	FF	SN	EN
C. confertiflora (Crowded cryptantha)	Y	M	TA	SN WH GB	WNA
C. glomeriflora (Truckee cryptantha)	W	M	TA T	SN WH GB	WNA
C. hoffmannii (Hoffmann's cryptantha)	W	M	R	SN WH	EN
C. jamesii var. *abortiva* (James' cryptantha)	W	M	FF	WH	WNA
C. nubigena (Alpine cryptantha)	W	M	FF	SN	EN
Cryptogramma crispa ssp. *acrostichoides* (American rockbrake)	N	N	R	RM SN WH SNC OR	WNA
Cudweed: see *Gnaphalium*					
Currant: see *Ribes*					
Cymopterus cinerarius (Gray's parsley)	W	M	R	SN WH GB	EN
Cystopteris fragilis (Brittlefern)	N	N	R	RM SN WH	NA CP
Daisy: see *Erigeron*					
Dandelion: see *Taraxacum*					
Danthonia intermedia (Timber danthonia)	G	M	T	SN SNC	WNA
Death camas: see *Zigadenus*					
Deer's hair: see *Scirpus*					
Delphinium alpestre (Alpine larkspur)	B	M	SC	RM	EN
D. glareosum (Flathead larkspur)	PR	M	SC	OR	EN
D. polycladon (Larkspur)	B-PR	M	M	SN WH	WNA

Scientific and Common Names	Color	Bloom	Community	U.S. distribution	World distribution
Deschampsia alpicola (Alpine hairgrass)	G	M	D	RM	EN
D. caespitosa (Tufted hairgrass)	G	M	S M	RM SN WH SNC OR GB PR	AA CP BP
D. flexuosa (Nodding hairgrass)	G	M	T	PR	ENA CP
Descurainia californica (Sierra tansy-mustard)	Y	E	SC	SN WH GB	WNA
D. richardsonii (Mountain tansy-mustard)	Y	E	FF	RM SN WH SC NRM	WNA
Diapensia lapponica (Diapensia)	W	E	F FF B	PR	ENA AA CP
Dicentra pauciflora (Few-flowered bleedingheart)	W-O	M	SC	SN SC	WNA
D. uniflora (Steer's head)	P	M	SC TA B	SN SNC NRM	WNA
Dock: see *Rumex*					
Dodecatheon alpinum (Alpine shooting star)	P-PR	M	ST	SN SC GB	WNA
D. redolens (Sierra shooting star)	P-PR	M	ST	SN WH GB	WNA
Douglasia laevigata (Cliff douglasia)	P-PR	M	SC	SC OR	EN
D. nivalis (Snow douglasia)	P-PR	M	TA	NC NRM GB	WNA
Draba albertina	Y	M	S	RM SN WH SNC OR GB	WNA
D. aurea (Golden draba)	Y	M	T	RM	WNA AA
D. aureola (Mount Lassen draba)	Y	E	B	SC	EN
D. breweri (Brewer's whitlowgrass)	W	M	SC	SN WH SC	WNA

Scientific and Common Names	Color	Bloom	Community	U.S. distribution	World distribution
Draba cana (White draba)	W	M	T	RM GB	NA AA CP
D. cascadensis (Cascade draba)	?	E	M	NC	EN
D. crassa (Thick draba)	Y	M	TA	RM	WNA AA
D. cruciata (Cross-like draba)	Y	M	FF	SN	EN
D. densifolia (Dense-leaved draba)	Y	M	FF	RM SN SNC GB	WNA
D. exunguiculata (Clawless draba)	Y	M	FF	RM	EN
D. fladnizensis (White arctic draba)	W	M	TA F	RM SN WH GB	WNA AA CP
D. graminea (Whitlowgrass)	Y	M	TA	RM	EN
D. grayana (Gray's Peak draba)	Y	M	B	RM	EN
D. howellii (Howell's draba)	Y	M	B	SC	EN
D. lemmonii (Lemmon's draba)	Y	E	FF	SN	EN
D. nivalis (Snow draba)	W	M	R	RM SN	WNA CP
D. novolympica (Olympic draba)	Y	M	R	SNC OR	EN
D. oligosperma (White Mountain draba)	Y	E	FF	SN WH SNC NRM	WNA
D. oligosperma var. *subsessilis*	Y	E	B	SN WH	EN
D. paysonii var. *treleasii* (Payson's draba)	Y	E	FF	SN SNC NRM GB	WNA
D. praealta (Tall draba)	W	E	M	SN SNC NRM	WNA
D. ruaxes (Volcano draba)	Y	M	SC	NC	EN

Scientific and Common Names	Color	Bloom	Community	U.S. distribution	World distribution
Draba sierrae (Sierra draba)	Y	E	FF	SN WH	EN
D. spectabilis (Showy draba)	Y	M-L	T	RM	EN
D. stenoloba var. *nana* (Narrow-lobed draba)	Y	E	M	RM SN WH SNC NRM	WNA AA
D. streptocarpa (Twisted-pod draba)	Y	E	FF T	RM	EN
Drosera rotundifolia (Sundew)	W	M	M	PR	NA AA
Dryad: see *Dryas*					
Dryas drummondii (Drummond's mountain dryad)	Y	M	G	SNC NRM GB	WNA AA
D. octopetala ssp. *hookeriana* (Alpine dryad)	W	M	FF SC D	RM SNC	AA CP
Dryopteris spinulosa (Mountain woodfern)	N	N	K	PR	NA
Dusty maiden: see *Chaenactis, Orochaemactis* Easter-daisy: see *Townsendia* Elderberry, Elder: see *Sambucus*					
Eleocharis acicularis (Needle-like spike-rush)	BR	L	M	RM	CP
E. pauciflora (Few-flowered spike-rush)	BR	M	M	RM SN WH SNC OR	NA CP BP
Elephantella, Elephant head, Elephant snout: see *Pedicularis*					
Elmera racemosa (Elmera)	Y-W	M	R SC	SNC OR	WNA
Empetrum atropurpureum (Purple crowberry)	W	E	FF	PR	AA
E. eamesii ssp. *hermaphroditum* (Rockberry)	W	E	FF	PR	EN

Scientific and Common Names	Color	Bloom	Community	U.S. distribution	World distribution
Empetrum nigrum (Black crowberry)	W	E	FF	SNC OR PR	AA CP
Epilobium anagallidifolium (Alpine willowherb)	P	M	ST	RM SN WH SNC OR PR	CP
E. clavatum (Clavate-fruited willowherb)	PR	M	TA	RM SNC NRM	WNA
E. glaberrimum (Glaucous willowherb)	W-PR	M	ST	SN	WNA
E. hornemannii (Hornemann's willowherb)	W	M	M	RM SN WH SNC PR	NA CP
E. lactiflorum (White-flowered willowherb)	W	M	ST	RM SN SNC PR	NA CP
E. luteum (Yellow willowherb)	Y	M	ST	SNC OR	EN
E. obcordatum (Rock fringe)	P-PR	M	D SC	SN SC GB	WNA
E. oregonense (Oregon willowherb)	Y-PR	M	M	SN SNC NRM GB	WNA
E. palustre (Marsh willowherb)	P W	M	M	NC PR	NA CP
Equisetum sylvaticum var. *pauciramosum* (Wood horsetail)	N	N	K	PR	ENA
Eriastrum wilcoxii (Wilcox's eriastrum)	Y W	M	SC	SN	EN
Erigeron aureus (Alpine yellow daisy)	Y	M-L	T	SNC NRM	WNA
E. breweri (Brewer's daisy)	P-PR	L	TA	SN GB	WNA
E. clokeyi (Clokey's daisy)	P B	L	TA	SN WH GB	WNA
E. compositus var. *discoideus* (Cut-leaved daisy)	W	L	FF	RM SN WH OR GB	WNA

Scientific and Common Names	Color	Bloom	Community	U.S. distribution	World distribution
Erigeron compositus var. *glabratus*	W	M	FF	RM SN WH OR GB	WNA
E. flettii (Olympic daisy)	W	L	R	OR	EN
E. grandiflorus (Large daisy)	P	M	FF	RM	EN
E. leiomerus (Rockslide daisy)	P-PR	M	S	RM	EN
E. melanocephalus (Black-headed daisy)	W	L	S	RM	EN
E. peregrinus ssp. *callianthemus* (Wandering daisy)	PR	M	T	RM SN SC OR	WNA
E. petiolaris (Sierra daisy)	P-PR	L	TA T	SN	EN
E. pinnatisectus (Pinnate-leaved daisy)	PR	M	FF	RM	EN
E. pygmaeus (Dwarf daisy)	B-PR	L	FF	SN WH GB	EN
E. simplex (One-headed daisy)	P-B	M	T	RM NRM GB	WNA
E. tener (Slender daisy)	P-B	L	R	SN SC NRM GB	WNA
E. ursinus	B-PR	L	T	RM	EN
E. vagus	W P	L	TA	RM SN WH SC GB	WNA
Eriogonum alpinum (Alpine buckwheat)	Y	M	SC TA	SC	EN
E. flavum ssp. *xanthum* (Alpine golden buckwheat)	Y-O	M	FF	RM	EN
E. kennedyi (Kennedy's buckwheat)	R-Y	M	FF	SN WH GB	WNA
E. latens (Onion-flowered buckwheat)	W-P	M	SC	SN WH GB	WNA

Scientific and Common Names	Color	Bloom	Community	U.S. distribution	World distribution
Eriogonum latifolium ssp. *nudum* (Broad-leaved buckwheat)	P-Y	M	FF	SN	EN
E. lobbii (Lobb's buckwheat)	Y P	M	FF	SN GB	WNA
E. marifolium var. *incanum*	Y	M	SC FF	SN	EN
E. microthecum (Great Basin buckwheat)	Y-W P	M	FF	SN WH SNC NRM	WNA
E. ochrocephalum ssp. *agnellum* (Ochre-flowered buckwheat)	Y O	M	FF	SN	EN
E. ovalifolium var. *nivale*	W-P	M	FF	SN	EN
E. ovalifolium ssp. *vineum* (Oval-leaved buckwheat)	Y-W P-R	M	FF	RM SN WH SNC OR NRM GB	WNA
E. piperi (Piper's buckwheat)	Y	M	SC	NRM GB	WNA
E. polypodum	W R	M	FF	SN	EN
E. pyrolaefolium var. *coryphaeum* (Pyrola-leaved buckwheat)	W-P	M	FF SC	SN SNC NRM	WNA
E. umbellatum ssp. *covillei* (Sulphurflower)	Y	M	FF SC	SN SC GB	WNA
E. wrightii ssp. *subscaposum* (Wright's buckwheat)	W P	M	SC TA	WH	EN
Eriophorum chamissonis (Russet cottongrass)	G	E	M	SNC NRM	AA CP
E. scheuchzeri (Scheuchzer's cottongrass)	W	L	M	RM	CP
E. spissum (Hare's-tail)	G	E	M	PR	ENA CP
Eriophyllum lanatum var. *monoense* (Common woolly sunflower)	Y	L	FF	SN WH SC	WNA

Scientific and Common Names	Color	Bloom	Community	U.S. distribution	World distribution
Eritrichium aretioides (Alpine forget-me-not)	B W	E	T	RM	CP
Erysimum amoenum (Lavender alpine wallflower)	PR	M	T	RM	EN
E. nivale (Alpine wallflower)	Y-O-R	E	FF T	RM	EN
E. perenne (Sierra wallflower)	Y	E	FF	SN SC	WNA
Erythronium grandiflorum (Glacier lily)	Y	E	S	RM SNC OR GB	WNA
E. montanum (Avalanche lily)	W	E	S	SNC	EN
Euphrasia oakesii (Eyebright)	W-PR	L	ST	PR	ENA
E. williamsii (Eyebright)	BR-PR	L	ST	PR	ENA

Everlasting: see *Anaphalis*
Eyebright: see *Euphrasia*
False dandelion: see *Agoseris*
False lily-of-the-valley: see *Maianthemum*
False Solomonseal: see *Smilacina*
Fern: see *Asplenium, Athyrium, Botrychium, Carpogymnia, Cryptogramma, Cystopteris, Dryopteris, Pellaea, Phegopteris, Polystichum, Woodsia*
Fescue: see *Festuca*

Festuca baffinensis (Baffin fescue)	G	M	T	RM NRM	AA
F. brachyphylla (Alpine fescue)	G	M	E	RM SN WH SNC OR GB PR	NA AA

Scientific and Common Names	Color	Bloom	Community	U.S. distribution	World distribution
Festuca hallii (Hall's fescue)	G	M	T	RM	EN
F. rubra ssp. *richardsonii* (Red fescue)	G	M	M B	PR	ENA
F. thurberi (Thurber fescue)	G	M	T	RM	EN

Fireweed: see *Chamerion*
Five-finger: see *Potentilla*
Flax: see *Linum*
Forget-me-not: see *Eritrichium; Myosotis*

Scientific and Common Names	Color	Bloom	Community	U.S. distribution	World distribution
Fragaria virginiana var. *terranovae* (Wild strawberry)	W	M	K	PR	ENA
Galium hypotrichium ssp. *subalpinum* (Alpine bedstraw)	Y-P	M	B	SN WH GB	WNA
G. munzii var. *subalpinum* (Munz's bedstraw)	G BR	M	B	SN	EN
Gaultheria hispidula (Creeping snowberry)	W-P	M	S	PR	NA AA
G. humifusa (Creeping wintergreen)	W-P	M	S K	RM SNC	WNA
Gayophytum nuttallii (Nuttall's gayophytum)	W-R	M	FF	SN SNC	WNA BP
G. racemosum (Black-foot gayophytum)	W-R	M	FF	SN	WNA

Gentian: see *Gentiana*. We prefer to maintain the single genus *Gentiana*, rather than divide it into 8 genera as W.A. Weber has.

Scientific and Common Names	Color	Bloom	Community	U.S. distribution	World distribution
Gentiana algida (Arctic gentian)	W-G	L	T	RM	CP
G. amarella (Rose gentian)	P	M-L	T	RM SNC OR	WNA
G. amarella var. *acuta* (Northern gentian)	P	M-L	T	SN	EN

Scientific and Common Names	Color	Bloom	Community	U.S. distribution	World distribution
Gentiana barbellata (Fragrant gentian)	B	L	T	RM NRM	EN
G. calycosa (Explorer's gentian)	B	M-L	T	RM SN SNC OR	WNA
G. holopetala (Sierra gentian)	B	L	T	SN	EN
G. newberryi (Newberry's gentian)	W	L	T	SN WH SC	WNA
G. nutans (Stiped gentian)	B	L	T	RM	CP
G. plebeia (Dwarf rose gentian)	P-B	L	T	RM NRM	AA
G. prostrata (Moss gentian)	B	L	T	RM WH	CP BP
G. simplex (Hiker's gentian)	B	L	T	SN	EN
G. tenella (Dane's gentian)	B	L	S	RM SN WH	CP
G. thermalis (Fringed gentian)	B	L	M	RM	EN
Geum peckii (Mt. Washington avens)	Y	M	H	PR	EN
G. rivale (Brook avens)	P-PR	M	K	PR	NA CP
Gilia: see *Ipomopsis; Leptodactylon; Linanthus*					
Glacier lily: see *Erythronium*					
Globeflower: see *Anemone; Trollius*					
Gnaphalium supinum (Mountain cudweed)	W	L	S	PR	CP
Goldenrod: see *Solidago*					
Goldenweed: see *Haplopappus*					
Goldflower: see *Hymenoxys*					
Goldthread: see *Coptis*					
Grapefern: see *Botrychium*					
Grassfern: see *Asplenium*					
Grass-of-Parnassus: see *Parnassia*					

417 ALPINE PLANTS

Scientific and Common Names	Color	Bloom	Community	U.S. distribution	World distribution
Groundcedar, Groundfir, Groundpine: see *Lycopodium*					
Groundsel: see *Ligularia; Senecio*					
Hackelia jessicae (Jessica's stickseed)	B	M	M	SNC	WNA
H. sharsmithii (Sharsmith's stickseed)	W-B	M	R	SN	EN
Hairgrass: see *Deschampsia, Vahlodea*					
Haplopappus acaulis (Dwarf goldenweed)	Y	L	FF	WH GB	WNA
H. apargioides (Dana goldenweed)	Y	M	FF	SN WH	EN
H. lyallii (Lyall's goldenweed)	Y	M	FF	RM SNC GB	WNA
H. macronema (Western goldenweed)	Y	M	TA	RM SN WH NRM GB	WNA
H. peirsonii (Inyo goldenweed)	Y	M	B	SN	EN
H. pygmaeus (Alpine goldenweed)	Y	L	FF	RM	EN
H. suffruticosus (Big-head goldenweed)	Y	L	FF	SN WH NRM GB	WNA
H. uniflorus (Giant sunspot)	Y	M	FF	RM NRM	EN
Harebell: see *Campanula*					
Hare's-tail: see *Eriophorum*					
Hawksbeard: see *Crepis*					
Hawkweed: see *Hieracium*					
Heath, Heather: see *Cassiope, Phyllodoce*					
Hedysarum occidentale (Western sweetbroom)	P-PR	M	SC	OR	EN
Helictotrichon mortonianum (Alpine oat)	G	M	T	RM	BA

Scientific and Common Names	Color	Bloom	Community	U.S. distribution	World distribution
Heuchera duranii (Duran's alumroot)	Y-P	M	TA	WH	EN
H. glabra (Alpine alumroot)	W	M	R	SNC OR	WNA
H. nivalis (Snow alumroot)	W	M	R	RM	EN
H. parviflora (Common alumroot)	W	M	R	RM	EN
H. rubescens var. *alpicola* (Pink alumroot)	P	M	FF	SN WH	EN
Hieracium gracile (Slender hawkweed)	Y	L	S	RM SN SC OR	WNA
H. horridum (Shaggy hawkweed)	Y	L	B	SN SC	WNA
Hierochloe alpina (Alpine holygrass)	Y	M	T H	PR	CP
H. monticola (Mountain holygrass)	G	M	T H	PR	ENA
H. odorata (Sweetgrass)	G	M	T	PR	NA
Hollyfern: see *Polystichum* Holygrass: see *Hierochloe* Honeysuckle: see *Lonicera*					
Horkelia fusca (Dusky horkelia)	W	M	M T	SN SC	WNA
H. hispidula (White Mountains horkelia)	W	M	SC	WH	EN
Horsetail: see *Equisetum*					
Houstonia caerulea var. *faxonorum* (Alpine bluets)	W	E-M	M	PR	EN
Huckleberry: see *Vaccinium*					
Hulsea algida (Alpine hulsea)	Y	L	TA	SN WH NRM GB	WNA

Scientific and Common Names	Color	Bloom	Community	U.S. distribution	World distribution
Hulsea nana (Dwarf hulsea)	Y	L	SC	SNC GB	WNA
H. vestita (Clothed hulsea)	Y	L	FF	SN	WNA
Huperzia selago (Fir clubmoss)	N	N	F	PR RM	NA AA CP
Hutchinsia procumbens (Prostrate hutchinsia)	W	M	M	SN	EN
Hymenoxys acaulis (Goldflower)	Y	E	FF	RM	WNA
H. acaulis var. *caespitosa*	Y	E	FF	RM	EN
H. cooperi var. *canescens* (Cooper's goldflower)	Y	L	TA	WH NRM GB	WNA
H. grandiflora (Rydbergia; Old-man-of-the-mountains)	Y	E-M	T	RM	EN
Icegrass: see *Phippsia* Indian paintbrush: see *Castilleja* Indian poke: see *Veratrum*					
Ipomopsis globularis (Globe gilia)	W	M	FF	RM	EN
Isoetes setacea ssp. *muricata* (Alpine quillwort)	N	N	P	PR	EN
Ivesia gordonii (Gordon's ivesia)	Y	M	FF	RM SN WH SNC NRM GB	WNA
I. lycopodioides (Clubmoss ivesia)	W-Y	M	B	SN WH	EN
I. muirii (Muir's ivesia)	Y	M	B	SN	EN
I. pygmaea (Dwarf ivesia)	Y	M	SC	SN WH	EN
I. shockleyi (Shockley's ivesia)	Y	M	FF	SN WH	EN

Scientific and Common Names	Color	Bloom	Community	U.S. distribution	World distribution
Ivesia tweedyi (Tweedy's ivesia)	Y	M	FF	NRM GB	EN
Jacob's ladder: see *Polemonium*					
Jamesia americana var. *californica* (Cliffbush)	P	M	R	SN GB	EN
Juncus arcticus ssp. *ater* (Arctic rush)	BR	M	M	RM SNC OR	WNA CP
J. biglumis (Two-glumed rush)	BR	M	ST F	RM	AA CP
J. brevicaudatus (Short-tailed rush)	BR	M	ST	PR	ENA
J. castaneus (Chestnut rush)	BR	M	ST	RM NRM	AA CP
J. drummondii (Drummond's rush)	BR	L	S	RM SN SNC OR	WNA
J. filiformis (Thread-like rush)	BR	M	M	RM SNC OR PR	NA
J. mertensianus (Subalpine rush)	BR	M	M S	RM SN WH SNC OR	WNA
J. mexicanus (Mexican rush)	G-Y	M	M	SN WH	NA CA
J. nevadensis (Nevada rush)	BR	M	M	SN	WNA
J. parryi (Parry's rush)	BR	M	M S	RM SN WH SNC GB	WNA
J. trifidus (Highland rush)	G	M	T H	PR	ENA AA CP
J. triglumis (Three-glumed rush)	BR	M	ST F	RM	AA CP
Juneberry: see *Amelanchier* Junegrass: see *Koeleria* Juniper: see *Juniperus*					
Juniperus communis (Dwarf juniper)	N	N	K	RM SNC OR PR	CP

Scientific and Common Names	Color	Bloom	Community	U.S. distribution	World distribution
Kalmia polifolia ssp. *microphylla* (Bog laurel)	P	M	M	SN PR	NA AA
King's crown: see *Rhodiola*					
Kinnikinnik: see *Arctostaphylos*					
Kittentail: see *Besseya, Synthris*					
Knotweed: see *Polygonum*					
Kobresia myosuroides (Kobresia)	BR	M	T	RM SN NRM	CP
K. sibirica	BR	M-L	M	RM	EN
K. simpliciuscula	BR	L	M	RM	CP
Koeleria macrantha (Junegrass)	BR	M	FF	SN WH	WNA
Koenigia islandica (Koenigia)	W	M	ST F	RM NRM	AA CP
Labrador tea: see *Ledum*					
Ladies' tresses: see *Spiranthes*					
Ladyfern: see *Athyrium*					
Lake-agoseris: see *Nothocalais*					
Larkspur: see *Delphinium*					
Lathyrus sulphureus (Brewer's pea)	Y-O	M	SC	SN	EN
Laurel: see *Kalmia*					
Ledum groenlandicum (Labrador tea)	W	M	H	PR	NA AA
Leptodactylon pungens (Prickly gilia)	W-P-Y	M	FF	SN WH SC NRM	WNA
Lesquerella alpina (Alpine bladderpod)	Y	M	TA FF F	RM NRM	EN
L. kingii var. *cordiformis* (King's bladderpod)	Y	M	SC TA	SN WH	EN
Lewisia nevadensis (Nevada bitterroot)	P	M	SC	RM SN SNC	WNA
L. pygmaea (Pygmy bitterroot)	P W	E-M	S	RM SN WH SNC OR PR	NA

Scientific and Common Names	Color	Bloom	Community	U.S. distribution	World distribution
Lewisia pygmaea ssp. *glandulosa* (Alpine bitterroot)	W	M	S	SN	EN
L. rediviva (Montana bitterroot)	P-PR	M	G	SN	WNA
L. sierrae (Sierra bitterroot)	P-PR	M	G ST	SN	EN
Ligularia amplectens (Daffodil ragwort)	Y	L	T	RM NRM GB	WNA
L. holmii (Alpine groundsel)	Y	M-L	D SC	RM	EN
L. soldanella (Nodding ragwort)	Y	M-L	B SC	RM	EN
L. taraxacoides (Dandelion butterweed)	Y	M	SC FF	RM	EN
Lily: see *Clintonia, Erythronium, Lloydia, Veratrum, Zygadenus*					
Limnorchis dilatata ssp. *albiflora* (White bog orchid)	W	M	S	PR	NA
Linanthus nuttallii (Nuttall's gilia)	W	E	FF	RM SN WH SC	WNA
Linnaea borealis (Twinflower)	P	M	K	PR	NA CP
Linum perenne ssp. *lewisii* (Western blue flax)	B	M	FF	SN WH SNC	WNA AA
Lithophragma bulbifera (Rockstar)	W	E	R	SN SNC	WNA
Lloydia serotina (Alplily)	W	E	T	RM SNC OR	AA CP
Locoweed: see *Astragalus; Oxytropis*					
Loiseleuria procumbens (Alpine azalea)	P	N	R B H	SNC PR	AA CP
Lomatium angustatum (Cascade lomatium)	W Y	L	FF	SC OR	WNA
L. cusickii (Cusick's lomatium)	W PR	L	B	NRM GB	WNA

Scientific and Common Names	Color	Bloom	Community	U.S. distribution	World distribution
Lomatium torreyi (Torrey's lomatium)	Y	L	SC	SN	EN
Lonicera villosa (Mountain fly honeysuckle)	Y	E	M	PR	ENA
Lousewort: see *Pedicularis*					
Luetkea pectinata (Luetkea, Partridge foot)	W-Y	M-L	SC	SNC OR	EN
Luina stricta (Tongue-leaf luina)	L	M	M	SC	EN
Lupine: see *Lupinus*					
Lupinus adsurgens var. *undulatus* (Drew's silky lupine)	Y B PR	M	SC	SN SC	WNA
L. alpestris (Alpine lupine)	B	M	SC	NRM GB	WNA
L. argenteus var. *tenellus* (Silvery lupine)	B	M	TA	WH GB	WNA
L. breweri (Brewer's lupine)	PR W	M	FF	SN WH SC GB	WNA
L. caespitosus (Stemless lupine)	B	M	SC	WH GB	EN
L. hypolasius (Woolly lupine)	PR B	M	TA SC	SN	EN
L. lobbii (Lobb's lupine)	B-PR	M	FF	SN	EN
L. lyallii (Lyall lupine)	B	M	FF	SN SC OR	WNA
L. lyallii var. *danaus* (Dana lupine)	W-PR	M	FF	SN GB	EN
L. pratensis (Inyo meadow lupine)	B-PR	M	M	SN	EN
L. volcanicus (Mount Rainier lupine)	B-Y	M	SC	SNC	EN
Luzula confusa (Northern woodrush)	BR	M	T	PR	AA CP
L. divaricata (Forked woodrush)	BR	M	S B	SN SNC	WNA AA

Scientific and Common Names	Color	Bloom	Community	U.S. distribution	World distribution
Luzula multiflora (Many-flowered woodrush)	BR	M	B	PR	NA
L. orestera (Sierra woodrush)	BR	M	M	SN	EN
L. parviflora (Small-flowered woodrush)	BR	M	ST	SN SNC OR PR	NA CP
L. parviflora var. *melanocarpa*	BR	M	ST	PR	EN
L. spicata (Spike woodrush)	BR	M	T FF	RM SN SNC OR PR	AA CP
L. subcapitata (Tundra woodrush)	BR	L	S	RM	EN
L. subcongesta (Donner woodrush)	BR	M	FF	SN SC	WNA
Lycopodium alpinum (Alpine groundfir)	N	N	K	NRM PR	NA AA CP
L. annotinum var. *alpestre*	N	N	K	PR	ENA AA
L. annotinum var. *pungens* (Bristly clubmoss)	N	N	K	PR	NA AA CP
L. clavatum (Runningpine)	N	N	K	PR	NA
L. complanatum ssp. *flabelliforme* (Groundcedar)	N	N	S	PR	CP
L. obscurum (Bunch evergreen)	N	N	S K	NRM PR	ENA AA BA
Maianthemum canadense (False lily-of-the-valley)	W	M	K	PR	ENA
Marmot-tail grass: see *Trisetum*					
Marsh-marigold: see *Caltha*					
Meadowrue: see *Thalictrum*					
Meadowsweet: see *Spiraea*					
Melampyrum lineare (Cow-wheat)	W Y	M	M	PR	NA AA
Melandrium apetalum (Petalless campion)	G	M	FF T	RM NRM	AA CP

Scientific and Common Names	Color	Bloom	Community	U.S. distribution	World distribution
Melandrium kingii (Alpine campion)	W	M	T FF	RM	AA
Melica bulbosa (Western oniongrass)	G	M	T M	SN SC GB	WNA
M. stricta (Nodding oniongrass)	G	M	TA	SN WH SC	WNA
Mertensia alpina (Alpine chiming bells)	B	M	TA S	RM NRM	EN
M. ciliata (Tall chiming bells)	B	M	ST	RM	WNA
M. ciliata var. *stomatechoides*	B P	M	ST	SN	EN
M. viridis (Green-leaf chiming bells)	B	E-M	FF T D B	RM GB	WNA
Milkvetch: see *Astragalus*					
Mimulus breweri (Brewer's monkey-flower)	P	M	G	SN SNC NRM GB	WNA
M. coccineus (Sierra monkeyflower)	PR	M	FF	SN WH	WNA
M. guttatus (Common yellow monkeyflower)	Y	M	ST	RM SN	WNA
M. leptaleus (Least monkeyflower)	PR	M	FF	SN	EN
M. primuloides var. *pilosellus* (Primrose monkey-flower)	Y	M	M D	SN WH	WNA
M. suksdorfii (Suksdorf's monkey-flower)	Y	M	SC	RM SN WH SC NRM	WNA
M. tilingii (Subalpine monkey-flower)	Y	M	SC	RM SN SNC OR	WNA
M. veronicifolius (Olympic monkeyflower)	Y	M	ST	OR	EN
Mint: see *Monardella*					

Scientific and Common Names	Color	Bloom	Community	U.S. distribution	World distribution
Minuartia biflora (Siberian sandwort)	W	L	S	RM SN GB	NA AA CP
M. macrantha (Large-flowered sandwort)	W	M	FF	RM	EN
M. obtusiloba (Alpine sandwort)	W	E	FF	RM SN SNC OR GB	WNA AA
M. rubella (Red sandwort)	W	M	D F	RM SN SNC OR	AA CP
M. stricta	W	L	S F	RM	NA AA
Monardella odoratissima var. *parvifolia* (Alpine mint)	PR	M	SC	SN	EN
Monkeyflower: see *Mimulus*					
Montia chamissoi (Water springbeauty)	W	M	M	SN WH SNC	WNA
Moss campion, Moss pink: see *Silene*					
Moss heath, Moss plant: see *Cassiope*					
Mountain ash: see *Sorbus*					
Mountain pride: see *Penstemon*					
Mouse-ear: see *Cerastium*					
Mousetail: see *Myosurus*					
Mugwort: see *Artemisia*					
Muhlenbergia richardsonis (Richardson's muhly)	G	M	T	SN WH	NA
Muhly: see *Muhlenbergia*					
Muskroot: see *Adoxa*					
Muttongrass: see *Poa*					
Myosotis alpestris ssp. *asiatica* (Alpine forget-me-not)	B	M-L	T	RM GB	WNA CP
Myosurus minimus ssp. *montanus* (Mousetail)	Y-G	M-L	ST	SN WH SNC NRM	WNA
Nailwort: see *Paronychia*					
Nama densum (Matted nama)	PR	M	SC	SN WH SC GB	WNA

Scientific and Common Names	Color	Bloom	Community	U.S. distribution	World distribution
Navarretia breweri (Brewer's navarretia)	Y	M	T S	SN WH SNC NRM	WNA
Needlegrass: see *Stipa*					
Nothocalais alpestris (Alpine lake-agoseris)	Y	M	T SC	SN WH SNC NRM	WNA
Oakfern: see *Carpogymnia*					
Oat: see *Avenochloa; Helictotrichon*					
Old man's beard: see *Senecio*					
Old-man-of-the-mountains: see *Hymenoxys*					
Onion: see *Allium*					
Oniongrass: see *Melica*					
Orchid: see *Limnorchis*					
Oreonana clementis (Clements' carrot)	W PR	M	FF	SN	EN
Oreoxis alpina (Alpine parsley)	Y	E	FF T	RM	EN
O. bakeri (Baker's parsley)	W-Y	M	TA	RM	EN
O. humilis (Dwarf parsley)	W-Y	M	TA	RM	EN
Orochaenactis thysanocarpa (Mountain dusty maiden)	G-Y	L	FF	SN	EN
Orthocarpus imbricatus (Owlclover)	P-PR	M	T	SC OR	EN
Oryzopsis exigua (Little ricegrass)	G	M	FF	SC NRM GB	WNA
O. hymenoides (Indian ricegrass)	G-Y	M	SC FF	SN WH SNC	WNA
O. kingii (King's ricegrass)	G	M	ST T	SN	EN
Owlclover: see *Orthocarpus*					
Oxalis acetosella ssp. *montana* (Common woodsorrel)	W-P	M	K	PR	ENA CP

Scientific and Common Names	Color	Bloom	Community	U.S. distribution	World distribution
Oxyria digyna (Alpine sorrel)	P	M	G B SC R	RM SN SNC OR GB PR	CP
Oxytropis cusickii (Cusick's locoweed)	Y-W	M	FF T	SNC OR NRM	WNA
O. deflexa (Pendant-pod locoweed)	W B	M	M	SN	WNA BA
O. luteola (Yellow locoweed)	Y	M	FF B	SNC OR NRM	WNA
O. oreophila (Rock-loving locoweed)	P	M	TA	WH GB	WNA
O. parryi (Parry's locoweed)	PR	M	FF	RM SN WH	WNA
O. podocarpa (Alpine locoweed)	P-PR	M	FF T	RM NRM	AA
O. viscida (Sticky locoweed)	W PR	M	T	RM SN WH NC OR	WNA
Paintbrush: see *Castilleja*					
Papaver kluanense (Alpine poppy)	Y-W	M	TA B	RM	EN
Parnassia kotzebuei	W	L	R	RM	AA
P. palustris var. *californica* (California grass-of-Parnassus)	W	L	ST	SN	WNA CP
Paronychia argyrocoma var. *albi-montana* (Mt. Washington whitlowwort)	Y-G	L	TA B	PR	EN
P. pulvinata (Alpine nailwort)	Y-G	E	FF	RM	EN

Parrya: see *Phoenicaulis*
Parsley: see *Cymopterus,*
   Oreoxis, Podistera,
   Pseudocymopterus
Partridge foot: see *Luetkea*
Pasqueflower: see *Pulsatilla*
Pearlwort: see *Sagina*

Scientific and Common Names	Color	Bloom	Community	U.S. distribution	World distribution
Pedicularis attollens (Elephant snout)	P	M	M	SN WH SC	WNA
P. contorta (Coiled-beak lousewort)	W-Y	M	T FF	SNC NRM	WNA
P. groenlandica (Little red elephant, Elephant head, Elephantella)	PR	M	M	RM SN SNC OR NRM	NA AA
P. groenlandica ssp. *surrecta*	PR	M	M	RM SN SNC NRM GB	WNA
P. ornithorhyncha (Bird's beak lousewort)	PR	M	M	SNC	WNA AA
P. paddoensis (Mt. Adams lousewort)	Y PR	M	T	SC	EN
P. parryi (Parry's lousewort)	W	E	FF	RM	EN
P. rainieriensis (Mt. Rainier lousewort)	Y	M	M T	SC	EN
P. sudetica ssp. *scopulorum* (Rocky Mountain lousewort)	P	M	M	RM	CP
P. thompsonii (Thompson's lousewort)	PR	M	T	NC NRM	WNA
Pellaea breweri (Brewer's cliffbrake)	N	N	R	SN WH SNC GB	WNA
Penstemon davidsonii (Creeping penstemon)	PR-B	M	B TA FF R	SN SC	WNA
P. hallii (Hall's penstemon)	B-PR	M	SC B	RM	EN
P. harbourii (Harbour's penstemon)	B	M	SC	RM	EN
P. heterodoxus (Sierran penstemon)	B PR	M	TA T	SN WH GB	EN
P. newberryi (Mountain pride)	P-PR	M	SC TA R	SN	EN

Scientific and Common Names	Color	Bloom	Community	U.S. distribution	World distribution
Penstemon speciosis ssp. *kennedyi* (Showy penstemon)	B PR	M	SC	SN WH	EN
P. tolmiei (Alpine penstemon)	B-PR Y	M	T TA	SNC	EN
P. whippleanus (Dark beardtongue)	W PR	M	D K	RM	EN
Perideridia gairdneri (Gairdner's squaw-root)	W P	M	M	SN SNC	WNA
P. parishii (Parish's squaw-root)	W P	M	M	SN GB	EN
Petasites frigidus var. *nivalis* (Sweet coltsfoot)	W	L	ST	SNC OR NRM	WNA
Petrophytum hendersonii (Henderson's rockspiraea)	W	M	R	OR	EN
Phacelia frigida (Timberline scorpionweed)	PR-W	M	TA G	SN WH SC	WNA
P. glandulosa (San Juan scorpionweed)	PR	M	SC	RM	EN
P. sericea (Purple fringe)	PR	M	D K	RM SNC OR	WNA
Phegopteris connectilis (Long beechfern)	N	N	S	PR	NA
Phippsia algida (Icegrass)	G	M	F-ST	RM	AA CP
Phleum alpinum (Alpine timothy)	G	M	T	RM SN SNC OR PR	CP
Phlox condensata (Alpine phlox)	W-PR	M	FF	RM SN WH GB	WNA
P. covillei (Coville's phlox)	PR	M	FF	SN WH	EN
P. diffusa (Spreading phlox)	PR	M	FF	SN WH SNC	WNA
P. diffusa ssp. *subcarinata*	W-PR	M	FF SC	SN WH SNC	WNA
P. dispersa	W	M	FF	SN	EN

Scientific and Common Names	Color	Bloom	Community	U.S. distribution	World distribution
Phlox stansburyi (Stansbury's phlox)	P W	M	FF SC	SN WH SRM	WNA
Phoenicaulis cheiranthoides (Common parrya)	?	M	SC	SN SC NRM GB	WNA
P. eurycarpa (Broad-podded parrya)	Y	M	SC	SN WH NRM	WNA
Phyllodoce breweri (Brewer's mountain heather)	P	M	ST S	SN	EN
P. caerulea (Mountain heath)	P	E	S	PR	ENA CP
P. empetriformis (Pink mountain heather)	P	M	S	SNC OR NRM GB	WNA AA
P. glanduliflora (Ivory or Yellow mountain heather)	W	M	S	SNC OR NRM GB	WNA AA
Physaria alpestris (Alpine double bladderpod)	Y	M	SC	RM SNC	WNA
Pinguicula vulgaris (Common butterwort)	PR	M	ST	SNC OR	CP
Pink: see *Silene*					
Poa alpigena (Speargrass)	G	M	T F M	PR	AA CP
P. alpina (Alpine bluegrass)	G	M	T	RM SNC PR	AA CP
P. arctica (Arctic bluegrass)	G	L	S	RM	AA CP
P. compressa (Canada bluegrass)	G	M	FF	PR	AA
P. epilis (Skyline bluegrass)	G	M	T	RM SN SNC NRM	WNA
P. fendleriana (Muttongrass)	G	M	D SC	RM	WNA
P. fernaldiana (Wavy bluegrass)	G	M	B TA FF	PR	AA

Scientific and Common Names	Color	Bloom	Community	U.S. distribution	World distribution
Poa glauca (Rock bluegrass)	G	M	T FF D	RM SN WH NRM GB PR	AA CP
P. gracillima (Pacific bluegrass)	G	M	TA	SN SNC NRM	WNA
P. grayana (Gray's bluegrass)	G	M	T	RM SNC	WNA
P. hanseni (Hansen's bluegrass)	G	M	M SC	SN WH	EN
P. incurva (Incurved bluegrass)	G	M	B FF	SN WH	EN
P. juncifolia (Rush-leaved bluegrass)	G	M	M	SN WH NRM	WNA
P. lettermanii (Letterman's bluegrass)	G	M	FF SC	RM SN WH SNC NRM	WNA
P. nervosa (Nerved bluegrass)	G	M	T	SNC	WNA
P. pattersonii (Patterson's bluegrass)	G	M	F ST	RM SN SC	WNA
P. pringlei (Pringle's bluegrass)	G	M	SC TA	SN WH SC	WNA
P. reflexa (Nodding bluegrass)	G	L	S	RM	EN
P. saltuensis	G	M	S T	PR	ENA
P. sandbergii (Sandberg's bluegrass)	G	M	D K	RM SNC OR NRM	WNA AA
Podagrostis humilis	G	L	S	RM SNC	WNA
Podistera eastwoodii (Eastwood's parsley)	Y	M	T	RM	EN
P. nevadensis (Sierra parsley)	Y	M	FF	SN WH	EN
Polemonium brandegei (Honey sky pilot)	W	M	B SC TA	RM	EN
P. caeruleum ssp. *amygdalinum* (Western Jacob's ladder)	B	E-M	ST	SN SNC NRM	WNA

Scientific and Common Names	Color	Bloom	Community	U.S. distribution	World distribution
Polemonium chartaceum (Mason's polemonium)	B	M	FF	WH SC GB	WNA
P. delicatum (Subalpine Jacob's ladder)	B	M	K B	RM	WNA
P. elegans (Elegant polemonium)	B	M	T	SNC GB	EN
P. eximium (Sierra sky pilot)	B W	M	FF	SN	EN
P. viscosum (Sticky sky pilot)	B	E-M	D T	RM NC GB NRM	WNA
Polygonum davisiae (Davis' bistort)	G W	M	FF	SN SC	WNA
P. douglasii var. *johnstonii* (Douglas' knotweed)	G	M	FF	SN	WNA
P. minimum (Dwarf knotweed)	W	M	R	SNC NRM	WNA
P. newberryi (Newberry's knotweed)	Y	M	SC	SNC OR	WNA
Polystichum lonchitis (Mountain hollyfern)	N	N	R	SNC OR	NA CP
Poppy: see *Papaver*					
Potentilla brevifolia (Short-leaved cinquefoil)	?	M	T	NRM GB	EN
P. breweri (Brewer's cinquefoil)	Y	M	FF	SN WH	WNA
P. concinna (Alpine five-finger)	Y	M	T	RM	WNA
P. diversifolia (Blueleaf cinquefoil)	Y	M	S D	RM SN SNC OR	WNA
P. drummondii (Drummond's cinquefoil)	Y	M	M	SN WH SNC OR	WNA
P. flabellifolia (Mt. Rainier cinquefoil)	Y	M	M	SN SNC OR	WNA

Scientific and Common Names	Color	Bloom	Community	U.S. distribution	World distribution
Potentilla fruticosa (Shrubby cinquefoil)		M	M SC	RM SN WH SNC OR NRM GB PR	NA CP
P. glandulosa ssp. *nevadensis* (Sticky cinquefoil)	W-Y	M	FF	SN SNC	WNA
P. hookeriana	Y	M	T	RM	EN
P. hyparctica (Arctic cinquefoil)	W-Y	M	F	PR	AA CP
P. labradorica (Rough cinquefoil)	Y	M	H F B FF	PR	ENA AA
P. ledebouriana (Alpine cinquefoil)	Y	M	FF	RM	AA
P. nivea (Snow cinquefoil)	Y	M	FF	RM	AA CP
P. ovina	Y	M	FF	RM	EN
P. pensylvanica (Pennsylvania cinquefoil)	Y	M	T	WH	NA AA
P. pseudosericea (Strigose cinquefoil)	Y	M	T	RM SN WH NRM	WNA
P. quinquifolia	Y	M	T	RM NRM	EN
P. robbinsiana (Dwarf cinquefoil)	Y	E	F	PR	EN
P. rubricaulis (Red-stemmed cinquefoil)	Y	M	T	RM SN	AA
P. rupincola (Rock cinquefoil)	Y	M	R	RM	EN
P. subjuga	Y	M	T	RM	EN
P. tridentata (Three-toothed cinquefoil, Sibbaldiopsis)	W	M	B	PR	AA
P. villosa (Villous cinquefoil)	Y	M	FF	NC OR	BA

Scientific and Common Names	Color	Bloom	Community	U.S. distribution	World distribution
Prenanthes boottii (Boott's rattlesnake root)	P	L	ST	PR	EN
P. trifoliolata var. *nana*	?	L	B H	PR	ENA
Primrose: see *Primula*					
Primula angustifolia (Alpine primrose)	P-PR	E	FF T	RM	EN
P. parryi (Parry's primrose)	P-PR	M	M	RM	EN
P. suffrutescens (Sierra or Muir's primrose)	P-PR	M	FF	SN	EN
Prunella vulgaris var. *lanceolata* (Selfheal)	P-PR	M	K	PR	NA
Pseudocymopterus montanus (Yellow mountain parsley)	Y	M	T K	RM	WNA
Ptilagrostis porteri	G	L	B	RM	EN
Pulsatilla patens ssp. *multifida* (Pasqueflower)	W-PR	E	S	RM	WNA
P. occidentalis (Western pasqueflower)	W	E	T	SN SNC NRM	WNA
Purple fringe: see *Phacelia*					
Pussypaws: see *Calyptridium*					
Pussytoes: see *Antennaria*					
Quillwort: see *Isoetes*					
Rabbitbrush: see *Chrysothamnus*					
Ragwort: see *Ligularia; Senecio*					
Raillardella argentea (Silky raillardella)	Y	M	FF	SN WH SC	AA
Ranunculus adoneus (Snow buttercup)	Y	E	S	RM	EN
R. alismaefolius (Caltha-flowered buttercup)	Y	E	S	RM SN WH NRM	WNA

Scientific and Common Names	Color	Bloom	Community	U.S. distribution	World distribution
Ranunculus cooleyae (Cooley's buttercup)	Y	M	S	OR	WNA AA
R. eschscholtzii (Snowbed buttercup)	Y	M	S	RM SN WH SNC OR	WNA
R. gelidus (Alpine buttercup)	Y	M	B	RM	EN
R. glaberrimus (Sagebrush buttercup)	Y	E	FF	WH	WNA
R. macauleyi (Black-headed buttercup)	Y	M	S	RM	EN
R. pedatifidus (Birdfoot buttercup)	Y	E	T	RM	CP
R. pygmaeus (Pygmy buttercup)	Y	M	S	RM	CP
R. verecundus (Timberline buttercup)	Y	M	SC	SC NRM	WNA
Raspberry: see *Rubus* Rattle: see *Rhinanthus* Rattlesnake root: see *Prenanthes* Rattleweed: see *Astragalus* Reedgrass: see *Calamagrostis*					
Rhinanthus borealis (Yellow rattle)	Y	L	T	PR	ENA AA
Rhodiola integrifolia (King's crown)	P Y	M	T	RM SN WH SNC OR	CP
Rhododendron canadense (Rhodora)	P-W	E	M	PR	ENA
R. lapponicum (Lapland rosebay)	PR	E	FF	PR	AA CP
Rhodora: see *Rhododendron*					
Ribes acerifolium (Maple-leaved currant)	R	M	TA	SNC OR	EN
R. cereum (Wax currant)	P	M	B	RM SN WH	WNA
R. glandulosum (Sticky currant)	W-P	M	B	PR	ENA AA

Scientific and Common Names	Color	Bloom	Community	U.S. distribution	World distribution
Ribes lacustre (Swamp black currant)	?	M	M	PR	NA
R. montigenum (Mountain currant)	P	M	B	RM SN SNC	WNA
Ricegrass: see *Oryzopsis*					
Rockberry: see *Empetrum*					
Rockbrake: see *Cryptogramma*					
Rockcress: see *Arabis*					
Rock fringe: see *Epilobium*					
Rockjasmine, Rockprimrose: see *Androsace*					
Rockspiraea: see *Petrophytum*					
Rockstar: see *Lithophragma*					
Romanzoffia sitchensis (Sitka romanzoffia)	?	E-M	FF TA	SNC NRM	WNA AA
Rosebay: see *Rhododendron*					
Rose crown: see *Clementsia*					
Rubus chamaemorus (Baked-apple berry)	W	M	M	PR	AA CP
R. pubescens (Dwarf raspberry)	W-P	M	ST K	PR	NA AA
Rumex californicus (Willow dock)	BR-R	M	M	SN	EN
R. paucifolius ssp. *gracilescens* (Few-leaved dock)	R	L	FF	SN	EN
R. triangulivalvis	Y	M	FF	SN	EN
Rush: see *Juncus*					
Rydbergia: see *Hymenoxys*					
Runningpine: see *Lycopodium*					
Sage, Sagebrush, Sagewort: see *Artemisia*					
Sagina saginoides (Arctic pearlwort)	W	M	F	RM SN SNC NRM GB	AA CP

Scientific and Common Names	Color	Bloom	Community	U.S. distribution	World distribution
Salix arctica (Arctic willow)	G-BR	E-M	S	RM SN SNC PR	AA BA
S. arctophila (Arctic-loving willow)	G-BR	M	G T	PR	ENA AA
S. argyrocarpa (Silver willow)	G-BR	M	B	PR	EN
S. brachycarpa (Short-fruited willow)	W	E-M	B W	RM SN WNA	NA AA
S. cascadensis (Cascade willow)	G-BR	E-M	S	RM SN SNC	WNA
S. commutata	G-BR	E	ST	SNC OR NRM GB	WNA AA
S. eastwoodiae (Eastwood's willow)	G-BR	M	ST	SN SC	WNA
S. glauca (Blue willow)	G	M	B SC	RM SC	WNA
S. herbacea (Dwarf willow)	R-BR	E	S F	PR	AA CP
S. jepsoni (Jepson's willow)	G-BR	E	W	SN	EN
S. nivalis (Snow willow)	P-Y	M	S T	RM SN SNC OR	WNA
S. orestera (Sierra willow)	G-BR	M	ST	SN GB	EN
S. planifolia (Tea-leaved willow)	BR	E	ST	PR	ENA
S. phylicifolia ssp. *planifolia* (Plain-leaved or Nelson's willow)	BR	E	ST F W	RM SN SNC NRM	WNA
S. uva-ursi (Bearberry willow)	G-BR	M	B	PR	ENA AA
Sambucus microbotrys (Mountain red elderberry)	W	M	FF	SN NRM	WNA
S. racemosa (Red-berried elder)	W	M	B	SN	WNA

Scientific and Common Names	Color	Bloom	Community	U.S. distribution	World distribution
Sandwort: see *Arenaria, Minuartia*					
Saussurea weberi (Weber's saussurea)	Y	M	S	RM	EN
Saxifraga: We are leaving all species in the genus *Saxifraga,* rather than putting them in the genera used by W. A. Weber.					
Saxifraga adscendens (Wedge-leaved saxifrage)	W	M	T	RM SNC NRM GB	CP
S. aestivalis (Summer saxifrage)	W	M	ST	SNC	AA BA
S. aizoides (Yellow mountain saxifrage)	Y	L	M	NC NRM PR	AA CP
S. aizoon var. *neogaea* (White mountain saxifrage)	W	M	B	PR	AA CP
S. aprica (Sierra saxifrage)	W	M	FF	SN SC GB	WNA
S. bronchialis (Dotted saxifrage)	W	M	B	RM SNC NRM	WNA
S. bryophora (Bud saxifrage)	W	M	D R	SN	EN
S. caespitosa (Tufted saxifrage)	W	M	T FF	RM SNC OR	AA CP
S. cernua (Nodding saxifrage)	W	M	B	RM NC	AA CP
S. debilis (Weak-stemmed saxifrage)	W	M	B	RM SN SNC	WNA
S. ferruginea (Alaska saxifrage)	W	M	ST	SNC OR NRM	WNA AA
S. flagellaris (Whiplash saxifrage)	Y	M	F SC	RM	AA CP
S. foliolosa (Leafy saxifrage)	G	M-L	M	RM PR	AA CP
S. hirculus (Arctic saxifrage)	Y	M-L	M	RM	AA CP

Scientific and Common Names	Color	Bloom	Community	U.S. distribution	World distribution
Saxifraga lyallii (Red-stemmed saxifrage)	W	M	B	NC NRM	WNA
S. occidentalis (Rusty saxifrage)	W	E	R	SNC OR NRM	WNA
S. odontoloma (Brook saxifrage)	W	M	M	RM SN SNC OR	WNA
S. oppositifolia (Purple saxifrage)	PR	M	R	SNC OR NRM PR	AA CP
S. oregana var. *montanensis* (Oregon saxifrage)	W	M	M	RM SN SNC	WNA
S. rhomboidea (Snowball saxifrage)	W	E	T	RM	WNA
S. rivularis (Alpine brook saxifrage)	W	L	B	RM PR	CP
S. serpyllifolia (Goldbloom saxifrage)	Y	E	FF R	RM	CP
S. tolmiei (Tolmie's saxifrage)	W	M	R S	SN SNC OR	WNA
Saxifrage: see *Chrysosplenium, Saxifraga, Telesonix*					
Scirpus atrocinctus (Dark-girdled bulrush)	B	M	T	PR	NA AA
S. caespitosus (Deer's hair)	G	M	T S	SNC NRM PR	NA AA CP
S. clementis (Clements' bulrush)	B	M	T	SN	EN
S. criniger (Fringed bulrush)	B	M	S T	SN	WNA
S. pumilus (Low clubrush)	G-BR	M	T	SN	WNA CP
Scorpionweed: see *Phacelia*					
Sedge: see *Carex; Kobresia*					
Sedum lanceolatum (Yellow stonecrop)	Y	M-L	FF T	RM SN OR	WNA
S. obtusatum (Sierra stonecrop)	P	M	R	SN SNC	WNA

Scientific and Common Names	Color	Bloom	Community	U.S. distribution	World distribution
Sedum stenopetalum (Narrow-petaled stonecrop)	Y	M	B	SN SNC OR	WNA
Selaginella densa (Rock clubmoss)	N	N	FF T	RM SNC NRM GB	WNA
S. watsonii (Alpine clubmoss)	N	N	FF	SN WH NRM GB	WNA
Selfheal: see *Prunella*					
Senecio canus (Woolly butterweed)	Y	L	SC FF	RM SN WH SNC	WNA
S. crassulus (Thick ragwort)	Y	L	M	RM	EN
S. crocatus (Saffron ragwort)	O	L	S	RM	EN
S. cymbalarioides (Rocky Mountain butterweed)	Y	M	M ST	RM SNC SN	WNA
S. dimorphophyllus (Two-leaved ragwort)	Y	L	S	RM	EN
S. fremontii var. *blitoides* (Dwarf mountain butterweed)	Y	L	TA	RM SN SNC	WNA
S. integerrimus var. *major* (Lambstongue groundsel)	Y	M	TA SC	WH	WNA
S. lugens (Black-tipped butterweed)	Y	M	T	OR NRM	WNA AA
S. neowebsteri (Olympic butterweed)	Y	L	TA	OR	EN
S. pattersonianus (Mono butterweed)	Y	L	B	SN GB	EN

Scientific and Common Names	Color	Bloom	Community	U.S. distribution	World distribution
Senecio pauciflorus (Rayless alpine butterweed)	O-R	L	T	SN SNC	WNA
S. porteri (Porter's butterweed)	Y	L	G B	RM GB	WNA
S. resedifolius (Arctic butterweed)	Y O	M	B	SNC NRM	AA CP
S. scorzonella	Y	L	T	WH	EN
S. triangularis (Old man's beard)	Y	M	ST	SN SNC OR	WNA
S. werneriaefolius	Y	M	SC FF	RM SN WH	WNA
Shooting star: see *Dodecatheon*					
Sibbaldia procumbens (Sibbaldia)	Y	M	S	RM SN WH SNC OR GB PR	CP
Sibbaldiopsis: see *Potentilla*					
Silene acaulis ssp. *acaulescens* (Moss campion, Moss pink)	P	E-M	FF	RM SNC OR GB	CP
S. acaulis var. *arctica* (Moss campion)	P	E-M	FF	PR	CP
S. grayii (Gray's campion)	P	M	S	SC	EN
S. montana ssp. *bernardina* (Mountain catchfly)	W-P	M	TA SC	SN	WNA
S. parryi (Parry's catchfly)	G-W-PR	M	TA SC	SNC OR NRM GB	WNA
S. sargentii (Sargent's catchfly)	W-PR	M	R TA	SN WH	EN

Scientific and Common Names	Color	Bloom	Community	U.S. distribution	World distribution
Sitanion hanseni (Hansen's squirreltail)	G	M	FF	SN WH SC NRM GB	WNA
S. hystrix (Bottlebrush squirreltail)	G	M	D	SN WH SC	WNA
Sky pilot: see *Polemonium*					
Smelowskia calycina (Fernleaf candytuft)	W	M	FF SC	RM NC OR NRM GB	WNA BA
S. ovalis (Olympic fernleaf candytuft)	W	E	FF T	SNC OR	EN
Smilacina trifolia (Three-leaved false Solomonseal)	W	M	M	NRM PR	BA
Snowberry: see *Gaultheria* Snowlover: see *Chionophila*					
Solidago cutleri (Alpine goldenrod)	Y	L	FF	PR	ENA
S. decumbens (Dwarf goldenrod)	Y	M	TA SC	RM SNC	WNA
S. macrophylla (Large-leaved goldenrod)	Y	L	K	PR	ENA
S. multiradiata (Many-rayed goldenrod)	Y	L	FF M	RM SN WH SNC	NA BA
S. randii (Rand's goldenrod)	Y	L	B	PR	ENA
S. spathulata var. *nana* (Alpine goldenrod)	Y	L	M T	RM SC	WNA
Solomonsplume, Solomonseal, false: see *Smilacina*					
Sorbus scopulina (Mountain ash)	W	M	K B TA	SNC OR	WNA
Sorrel: see *Oxalis; Oxyria* Speargrass: see *Poa*					

Scientific and Common Names	Color	Bloom	Community	U.S. distribution	World distribution
Speedwell: see *Veronica*					
Spikerush: see *Eleocharis*					
Spiraea latifolia (Spiraea or Meadowsweet)	P	M	K	PR	ENA
S. septentrionalis (Northern meadowsweet)	W	M	K	PR	ENA AA
Spiranthes romanzoffiana (Hooded ladies' tresses)	W	M	T M	SNC	NA
Springbeauty: see *Claytonia; Montia*					
Squashberry: see *Viburnum*					
Squawroot: see *Perideridia*					
Squirreltail: see *Sitanion*					
Starflower: see *Trientalis*					
Starwort: see *Callitriche; Stellaria*					
Steer's head: see *Dicentra*					
Stellaria calycantha (Northern stitchwort)	W	M	M	RM SNC OR PR	NA CP
S. crispa (Chamisso's starwort)	W-G	M	R B	SN SNC	WNA AA
S. irrigua (Siberian starwort)	W	M	FF T	RM	BA
S. laeta (Alpine chickweed)	W	M	T	RM	CP
S. longipes (Long-stalked stitchwort)	W	M	T	RM SN WH SNC OR	CP
S. umbellata (Umbrella starwort)	G	M	M T	RM SN SNC	WNA BA
Stickseed: see *Hackelia*					
Stitchwort: see *Stellaria*					
Stipa columbiana (Columbia needlegrass)	G	M	TA SC	SN	WNA AA
S. elmeri (Elmer's needlegrass)	G	M	B	SN SNC	WNA

Scientific and Common Names	Color	Bloom	Community	U.S. distribution	World distribution
Stipa lettermanii (Letterman's needlegrass)	G	M	FF	SN SC NRM	WNA
S. occidentalis (Western needlegrass)	G	M	FF	SN WH SNC GB	WNA
S. pinetorum (Pine needlegrass)	G	M	B	RM SN WH NRM	WNA
Stonecrop: see *Sedum*					
Strawberry: see *Fragaria*					
Streptanthus cordatus (Perennial twistflower)	PR	M	TA SC	RM SN WH NRM	WNA
Streptopus amplexifolius var. *americanus* (Clasping-leaved twisted-stalk)	G-W	M	K	PR	NA
S. oreopolus (Mountain twisted-stalk)	W	M	K	PR	ENA
S. roseus var. *perspectus* (Rosy twisted-stalk)	PR	M	K	PR	ENA
Sulphurflower: see *Eriogonum*					
Sundew: see *Drosera*					
Sunflower: see *Eriophyllum*					
Sunspot: see *Haplopappus*					
Sweetbroom: see *Hedysarum*					
Sweetgrass: see *Hierochloe*					
Sweetvetch: see *Hedysarum*					
Swertia perennis (Star gentian)	B	M	M	RM	WNA CP
Synthris lanuginosa (Woolly kittentail)	PR B	M	T	OR	EN
S. missurica (Lewis & Clark's kittentail)	PR	M	R FF	NRM GB	WNA
Tanacetum canum (Gray tansy)	Y	L	B	SN	EN
Tansy: see *Tanacetum*					
Tansy-mustard: see *Descurainia*					

Scientific and Common Names	Color	Bloom	Community	U.S. distribution	World distribution
Taraxacum ceratophorum (Tundra dandelion)	Y	M	T	RM SNC OR	WNA BA
T. eriophorum (Rocky Mountain dandelion)	Y	M	T	RM SNC OR NRM	WNA AA
T. lyratum (Alpine dandelion)	Y	M	B F	RM SNC OR	NA AA BA
T. officinale (Common dandelion)	Y	M	D	RM SN WH SNC OR	NA CP
T. phymatocarpum	Y	M	SC	RM	EN
Telesonix jamesii (Pink saxifrage, Boykinia)	P	E-M	R	RM	BA
Thalictrum alpinum (Alpine meadowrue)	G	E-M	T M	RM SN WH	CP
T. polygamum (Tall meadowrue)	W PR	M	TA	PR	ENA
Thistle: see *Cirsium*					
Thlaspi alpestre (Alpine candytuft)	W	E	FF T	RM SC NRM	CP
Thoroughwort: see *Bupleurum*					
Thrift: see *Armeria*					
Ticklegrass: see *Agrostis; Podagrostis; Ptilagrostis*					
Timothy: see *Phleum*					
Toadflax: see *Comandra*					
Townsendia condensata (Cushion Easter-daisy)	PR	M	FF	WH NRM GB	WNA
T. leptotes (Alpine Easter-daisy)	W-P	M	TA SC	RM WH NRM	WNA
T. rothrockii (Rocky Mountain Easter-daisy)	PR	M	T	RM	EN
Trientalis borealis (Starflower)	W	M	D	PR	ENA

Scientific and Common Names	Color	Bloom	Community	U.S. distribution	World distribution
Trifolium dasyphyllum (Alpine clover)	P	E-M	FF	RM	EN
T. monanthum (Carpet clover)	W	M	S	SN WH GB	EN
T. monoense (Mono clover)	P	M	B TA	SN WH	EN
T. nanum (Dwarf clover)	P	E	FF	RM	EN
T. parryi (Parry's clover)	P	M	S D	RM	EN
T. stenolobum (San Juan clover)	P	M-L	T SC S	RM	EN
Trisetum spicatum ssp. *spicatum* (Spike trisetum; Marmot-tail grass)	G	M	T FF	RM SN WH SNC OR NRM GB PR	CP BP
T. triflorum (Three-flowered trisetum)	G	M	B	RM SN SNC NRM PR	CP BP
Trollius laxus (Globeflower)	W	M	M	RM SNC OR	NA
Twinflower: see *Linnaea* Twistflower: see *Streptanthus* Twisted-stalk: see *Streptopus*					
Vaccinium angustifolium (Sweet blueberry)	W	M	B	PR	ENA CP
V. cespitosum (Dwarf bilberry)	P	M	D	RM SN SNC OR PR	NA
V. deliciosum (Rainier huckleberry)	P	M	T	SNC OR	CP
V. myrtilloides (Velvet-leaf blueberry)	Y-G	E	TA SC	PR	ENA
V. oxycoccos (Small cranberry)	P	M	S	PR	AA CP
V. uliginosum (Bog bilberry)	P	M	T	PR	NA CP
Vaccinium vitis-idaea var. *minus* (Mountain cranberry)	P	M	R	PR	CP

Scientific and Common Names	Color	Bloom	Community	U.S. distribution	World distribution
Vahlodea atropurpurea ssp. *latifolia* (Mountain hairgrass)	G	M-L	S	RM SNC OR PR	CP
Valerian: see *Valeriana*					
Valeriana capitata ssp. *acutiloba* (Globe valerian)	W	M	T	RM	WNA
V. edulis (Edible valerian)	W	M	T	RM	WNA
Veratrum californicum (Cornlily)	G-W	M	ST	RM SN SNC GB	WNA CA
V. viride (Indian poke)	Y-G	L	M	PR	ENA
Veronica wormskjoldii (Alpine speedwell)	B	M	M	RM SNC OR PR	AA CP
Viburnum edule (Squashberry, Highbush cranberry)	W	L	D	PR	NA AA BA
Viola adunca ssp. *bellidifolia* (Mountain blue violet)	P	M	T	RM SN SNC	NA
V. biflora (Twinflower violet)	Y	M	B	RM	CP
V. cucullata (Blue marsh violet)	B	M	M	PR	ENA
V. flettii (Olympic violet)	PR	M	R	OR	EN
V. orbiculata (Round-leaved violet)	Y	M	D	SNC NRM	WNA
V. palustris (Alpine marsh violet)	W PR	M	ST	PR	NA CP
V. purpurea ssp. *xerophyta* (Mountain violet)	Y-PR-BR	M	TA SC	SN	EN
Violet: see *Viola*					
Wallflower: see *Erysimum*					
Wandlily: see *Zigadenus*					

Scientific and Common Names	Color	Bloom	Community	U.S. distribution	World distribution
Water springbeauty: see *Montia*					
Water-starwort: see *Callitriche*					
Wheatgrass: see *Agropyron*					
Whitlowgrass: see *Draba*					
Whitlowwort: see *Paronychia*					
Willow: see *Salix*					
Willowherb: see *Epilobium*					
Wintercress: see *Barbarea*					
Wintergreen: see *Gaultheria*					
Woodfern: see *Dryopteris*					
Woodrush: see *Luzula*					
Woodsia scopulina (Rocky Mountain woodsia)	N	N	D B	RM SNC	NA AA
Woollypod: see *Astragalus*					
Yarrow: see *Achillea*					
Zigadenus elegans (Wandlily, Death camas)	W	E-M	T	RM SNC OR NRM	WNA AA

Glossary

ANTHER: The pollen-producing part of the stamen in a flower.

ANTHOCYANIN: Water-soluble pigments, usually red, blue or violet, in the cell-sap of leaves, stems, flowers and fruits of plants.

BIPOLAR: Associated with both north and south polar regions. Certain organisms with a bipolar distribution are found around the North and South poles.

BRACT: A modified leaf, usually small and scalelike, sometimes large and brightly colored, growing at the base of a flower or on its stalk.

CALYX: The composite group of sepals.

CHROMOSOME: The thread- or rodlike bodies bearing genes (hereditary bodies) in the cells of plants and animals.

CIRCUMPOLAR: Around one of the terrestrial poles.

CIRQUE: A deeply eroded depression with steep slopes in areas which have been glaciated. Occurs at the point of origin of glaciers; therefore is usually close to the top of mountains.

CLIMAX VEGETATION: Vegetation that is mature, self-maintaining, self-reproducing and permanent. It is in balance with the prevailing climate.

COROLLA: The composite group of petals.

CRUSTOSE: Forming a thin, brittle crust; used in reference to a lichen on rock that cannot be pulled off.

CUSHION PLANT: A herbaceous perennial plant forming a dense, rounded, plump mass of short stems and many leaves, as in moss campion.

ECOSYSTEM: A community of interdependent, interacting living organisms within a specific environment, such as a marsh.

FELLFIELD: A type of tundra that is thirty-five to fifty percent bare rock, with cushion plants, mosses and lichens between.

FELSENMEER: A "sea of rocks," an assemblage of angular rock fragments completely mantling the surface, common in mountainous regions above the treelimit where slopes are not too steep to hold the loose debris. Caused by frost action.

FILAMENT: The stalk of an anther.

FIRN: Snow of more than a year old, in the process of becoming glacier ice.

FOLIOSE: Leafy.

FROST BOIL: An area of active annual churning caused by ice formation within soil, as in areas denuded by frost scars.

FROST SCAR: A break in vegetation produced by wind and snow action, leaving topsoil or mineral soil exposed to frost action.

FRUTICOSE: Shrubby; applied to a lichen with an erect, usually branched, body.

GLACIER: Unlike a snowbank, a glacier is a large body of ice moving slowly down a slope, plain or valley, carrying, pushing or depositing loose rock and eroding land forms.

GLEY: Soil formed under the influence of waterlogging and lack of oxygen; usually neutral gray in color and containing reddish-brown deposits of ferrous oxide. Typical of tundra soils.

GOPHER ESKER: Small narrow ridge of gravel and sand, resulting from the winter tunneling of pocket gophers. Resembles a glacial esker in being formed under snow in a long tubular shape.

GRAUPEL: Granular snow pellets, also called "soft hail."

INVOLUCRE: A number of closely associated bracts under a flower or inflorescence.

KRUMMHOLZ: Scrubby, stunted growth-form of trees, characteristically found at the limit of tree growth in mountains. From German meaning "crooked wood."

LICHEN: A single plant formed by the symbiotic relationship of an alga and a fungus, which forms crustose, foliose or fruticose bodies.

MAT: Plant growth form that is densely interwoven or felted, or growing in a thick tangle, such as dwarf clover.

MICROCLIMATE: Climatic conditions peculiar to a very small area, such as a space between clumps of grass.

MORAINE: The accumulation of rock material transported by a glacier, occurring in various topographic forms such as ridges, or more level areas.

NEEDLE ICE: Ice crystals that form just below the surface of the ground and vertical to it, raising the surface soil.

NIVATION: Process of forming gentle depressions; snow accumulation squeezes soil downslope during melting.

NIVATION DEPRESSION: An eroded sunken area caused by the action of snow accumulation.

NONVASCULAR PLANT: A plant that has no structures for transport of water and food. Lichens, algae and mosses are nonvascular.

NUNATAK: A body of land, such as a mountain top, projecting for some considerable time above a mass of ice and snow, or above a glacier. These "islands" of land formed refuges for animals and plants when glaciers were more extensive.

OVARY: Seed-producing part of the pistil.

PATTERNED GROUND: Characteristic land surface resulting from freeze-thaw processes that extrude buried rocks to the surface to form definite patterns.

PERIGYNIUM: The saclike bract below the pistillate flower of sedges of the genera *Carex* and *Kobresia* that, in fruit, becomes a flask-shaped envelope around the achene.

PERMAFROST: Permanently frozen ground, characteristic of arctic and subarctic regions and occasionally in alpine tundra.

PHOTOSYNTHESIS: The synthesis of carbohydrates from carbon dioxide and water by chlorophyll, using light as energy with oxygen as a by-product.

PINK SNOW: The effect of green algae (*Chlamydomonas nivalis*) with a high concentration of pink pigments (anthocyanins) growing in snow.

PISTIL: The seed-bearing organ of a flower, consisting of the ovary, stigma and style.

PLEISTOCENE: The geological epoch preceding the Recent in the Quaternary period of the Cenozoic era, which began about one or two million years ago and lasted for about one or two million years. Characterized by several glacial stages.

POLYPLOID: Having more than two sets of chromosomes; particularly frequent in tundra plants.

RHIZOME: An underground stem that produces shoots and roots at the nodes.

ROSETTE: A dense basal cluster of leaves arranged in circular overlapping fashion, as dandelion leaves. Arrangement assures maximum exposure to light.

SCREE: Accumulation of unsorted rock fragments, smaller pieces than on a talus slope, varying from the size of a fifty-cent piece to fist-size, resulting from in-place weathering.

SEPAL: A unit of the outer whorl of flower parts, usually green and resembling leaves or bracts, or with other colors in some flowers. The collective group of sepals is a calyx.

SNOWBED: Area where there is a perennial accumulation of snow.

SNOWLINE: A line, orographic or regional, marking the lower limit of perpetual snow.

SOIL HORIZON: A clearly visible zone in soil produced by hundreds of years of weathering and alteration by adding organic material.

SOIL PROFILE: A vertical section of the soil from the surface through all its horizons to the parent rock.

SOLIFLUCTION: The flow of saturated soil upon an impermeable layer of frozen ground or bedrock, under conditions of alternate freezing and thawing. Characteristic of tundra regions. Produces terraces and lobes making undulating landscape.

STAMEN: The part of a flower that produces pollen, consisting of an anther (containing the pollen) and a filament.

STIGMA: The upper part of the pistil of a flower, which receives the pollen and aids in its germination.

STYLE: The portion of the pistil between the stigma and the ovary in a flower.

TALUS: Accumulations of unstable rock fragments below steep slopes or cliffs; the fragments are sorted by gravity with the largest at the bottom.

THALLUS: A plant body not differentiated into leaves, stems and roots; one-to many-celled, as in lichens.

TIMBERLINE: The upper altitude or latitude at which erect marketable trees grow; not synonymous with treelimit.

TRANSPIRATION: The loss of water in vapor form from a plant, mostly through stomata and lenticels.

TREELIMIT: The point in altitude or latitude beyond which trees can no longer grow due to the interaction of their makeup with the complex of environment factors.

VASCULAR PLANT: A plant that has tubes in its stems for transport of water and food materials. Includes ferns and seed plants.

VENTURI: Refers to the increasing speed of wind and the drop in temperature and pressure, as air goes through a constriction.

VIVIPAROUS: Germinating while still attached to the parent plant, such as viviparous bistort.

References

Abrams, L. 1940–1960. Illustrated flora of the Pacific states: Washington, Oregon and California. Stanford Univ. Press, Palo Alto, Calif. 2771 pp., 4 vols. Illus.

Alexander, G. 1951. The natural history of high altitudes. Biol. 33 (3): 91–97.

Anderson, R. A. 1962. The lichen flora of the Dakota sandstone in north central Colorado. Bryol. 65 (3): 242–261.

Anonymous. 1962. Mount Washington. Mt. Washington Observatory, Inc. 1962. 12 pp.

Anonymous. 1964. Mountain flowers of New England. Appalachian Mountain Club, Boston. 147 pp. Illus.

Arnold, C. A. 1959. Some paleobotanical aspects of tundra development. Ecol. 40: 146–148.

Baker, M. 1961. The altitudinal distribution of mosquito larvae in the Colorado Front Range. Trans. of the Amer. Entomol. Soc. 231–246.

Bamberg, Samuel A. and J. Major. 1968. Ecology of the vegetation and soils associated with calcareous parent materials in three alpine regions of Montana. Ecol. Monogr. 38 (2): 127–169.

Bates, C. G. 1923. Physical requirements of Rocky Mountain trees. J. of Ag. Res. 24 (2): 97–164.

Beidleman, R. G. and W. A. Weber. 1958. Analysis of a pika hay pile. J. Mammal. 39: 599–600.

Benedict, James B. 1970. Downslope soil movement in a Colorado alpine region: rates, processes and climatic significance. Arctic and Alpine Res. 2 (3): 165–226.

Bent, Arthur B. (ed.). 1956. Winter on Mt. Washington. Mt. Washington Observatory, Gorham, N.H. 35 pp.

Billings, W. D. and L. C. Bliss. 1959. An alpine snowbank environment and its effects on vegetation, plant development and productivity. Ecol. 40 (3): 388–397.

———, E. E. C. Clebsch and H. A. Mooney. 1966. Photosynthesis and respiration rates of Rocky Mountain alpine plants under field conditions. The Amer. Midland Natur. 75 (1): 34–44.

—— and P. J. Godfrey. 1967. Photosynthetic utilization of internal carbon dioxide by hollow-stemmed plants. Sci. 158 (3797): 121–123.

—— and H. A. Mooney. 1959. An apparent frost hummock-sorted polygon cycle in the alpine tundra of Wyoming. Ecol. 40 (1): 16–20.

—— and H. A. Mooney. 1968. The ecology of arctic and alpine plants. Biol. Rev. 43: 481–530.

Bliss, L. C. 1956. A comparison of plant development in microenvironments of arctic and alpine tundras. Ecol. Monogr. 26: 303–337.

——. 1958. Seed germination in arctic and alpine species. Arctic. 11: 180–188.

——. 1960. Transpiration rates of arctic and alpine shrubs. Ecol. 41 (2): 386–389.

——. 1962. Adaptations of arctic and alpine plants to environmental conditions. Arctic. 15 (2): 117–144.

——. 1962. Caloric and lipid content in alpine tundra plants. Ecol. 43 (4): 753–757.

——. 1963. Alpine plant communities of the Presidential Range, N.H. Ecol. 44 (4): 678–697.

——. 1963. Alpine zone of the Presidential Range. Publ. by author, Edmonton, Canada. 62 pp.

——. 1966. Plant productivity in alpine microenvironments on Mt. Washington, N.H. Ecol. Monogr. 36: 125–155.

—— and E. B. Hadley. 1964. Photosynthesis and respiration of alpine lichens. Amer. J. of Bot. 51 (8): 870–874.

—— and G. M. Woodwell. 1964. An alpine podzol on Mt. Katahdin, Maine. Soil Sci. 2 (4): 274–279.

Bonde, E. K. 1968. Survival of seedlings on an alpine clover (*Trifolium nanum* Torr.). Ecol. 49: 1193–1195.

——. 1969. Plant disseminules in wind-blown debris from a glacier in Colorado. Arctic and Alpine Res. 1 (2): 135–140.

Bonham, Charles D. and R. T. Ward. 1970. Phytosociological relationships in alpine tufted hairgrass (*Deschampsia caespitosa* (L.) Beauv.) meadows. Arctic and Alpine Res. 2 (4): 267–275.

Braun, C. E. 1971. Habitat requirements of Colorado white-tailed ptarmigan. Reprint from Proc. Western Ass. State Game and Fish Comm. 51. 9 pp.

—— and R. K. Schmidt. 1971. Effects of snow and wind on wintering populations of white-tailed ptarmigan in Colorado. *In* Haugen, A.O. (ed.). Proceedings snow and ice symposium, Iowa State Univ., Ames. 280 pp.

Braun-Blanquet, J. 1932. Plant sociology. Trans. by G. D. Fuller and H. S. Conard. Hafner, N.Y. 439 pp. Illus., maps.

Boyd, W. L. 1959. Limnology of selected arctic lakes in relation to water supply problems. Ecol. 40 (1): 49–54.

Britton, M. E. 1967. Vegetation of the arctic tundra. *In* H. P. Hansen (ed.). Arctic Biology. pp. 67–130.

Brown, F. M., assisted by D. Eff and B. Rotger. 1957. Colorado butterflies. Denver Museum of Natural History, Denver. 368 pp. Illus., maps.

Burnett, A. L. and T. Eisner. 1964. Animal adaptation. Holt, Rinehart and Winston, N.Y. 136 pp. Illus.

Caldwell, M. M. 1968. Solar ultraviolet radiation as an ecological factor for alpine plants. Ecol. Monogr. 38: 243–268.

Campbell, J. B. 1970. New elevational records for the boreal toad (*Bufo boreas boreas*). Arctic and Alpine Res. 2 (2): 157–159.

Clausen, J. 1969. The Harvey Monroe Hall Natural Area. Carnegie Inst. Washington Department of Plant Biol. Publ. 459: 1–48.

———, D. Keck and W. M. Hiesey. 1940 and 1945. Experimental studies in the nature of species. Vol. 1 and 2. Carnegie Inst. of Washington Publ. 520 and 564, Washington, D.C. 626 pp. Illus.

Clements, F. E. and F. L. Long. 1923. Experimental pollination: an outline of the ecology of flowers and insects. Carnegie Inst. of Washington, Washington, D.C. 274 pp.

Conard, H. S. 1956. How to know the mosses and liverworts. W. C. Brown Co., Dubuque, Iowa. 226 pp. Illus.

Cox, C. F. 1933. Alpine plant succession on James Peak, Colorado. Ecol. Monogr. 3 (3): 300–372.

Craighead, J. J., F. C. Craighead and R. Y. Davis. 1963. A field guide to Rocky Mountain wildflowers, from northern Arizona and New Mexico to British Columbia. Houghton Mifflin, Cambridge. 277 pp. Illus.

Crandell, D. R. 1969. The geologic story of Mt. Rainier. Geol. Survey Bull. 1292. U.S. Government Printing Office, Washington, D.C. 43 pp.

Curry, R. R. 1966. Observation of alpine mudflows in the Tenmile Range, central Colorado. Geol. Soc. of Amer. Bull. 77: 771–776.

———. 1966. Glaciation about 3,000,000 years ago in the Sierra Nevada. Sci. 154 (3750): 770–771.

———. 1971. Glacial and Pleistocene history of the Mammoth Lakes Sierra. A geologic guidebook. Univ. of Montana Dept. of Geol., Series 11, Missoula. 49 pp. and map.

Dahl, E. 1958. Problems of amphiatlantic plant distribution. Saertrykk au Blyttia. 16: 93–121.

———. 1963. On the heat exchange of a wet vegetation surface and the ecology of *Koenigia islandica*. Oikos. 14 (2): 190–211.

———. 1966. The heat exchange of plants and its importance to plant morphology and distribution. Saertrykk au Blyttia, 24.

Danner, W. R. 1955. Geology of Olympic National Park. Univ. of Wash. Press, Seattle. 68 pp.

Dansereau, P. 1968. Alpine vegetation in eastern North America. Cranbrook Inst. of Sci. Newsletter. 37 (8): 95–107. Bloomfield Hills, Mich.

Daubenmire, R. F. 1967. Plants and environment. Harper and Row, N.Y. 300 pp. Illus.

————. 1969. Ecologic plant geography of the Pacific Northwest. Madroño. 20 (3): 111–128.

Duggar, B. M. (ed.). 1936. Biological effects of radiation. Vol. 2. McGraw-Hill, N.Y.

Eberhart, P. and P. Schmuck. 1970. The Fourteeners: Colorado's great mountains. Sage Books, Chicago. 126 pp. Illus., maps.

Evenson, C. D. 1962. Fauna from some high lakes. Mazama. 44: 48–54.

Faegri, K. and L. van der Pijl. 1966. The principles of pollination ecology. Pergamon, N.Y. 248 pp. Illus.

Fagerlund, G. O. 1954. Olympic National Park, Washington. Natural History Handbook I. Revised 1965. U.S. Government Printing Office, Washington, D.C. 60 pp.

Fernald, M. L. 1950. Gray's Manual of Botany: a handbook of the flowering plants and ferns of the central and northeastern United States and adjacent Canada. Corrected copy by R. C. Rollins, 1970. Van Nostrand Reinhold, N.Y. 1632 pp. Illus.

Fink, B. 1935. The lichen flora of the United States. (Completed for publication by J. Hedrick.) Revised 1960. Univ. of Mich. Press, Ann Arbor. 426 pp. Illus., pl.

Fiske, R. S., Clifford A. Hopson and A. C. Waters. 1963. Geology of Mt. Rainier National Park, Washington. Geol. Survey Prof. Paper 444. U.S. Government Printing Office, Washington, D.C. 93 pp.

Franklin, J. F. and N. A. Bishop. 1968. Notes on the natural history of Mt. Rainier National Park. Mt. Rainier Natural Hist. Assoc. Longmire, Wash. 24 pp.

———— and C. T. Dyrness. 1969. Vegetation of Oregon and Washington. U.S.D.A. Forest Service Res. Paper PNW–80. 216 pp.

Fries, M. A. 1970. Wildflowers of Mt. Rainier and the Cascades. Mt. Rainier Natur. Hist. Assoc. and the Mountaineers. Longmire, Washington. 208 pp.

Frost, S. W. 1959. Insect life and insect natural history. Dover, N.Y. 526 pp.

Gabrielson, I. N. 1932. Western American alpines. Macmillan, N.Y. 264 pp.

Gardner, J. 1970. Geomorphic significance of avalanches in the Lake Louise area, Alberta, Canada. Arctic and Alpine Res. 2 (2): 135–144.

Gates, D. M. 1968. Towards understanding ecosystems. In J. B. Cragg (ed.). Advances in ecological research. Academic Press, N.Y. 5: 1–34.

———— and R. Janke. 1965. The energy environment of the alpine tundra. Oecol. Planta. 1: 39–62.

Geiger, R. 1959. The climate near the ground. (Trans. by Scripta Technica [Das Klima der bodennahen Luftschicht].) Harvard Univ. Press, Cambridge. 611 pp. Illus.

Gleason, H. A. 1952. The new Britton and Brown illustrated flora of the northeastern United States and adjacent Canada: Pteridophyta, Gymnospermae, and Monocotyledonae. 3 vols. Hafner Publ. Co. for N.Y. Bot. Gardens. 1726 pp. Illus.

Goldthwait, R. P. 1970. Mountain glaciers of the Presidential Range in N.H. Arctic and Alpine Res. 2 (2): 85–102.

Gregg, R. E. 1947. Altitudinal indicators among the Formicidae. University of Colo. Stud. Ser. D. 2 (3).

Griggs, R. F. 1930. A contribution to the arctic-alpine problem. Ecol. 11 (3): 607–609.

―――. 1956. Competition and succession on a Rocky Mountain fellfield. Ecol. 37 (1): 8–20.

Grout, A. J. 1903–1910. Mosses with land-lens and microscope: Maryland. [A nontechnical handbook of the more common mosses of the northeastern U.S., 1903–1910.] Eric Lundberg, Ashton, Md. (imprint, 1965). 416 pp. Illus.

Hadley, E. B. and L. C. Bliss. 1964. Energy relationships of alpine plants on Mt. Washington, New Hampshire. Ecol. Monogr. 34: 331–357.

Hadley, N. F. 1969. Microenvironmental factors influencing the nesting sites of some subalpine fringillid birds in Colorado. Arctic and Alpine Res. 1 (2): 121–126.

Hansen, H. P. (ed.). 1967. Arctic biology. Oregon State Univ. Press, Corvallis, Oregon. 318 pp.

Harrington, H. D. 1954. Manual of the plants of Colo.: for the identification of the ferns and flowering plants of the state. Sage Books, Denver. 666 pp.

――― and L. W. Durrell. 1944. Key to some Colorado grasses in vegetative condition. Tech. Bull. 33, Colo. Agr. Exp. Sta., Fort Collins. 86 pp.

――― and L. W. Durrell. 1950. Colorado ferns and fern allies: Pteridophyta. Colo. Agr. Res. Found., Colorado A & M College, Fort Collins. 96 pp. Illus., maps.

Hayward, C. L. 1952. Alpine biotic communities of the Uinta Mountains, Utah. Ecol. Monogr. 22: 93–120.

Hermann, F. J. 1970. Manual of the Carices of the Rocky Mountains and Colorado Basin. Agr. Handbook 374, U.S.D.A., U.S. Forest Service, Washington, D.C. 397 pp. Illus.

Hitchcock, A. S. 1950. Manual of the grasses of the United States. 2nd ed. revised by A. Chase. U.S. Dept. of Agr. Misc. Publ. No. 200. 1051 pp. Illus.

Hopson, R. E. 1960. Collier Glacier—a photographic record. Mazama. 42 (13): 1–12.

―――. 1961. Collier Glacier, 1961. Mazama. 43 (13): 37–39.

―――. 1961. The arctic-alpine zone in the Three Sisters region. Mazama. 43 (13): 17–26.

————. 1962. Collier Glacier, 1962. Mazama. 44: 44–47.

Howard, G. E. 1950. Lichens of the state of Washington. Univ. of Wash. Press, Seattle. 191 pp. Plates, map.

Howell, J. T. 1951. The arctic-alpine flora of Three Peaks in the Sierra Nevada. Leafl. of Western Bot. 6 (7): 141–154.

Husted, W. M. 1962. A proposed archeological chronology for Rocky Mountain National Park based on projectile points and pottery. M.A. Thesis, Univ. of Colorado, Boulder. 109 pp.

Huxley, A. 1968. Mountain flowers in Colorado. Collier-Macmillan, N.Y. 428 pp. Illus.

Hylander, Clarence J. 1966. Wildlife communities from the tundra to the tropics in North America. Houghton Mifflin, Boston. 342 pp. Illus., maps.

Imshaug, H. A. 1957. Alpine lichens of western United States and adjacent Canada. I: the macrolichens. Bryol. 60: 177–272.

Jepson, W. L. 1925. A manual of the flowering plants of California. Ass. Stud. Store, Univ. of California, Berkeley. 1238 pp. Illus.

Johnson, D. R. and M. H. Maxwell. 1966. Energy dynamics of Colorado pikas. Ecol. 47: 1059–1061.

Johnson, P. L. and W. D. Billings. 1962. The alpine vegetation of the Beartooth Plateau in relation to cryopedogenic processes and patterns. Ecol. Monogr. 32: 105–135.

————— and J. J. Keeley, Jr. 1970. Dynamics of carbon dioxide and productivity in an arctic biosphere. Ecol. 51 (1): 73–80.

Johnson, R. and A. (with C. W. Ferguson). 1970. The ancient bristlecone pine forest. Chalfant Press, Bishop, Calif. 56 pp.

Johnson, W. M. 1964. Field key to the sedges of Wyoming. Rocky Mountain Forest Range Exp. Sta. with Agr. Exp. Sta. Bull. 419. Univ. of Wyoming, Laramie. 239 pp.

Jones, George N. 1938. Flowering plants and ferns of Mount Rainier. Univ. of Washington, Seattle. 192 pp. and 8 pp. of plates.

Jones, W. D. and L. O. Quam. 1938. Glacial land forms in Rocky Mountain National Park, Colorado. J. Geol. 52: 217–234.

Kiener, W. 1967. Sociological studies of the alpine vegetation on Longs Peak. Univ. of Nebraska Stud.: New Ser. 34, Lincoln. 75 pp.

Klikoff, L. G. 1965. Microenvironmental influence on vegetational pattern near timberline in the central Sierra Nevada. Ecol. Monogr. 35: 187–211.

Kruckeberg, A. R. 1969. Soil diversity and the distribution of plants, with examples from western North America. Madroño. 20 (3): 129–154.

LaChapelle, E. R. 1969. Field guide to snow crystals. Univ. of Washington Press, Seattle. 101 pp. Illus.

LaMarche, V. C. 1965. Distribution of Pleistocene glaciers in the White Mountains of California and Nevada. U.S. Geol. Surv. Prof. Paper 525-C: 144–146.

Lloyd, R. M. and R. S. Mitchell. 1966. Plants of the White Mountains, California and Nevada (revised edition). Dept. of Bot., White Mt. Res. Sta., Univ. of Calif., Berkeley. 60 pp.

Löve, A. 1967. The evolutionary significance of disjunctions. Taxon 16: 324–333.

—— and D. Löve. 1966. Cytotaxonomy of the alpine vascular plants of Mt. Washington. Univ. of Colorado Stud. Ser. in Biol. 24. 74 pp.

—— and D. Löve. 1967. Biosystematics of widely disjunctive taxa. Die Naturwiss. 54: 24–25.

—— and D. Löve. 1967. Continental drift and the origin of the arctic-alpine flora. Rev. Roumaine de Biol. 12 (2–3): 163–169.

—— and D. Löve. 1967. Polyploidy and altitude: Mt. Washington. Biol. Zentralblatt. 86: 307–312.

Löve, D. 1969. *Papaver* at high altitudes in the Rocky Mountains. Brittonia. 21 (1): 1–10.

Lund, T. 1969. Take care of the tundra. Colorado Outdoors. 18 (4): 31.

Lyons, C. P. 1956. Trees, shrubs and flowers to know in Washington. 5th edition, 1969. J. M. Dent, Toronto. 211 pp. Illus.

Macior, L. W. 1964. An experimental study of the floral ecology of *Dodecatheon media*. Amer. J. of Bot. 51 (1): 96–108.

——. 1966. Foraging behavior of *Bombus* (Hymenoptera: Apidae) in relation to *Aquilegia* pollination. Amer. J. of Bot. 53 (3): 302–309.

——. 1968. Pollination adaptation in *Pedicularis groenlandica*. Amer. J. of Bot. 55 (8): 927–932.

Madole, R. F. 1969. Pinedale and Bull Lake glaciation in upper St. Vrain drainage basin, Boulder County, Colo. Arctic and Alpine Res. 1 (4): 279–287.

Malde, H. E. 1964. Patterned ground in the Western Snake River plain, Idaho, and its possible cold-climate origin. Geol. Soc. of Amer. Bull. No. 75: 191–208.

Mani, M. S. 1962. Introduction to high altitude entomology: insect life above the timber-line in the northwest Himalaya. Methuen, London. 302 pp. Illus.

Marr, J. W. 1958. Technical progress report to the U.S. Atomic Energy Commission on Contract No. AT (11–1) 435 in Contrib. Inst. of Arctic and Alpine Res., pp. 1–15.

——. 1964. Utilization of the Front Range tundra, Colorado. Grazing in terrestrial and marine environments. *In* Blackwell's Sci. Publ., England.

——. 1967. Ecosystems of the East Slope of the Front Range in Colorado. Univ. of Colorado Stud. Ser. in Biol. 8. Boulder, Colo. 134 pp.

—— and B. E. Willard. 1970. Persisting vegetation in an alpine recreation area in the Southern Rocky Mountains, Colorado. Biol. Conserv. 2 (2): 97–104.

Marshall, N. L. 1910. Mosses and lichens: a popular guide to the identification and study of our commoner mosses and lichens, their uses, and methods of preserving. 1920. Doubleday, Page, N.Y. 327 pp. Illus.: 32 pl., 16 col. pl.

Martinelli, M., Jr. 1960. Creep and settlement in an alpine snowpack. Res. Notes, Rocky Mt. Forest and Range Exp. Sta., U.S.D.A., U.S. Forest Service. 43: 1–4.

———. 1960. Moisture exchange between the atmosphere and alpine snow surfaces under summer conditions (preliminary results). J. of Meteor. 17 (2): 227–231.

Meeuse, B. J. D. 1961. The story of pollination. Ronald Press Co., N.Y. 243 pp. Illus.

Moir, W. H. and H. M. Smith. 1970. Occurrence of an American salamander, *Aneides hardyi* (Taylor), in tundra habitat. Arctic and Alpine Res. 2 (2): 155–156.

Mooney, H. A. 1966. Influence of soil type on the distribution of two closely related species of *Erigeron*. Ecol. 47: 950–958.

——— and W. D. Billings. 1960. The annual carbohydrate cycle of alpine plants as related to growth. Amer. J. of Bot. 47: 498–594.

——— and W. D. Billings. 1961. Comparative physiological ecology of arctic and alpine populations of *Oxyria digyna*. Ecol. Monogr. 31: 1–29.

——— and A. W. Johnson. 1965. Comparative physiological ecology of an arctic and an alpine population of *Thalictrum alpinum* (L.) Ecol. 46 (5): 721–727.

———, G. St. Andre and R. D. Wright. 1962. Alpine and subalpine vegetation patterns in the White Mountains of California. The Amer. Midland Natur. 68 (2): 257–273.

Munz, P. A. 1969. California mountain wildflowers. Univ. of California Press, Berkeley. 122 pp. Illus.

——— and D. D. Keck. 1959. A California flora. Univ. of Calif. Press, Berkeley, Los Angeles. 1681 pp. Suppl., 1968, 224 pp. Illus.: col. pl., maps.

Nearing, G. G. 1962. The lichen book. Eric Lundberg, Ashton, Md. 648 pp.

Nelson, R. A. 1969. Handbook of Rocky Mountain plants. Dale Stuart King, Publ., Tucson, Arizona. 331 pp. Illus. (part col.), map.

———. 1970. Plants of Rocky Mountain National Park. 3rd edition. Rocky Mt. Natur. Assoc. 168 pp. Illus.

Osburn, W. S., Jr. 1961. The dynamics of fallout distribution in a Colorado alpine tundra snow accumulation ecosystem. *In* V. Schultz and W. W. Klement, Jr. (eds.). Radioecology. 1963, pp. 51–71.

———. 1961. Influence of four Rocky Mountain regional environments on pea plants grown from irradiated seeds. Inst. of Arctic and Alpine Res., Univ. of Colorado, pp. 319–324.

————. 1961. Variation in clones of *Penstemon* growing in natural areas of differing radioactivity. Sci. 134: 342–343.

Paulsen, H. A., Jr. 1960. Plant cover and forage use of alpine sheep ranges in the Central Rocky Mountains. Iowa State J. of Sci. 34 (4): 731–748.

Pennak, R. W. 1955. Comparative limnology of eight Colorado mountain lakes. Univ. of Colorado Stud. Ser. in Biol. 2. Boulder, Colorado. 75 pp.

————. 1968. Field and experimental winter limnology of three Colorado mountain lakes. Ecol. 49: 505–520.

Peterson, R. T. and M. McKenny. 1968. A field guide to wildflowers of northeast and northcentral North America. (A visual approach: arranged by color, form and detail.) Houghton Mifflin, Boston. 420 pp.

Pitelka, F. A. 1967. Some characteristics of microtine cycles in the Arctic. *In* H. F. Hansen (ed.). Arctic biology. Oregon State Univ. Press, Corvallis. pp. 153–183.

Polunin, N. 1959. Circumpolar arctic flora. Clarendon, Oxford. 514 pp. Illus., map.

————. 1960. Introduction to plant geography and some related sciences. McGraw-Hill, N.Y. 640 pp. Illus.

Porsild, A. E. 1955. Vascular plants of the western Canadian Arctic Archipelago. Nat. Museum of Canada, Bull. 135 (Biol. Ser. 45), Ottawa. 226 pp.

————. 1957. Illustrated flora of the Canadian Arctic Archipelago. Nat. Museum of Canada, Bull. 146. Ottawa. 209 pp.

Porter, C. L. 1962–1968. A flora of Wyoming. Parts 1–6. Agr. Exp. Sta., Univ. of Wyoming Bull. 402, 404, 418, 434; Res. J. 14, 20. Laramie. 261 pp.

Pusateri, S. J. 1963. Flora of our Sierran National Parks: Yosemite–Sequoia and Kings Canyon (including many valley and foothill plants). Publ. by author, Tulare, Calif. 170 pp.

Rall, G. and W. G. Solheim. 1963. The Melampsoraceae of the Rocky Mountains. Univ. of Wyoming, Laramie. 35 pp.

Ramaley, F. 1927. Colorado plant life. Univ. of Colo., Boulder. 299 pp. Illus. (part col.), maps.

Retzer, J. L. 1956. Alpine soils of the Rocky Mountains. J. of Soil Sci. 7: 22–32.

Rochow, T. F. 1970. Ecological investigations of *Thlaspi alpestre* L. along an elevational gradient in the central Rocky Mountains. Ecol. 51 (4): 649–656.

Rodeck, H. G. 1966. Guide to the mammals of Colorado. Univ. of Colorado Press, Boulder. 72 pp. Illus.

Rodin, R. J. 1960. Ferns of the Sierra. Yosemite Nat. History Assoc., Yosemite National Park, Calif. 124 pp.

Rogers, Glenn E. and C. E. Braun. 1967. Ptarmigan. Colorado Outdoors, July–August. pp. 22–28.

Sakai, A. and K. Otsuka. 1970. Freezing resistance of alpine plants. Ecol. 51 (4): 665–671.

Salisbury, F. B. and G. G. Spomer. 1964. Leaf temperatures of alpine plants in the field. Planta. 60: 497–505.

————, G. G. Spomer, M. Sobral and R. T. Ward. 1968. Analysis of an alpine environment. Bot. Gaz. 129 (1): 16–32.

Schimper, A. F. W. 1903. Plant geography upon a physiological basis. Trans. by W. R. Fisher, Eng. Rev. and ed. by P. Groom and I. B. Balfour. Reprint 1960. Clarendon Press, Oxford. 839 pp. 502 illus., 5 plates, 4 fold. maps.

Schofield, W. B. 1969. Phytogeography of northwestern North America: Bryophytes and vascular plants. Madroño. 20 (3): 157–207.

Smith, G. (ed.), with D. Rinehart, E. Vestal and B. Willard. 1969. The Mammoth Lakes Sierra. Wilderness Press, Berkeley. 145 pp. Illus. (3rd ed.).

Schuster, R. M. 1953. Boreal Hepaticae: a manual of the liverworts of Minnesota and adjacent regions. Amer. Midland Natur. 49: 257–684.

Scott, D. and W. D. Billings. 1964. The effect of environmental factors on the standing crop and productivity of an alpine tundra. Ecol. Monogr. 34: 243–270.

Sealander, J. A. 1962. Seasonal changes in blood valves of deer mice and other small mammals. Ecol. 43: 107–119.

Sharp, R. P. 1960. Glaciers. Univ. of Oregon, Oregon State System of Higher Educ., Eugene. 78 pp. Illus.

Spomer, G. G. 1964. Physiological ecology studies of alpine cushion plants. Physiol. Plant. 17: 717–724.

———— and F. B. Salisbury. 1968. Eco-physiology of *Geum turbinatum* and implications concerning alpine environments. Bot. Gaz. 129 (1): 33–49.

Stagner, Howard R. 1952. Behind the scenery of Mt. Rainier Nat'l. Park. Mt. Rainier Natur. History Assoc. Longmire, Wash. 64 pp.

Stebbins, G. L. 1950. Variation and evolution in plants. Columbia Univ. Press, N.Y. 643 pp. Illus., maps.

Stein, J. R. and C. C. Amundsen. 1967. Studies on snow algae and fungi from the Front Range of Colorado. Canad. J. of Bot. 45: 2033–2045.

Swan, L. W. 1961. The ecology of the high Himalayas. Sci. Amer. 205 (4): 68–78.

Tabor, R. W. 1969. Geological guide to the Hurricane Ridge area. Olympic Natur. History Assoc. Port Angeles, Washington. 19 pp.

Tanner, J. T. 1966. Effects of population density on growth rates of animal populations. Ecol. 47 (5): 733–745.

Terjung, W. H., R. N. Kiekert, G. L. Potter and S. W. Swarts. 1969. Energy and moisture balances of an alpine tundra in mid-July. Arctic and Alpine Res. 1 (4): 247–266.

Thomas, J. H. 1969. Botanical explorations in Washington, Oregon, California and adjacent regions. Huntia. 3: 5–92.

Toll, R. W. 1923. The mountain peaks of Colorado. Colo. Mountain Club. Boulder. 59 pp.

Troll, C. 1958. Structure, soils, solifluction, and frost climates of the earth. Trans. 43, U.S. Army Snow, Ice and Permafrost Estab. Corps of Engineers. 121 pp.

University of Washington Department of Botany. 1969. A check-list of vascular plants of west-central Washington, Pacific Coast to Columbia River. Prepared for delegates to the 11th International Botanical Congress, Seattle, Washington. Friends of the Univ. of Washington Arboretum, Inc. 33 pp.

Vasil'yev, I. M. 1961. Wintering of plants. Amer. Inst. of Biol. Sci. Washington, D.C. Trans. from Russian by Roger and Roger, Inc.

Veatch, F. M. 1969. Analysis of a 24-year photographic record of Nisqually Glacier, Mt. Rainier National Park, Washington. Geol. Surv. Prof. Paper 631, U.S. Government Printing Office, Washington, D.C. 52 pp.

Vose, R. N. and D. G. Dunlap. 1968. Wind as a factor in the local distribution of small mammals. Ecol. 49 (3): 381–386.

Wardle, Peter. 1968. Engelmann Spruce (*Picea engelmannii* Engel.) at its upper limits on the Front Range, Colorado. Ecol. 49 (3): 483–495.

Weber, W. A. 1955. The lichen flora of Colorado: *Cetraria, Cornicularia, Dactylina* and *Thamnolia*. Univ. of Colo. Stud. Ser. in Biol., Boulder, Colorado, 3: 115–134.

———. 1961. Studies of Colorado Bryophytes. Univ. of Colo. Stud. Ser. in Biol., Boulder, Colorado, 7: 27–52.

———. 1965. The lichen flora of Colorado: 2. *Pannariaceae*. Univ. of Colo. Stud. Ser. in Biol., Boulder, Colorado, 16: 1–10.

———. 1965. Plant geography in the southern Rocky Mountains. *In* H. E. Wright, Jr., and D. G. Frey (eds.). The Quaternary of the U.S. Princeton Univ. Press, Princeton, N.J. pp. 453–468.

———. 1966. Studies of Colorado Bryophytes. Univ. of Colorado Stud. Ser. in Biol., 23: 27–52. Boulder, Colorado.

———. 1967. Rocky Mountain flora. Univ. of Colorado Press, Boulder. 437 pp. Illus.

Webster, G. L. 1961. The altitudinal limits of vascular plants. Ecol. 42 (3): 587–590.

West, G. C. 1968. Bioenergetics of captive willow ptarmigan under natural conditions. Ecol. 49: 1035–1045.

Wiens, D. and D. K. Halleck. 1962. Chromosome numbers in Rocky Mountain Plants: I. Bot. Notiser. 115 (4): 455–464.

——— and J. A. Rechter. 1966. *Artemisia pattersonii:* a 14-chromosome species of alpine sage. Amer. J. of Bot. 53 (10): 981–986.

Willard, B. E. 1979. Plant sociology of the alpine tundra, Trail Ridge, Rocky

Mountain National Park, Colorado, Colo. Sch. of Mines Qtrly. 74 (4): 1–119.

———— and C. O. Harris. 1963. Alpine wildflowers of Rocky Mountain National Park. Rocky Mountain Nature Assoc., Estes Park, Colo. 24 pp.

———— and J. W. Marr. 1970. Effects of human activities on alpine tundra ecosystems in Rocky Mountain National Park, Colorado. Biol. Conserv. 2 (4): 257–265.

———— and J. W. Marr. 1971. Recovery of alpine tundra under protection after damage by human activities in the Rocky Mountains of Colorado. Biol. Conserv. 3 (3): 181–190.

Wright, H. E., Jr. and W. H. Osburn, eds. 1968. Arctic and Alpine Environments. Indiana Univ. Press. Bloomington. 308 pp.

Index

Italic figures refer to line drawings.

Achillea, see yarrow
Acomastylis, see avens
actinea *(Hymenoxys cooperi* var. *canescens),* 269
adaptation(s), 18, 96; physiological, 18–21, 41; plant, 18–40, 50, 53, 77, 96, 197, 212, 220, 273, 275, 296; succulence, 31–32; seed, 39–40; animal, 41–47; snowbed, 50, 53, 96; tree, 57; alga, 96; parallel, 117, 291
Adirondack Mountains, 381
agoseris, short-beaked *(Agoseris glauca* var. *dasycephala),* 282, *283,* 293, 316, 329
air, 5, 15, 28, 51, 56, 60, 94, 140, 157, 220, 237, 265, 275, 304; low pressure, 5; moist, 5, 15, 337; cold a. drainage, 15, 56; pressure, 15; near ground, 77, 140; temperature, 91, 94; dry, 94, 197, 281, 284, 304; masses, 252, 253; high pressure, 337
Alaska, 6, 58, 69, 272, 371; coast, 292
alder, mountain *(Alnus viridis* ssp. *crispa),* 73, 347, *348*
alga, algae, 22; with fungus, 22, 94, 183; "pink snow," 96; populations in water, 105
Allium, see onion
alluvial fans, 237
Alnus, see alder
alplily *(Lloydia serotina),* 40, *156,* 157
Alps, 40, 115, 383
altitude, 113, 120; high, higher, 3, 4, 6, 14, 18, 19, 20, 22, 31, 35, 45, 55, 56, 68, 77, 115, 119, 122, 123, 128, 206, 231, 243, 248, 253, 266, 275, 339, 384–85, 386; physiological effect of, 3,

altitude *(cont'd)*
384; disorientation at, 3, 384, 385; lack of oxygen, 3, 384; air, 4, 15; low, lower, 5, 20, 35, 42, 58, 116, 317, 318, 377, 340; wind at, 14; sunburn, 14; lack of moisture, dehydration, 31, 385; and trees, 57; and krummholz, 58; working at, 68, 384–85; physiological adjustment to, 68; atmosphere, 119, 275, 276; recovery rate at, 120; ultraviolet radiation, 275; cold at, 281; hypoxia, 384
alumroot *(Heuchera),* alpine *(H. glabra), 312,* 312, 377; snow *(H. nivalis), 124,* 124
Amargosa Mountains, 264
Amelanchier, see Juneberry
Androsace, see rockjasmine, rockprimrose
anemone *(Anemone),* 313; narcissus-flowered *(A. narcissiflora* ssp. *zephyra),* 157, *164;* Drummond's *(A. drummondii),* 288, *289;* globeflower *(A. multifida* var. *globosa),* 313, *324*
animals, 45, 55, 124, 128, 171, 380, 381; limited number of, 4, 48, 74, 77; mammals, 6, 44, 45, 131–32, 234–36, 269, 289–90, 343, 381; adaptations, 18, 41–47; metabolism, 41, 46; water, 43, 105; amphibians, 43; Bergmann's rule, 43; burrowing, 44; -controlled ecosystem, 44; warm-blooded, 45; boulder field, 49, 67–68, 69, 131–32; damage, 53, 77, 169; -disturbed communities, 50, 53, 97–100, 120, 200, 255; populations, 54, 105, 115,

bloodworm(s), 42
blueberry *(Vaccinium)*, 107; sweet *(V. angustifolium)*, **365,** 366; velvet-leaf *(V. myrtilloides)*, **365,** 366; *see also* bilberry, cranberry
bluegrass *(Poa)*, 35, 78, 80, 207, 213, 236, 266, 269, 331; arctic *(P. arctica)*, **163;** alpine *(P. alpina)*, **208;** Patterson's *(P. pattersonii)*, **221;** rock *(P. glauca)*, **212**
bluet, alpine *(Houstonia caerula* var. *faxonorum)*, 117, 340, **359,** 359
bog, 12, 117, 212; *see also* bilberry, laurel, marsh
boulder(s), 3, 5, 6, 17, 48, 62, 70, 86, 105, 122, 240, 262, 275, 285, 304, 330, 334, 335, 377; surface(s), 45, 51; field/pile, 49, 51, 53, 62–69, 70, 82, 88, 123–33, 239, 240, 303; weathering, 49, 70, 122–23; community, 62–69, 123–33; granite, 263; -fellfield
breccias, 287
Brewer, William, 256; *see also* mountain heather, whitlowgrass
buckwheat *(Eriogonum)*, 24, 74, 77, 113, 117, 243, 244, 256, 269, 281, 296, 303, 316, 329, 371; oval-leaved *(E. ovalifolium)*, 32, **33,** 244, 269, 271, **271;** onion-flowered *(E. latens)*, **245, 271,** 272; pyrola-leaved *(E. pyrolaefolium* var. *coryphaeum)*, **297;** sulphurflower *(E. umbellatum* ssp. *covillei)*, **279,** 280
Buckwheat family, 22, 116, 243
bulb, 35, 40, 99
bulblet(s), 35, **38,** 39, 213, 233
bumblebee(s), 42, 82, 142, 145, 216–20, 325, 366
bunchberry *(Cornus canadensis)*, **358,** 359
buttercup *(Ranunculus)*, 21, 183, 204, 269, 371; pygmy *(R. pygmaeus)*, **23,** 222, **233,** 233; black-headed *(R. macauleyi)*, 35, **186;** snow *(R. adoneus)*, 68, 117, 183–87, **186,** 188; birdfoot *(R. pedatifidus)*, 173, **177;** snowbed *(R. eschscholtzii)*, 269, **306,** 306; Cooley's *(R. cooleyae)*, 327
Buttercup family, 183
butterfly, -flies, 42, 77, 145, 200, 266, 286, 287; larvae, 83; mountain blue *(Agriades* sp.), 266; white cabbage

butterfly *(cont'd)* *(Pieris* sp.), 286; White Mountain *(Oeneis melissa semidea)*, 346
butterweed, Olympic *(Senecio neowebsteri)*, 313, **317;** *see also* ragwort
butterwort, 306
button lichen *(Lecidea atrobrunnea)*, **64**

caddisfly larvae, 42, 83
Calamagrostis, see reedgrass
California, 18, 24, 57, 113, 243, 237–276, 277; transplant experiments, 18–22
Calliergon sarmentosum, 226, 231, **231**
Caloplaca, see jewel lichen
Caltha, see marsh marigold
Calyptridium, see pussypaws
camas, death *(Zigadenus elegans)*, **123,** 123; *see also* wandlily
Campanula, see harebell
campion *(Melandrium)*, alpine *(M. kingii)*, 173, **175;** petalless *(M. apetalum)*, **175**
campion, moss *(Silene acaulis* ssp. *acaulescens)*, 25, **25,** 27, 77, 100, 144–45, **150,** 174, 381, 386
Canada, Canadian, 106, 236
Candellariella aurella, 263
candytuft; alpine, *(Thlaspi alpestre)*, **23,** 71, **72,** 142, **144;** *see also* fernleaf candytuft
capsule(s): seed, 172; moss, 192, 330
carbohydrate(s), 19, 21, 128
carbon dioxide, 46, 104, 385
Carex, see sedge
carnivore(s), 94
Cascade Mountains, 58, 69, 106, 119, 252, 300, 316, 325, 326, 327, 334, 375–376; Plateau, 277–79; Southern, 277–303
Cassiope, see bell heather, moss plant
Castilleja, see paintbrush
catchfly, Parry's *(Silene parryi)*, **318,** 323–24
caterpillar, 386
catkins, 91, 187, 348, 361
Cedar *(Libocedrus* sp.), 286, 288, 306
cells: plant, 19, 21, 32, 33, 56, 57, 93, 96, 162, 183, 192, 262; moss leaf, 192; nucleus, 272; division, 273; size, 273

Cerastium, see mouse-ear
Cetraria, see Iceland lichen
Chaenactis, see dusty maiden
Chamerion, see fireweed
Charleston Mountains, 264
chickweed *(Stellaria* sp.), 192
chill factor, 14, 47
chimingbells, green-leaf *(Mertensia viridis),* **34**, 35, 68, 200, ***206,*** 206, 377
Chionophila, see snowlover
chipmunks, 290
chlorophyll, 19, 83, 272, 275
chromosomes, 272–73
Chrysosplenium, see saxifrage, golden
cinquefoil *(Potentilla),* 192, 200, 243, 377; alpine *(P. ledebouriana),* 33, **36;** red-stemmed *(P. rubricaulis),* 33, **36,** snow *(P. nivea),* 33, **36;** blueleaf *(P. diversifolia),* 188, **191,** 192; Mount Rainier *(P. flabellifolia),* 301; shrubby *(P. fruticosa),* **316,** 317–18; three-toothed or sibbaldiopsis *(P. tridentata),* 340, 343, **345**
circumpolar plants, 27, 71, 113, 115, 116, 231
cirque(s), 6, 7, 88, 104, 119, 231, 237, 238, 248, 280, 307, 326, 337
Cirsium, see thistle
Cladonia, see pixie-cup lichen
Claytonia, see spring beauty
Clementsia, see queen's crown, rose crown
climate, 19, 22, 36, 40, 41, 43, 45, 51, 54, 55, 57, 60, 77, 106, 115, 119, 122, 162, 226, 243, 270, 275, 293, 296, 331, 335, 340; past, 7, 11, 51, 122, 265; California, 19, 243; and succession, 51; regions, 55; and treelimit, 56–58, 339; *microclimate,* 56, 58, 59, 145; change, 57–58, 119; continental, 57, 280; and soil formation, 76–77; Rocky Mountain, 106, 162; Great Basin, 265; maritime, 280; Mount Rainier, 296; Mount Washington, 331, 339–40, 370; Arctic, 384
climax: vegetation, 167; plants and animals, 171
Clintonia, see beadlily
cloud(s), 14, 16, 42, 172, 237, 273, 275, 286, 287, 304, 335, 337; cover, 276, 296, 362, 370

clover *(Trifolium),* 68, 94, 143–44, 160, 174, 188, 192; dwarf *(T. nanum),* **26,** 27, 77, 143, **149,** 157, 236; alpine *(T. dasyphyllum),* 53, 68, 157, **157;** Parry's *(T. parryi),* 188, **189;** carpet *(T. monanthum),* 248, **249;** Mono *(T. monoense),* 269
clubmoss, 22, 93, 143, 362, 364, 367, 386; rock *(Selaginella densa),* 143, **148,** 386; fir *(Huperzia selago),* 369; bristly *(Lycopodium annotinum* var. *pungens),* **369;** running *(L. clavatum),* **369; *see also*** running pine
collomia, talus *(Collomia larsenii),* 74, 117, **320,** 322
Colorado: alpine plant species, 24, 113, 120; tundra insects, 42; mountain ponds, 43; high plains, 118; plateau, 264; Front Range, 286; *see also* Rocky Mountains
Columbia River, 281
columbine, dwarf *(Aquilegia saximontana),* 119, **130,** 131
community (-ies), insect; water courses, 42; pool, 42–43; pond, 43
community (-ies): plant, 27, 48, 49, 51, 53, 54, 108, 117, 120, 179, 244, 255, 293, 303, 371; fellfield, 27, 49, 75–80, 120, 136–45, 256, 286, 303, 307, 334; scree and talus slope, 49, 70–74, 120, 133–34, 286, 307; snowbanks/snowbed, 49–50, 53, 88–96, 98, 104, 120, 183–98, 255, 272, 286, 303, 307, 353–62, 371, 376; boulder field, 49, 62–69, 120, 122–31, 303; meadow/turf, 49, 50, 81–87, 98, 120, 160–83, 286, 303, 307, 362; lowland, 50, 51, 53; animal-disturbed, 50, 53, 302–303, 379–81; marsh, 50, 53, 100–104, 120, 212–34, 255, 307, 348–53; health, 50, 106–109, 120, 303, 307, 329, 340–46, 363–71; snow, 96; lake, 104–105; rock sedge, 152–60; kobresia, 160–83; elk sedge, 162; hairgrass, 191–92; koenigia, 226; stream, 347–48, 371; diapensia, 362; krummholz, 371
competition: plant, 20, 27, 56, 68, 71, 78, 89, 116, 240, 300; animal, 236
coney, 67
Continental Divide, 5, 118, 119
Coptis, see goldthread

storm(s) *(cont'd)*
   afternoon, 14, 234; mountain, 16–18; west-east path, 57; winter, 57, 316; snow, 81, Pacific front, 290; fall, 92; affect on pollinating insects, 172; spring, 316; ice, 339; sleet, 339
stream(s), 44, 238, 277; needle ice near, 11; runoff, 102; plants of, 102, 119; outflow, 105; Rocky Mountain, 222–26, 231; Sierra Nevada, 238, 248; Mount Washington, 347–48; communities, 371; *see also* water courses
streamlets, 42, 376
stud lichen *(Buellia* sp.), *64, 65*
subalpine: valley, 15; forests, 56, 58, 75, 371, 376; zone, 58, 248; evergreens, 62; trees, 59
succession, plant: slowness of, 51; fellfield to meadow, 51, 53, 77–78, 81–82, 152; indicators of, 51, 89; boulder to fellfield to turf, 53; interruption of, 97–98; trends, 226
succulence, 31–32, 77, 212, 233, 260, 346
sugars, 21, 206
sulphurflower *(Eriogonum umbellatum* ssp. *covillei),* **279**, 280; *see also* buckwheat
summer, 17, 40, 44, 60, 88, 92, 94, 99, 104, 120, 132, 134, 157, 168, 187, 188, 192, 226, 272, 279, 288, 317, 325, 327, 354, 376, 377, 381, 385, 386, 387; snow storm, 4–6, 9, 198, 336; late-lying snow, 7, 75, 88, 122, 183, 231, 302, 375; needle ice, 11; warmth, 20, 142, 281; environmental conditions, 21; animal residents, 41, 290; insects, 42, 43; marmot feeding, 46; temporary water, 50, 53; cool, 54, 92, 220, 317, 326, 375; temperatures, 42, 56, 102, 128; animal activity, 68; drought, 76, 253, 281; rain, 77, 253, 254, 346; showers, 77, 284; wind, 77, 173, 316; fellfield, 80; meadow/turf, 81, 82, 161, 168; bloom, 82; soil temperatures, 91, 104; sheep grazing, 100; water temperatures, 102, 105, 240; wood production, 108; light, 197; marsh, 212; feeding grounds, 236; precipitation, 253, 254; growing season, 331; air moisture, 304; Mount

summer *(cont'd)*
   Washington, 335; snow storage, 375; water flow, 375–76; visitor pressure, 379
sunburn, 4, 14, 275
sunflower, alpine, *see* Rydbergia
sweetbroom, western *(Hedysarum occidentale),* **311**, 312

talus, 8, 49, 76; community, 70–74, 120, 133–34; slope, 280, 309; *see also* scree
taproot(s), 17, 25, 27, 31, 74, 77, 99, 100, 188, 282, 322, 346
Taraxacum, see dandelion
tarn, 53, 101, 102, 240–242
temperate: region, 20, 55; zone, 22
temperature, 18, 21, 220, 334; at altitude, 3, 4, 14, 83, 272; pattern, 7; and permafrost, 7; and needle ice, 11; freezing, 11, 56, 276; and wind, 14, 15; chill factor, 14, 47; body, 16, 43, 46; spring, 19; and photosynthesis, 20, 22, 51, 162; lower elevation, 20, 102; in cushion plants, 24; summer, 42, 56, 83, 102, 128; alpine night, 43; cold, low, 45, 47, 58, 60, 212, 339, 375; hibernation and, 46; soil, 49, 56, 91, 104; day, 56; range, 57; continental, 57, 280; fellfield, 9; in snowbed/snowbank, 91, 96; on snow surface, 94; air, 91, 94, 95; alpine lake, 105, 240; winter, 161; and koenigia, 226; and glaciers, 280–81
Texas, 298
Thalictrum, see meadowrue
thallus, lichen, 63, 93
thistle, edible *(Cirsium edule),* 313
Thlaspi, see candytuft
threadworms, 42
Three Sisters, 277, 375–76
Tibet, 38
timbering, 383
timberline, 55
timothy, alpine *(Phleum alpinum),* 207, *213*
Tolmie, William, 244, 285
Toninia, see flake lichen
Townsendia, see Easter daisy
Trail Ridge, 119, 377–80; Road, 379